PUBLIC DEBT AND FUTURE GENERATIONS

PUBLIC DEBT
AND
FUTURE GENERATIONS

EDITED BY

James M. Ferguson

The University of
North Carolina Press · Chapel Hill

Copyright © *1964 by*
THE UNIVERSITY OF NORTH CAROLINA PRESS

Library of Congress Catalog Card Number: 64-22528

PRINTED BY THE WILLIAM BYRD PRESS, INC., RICHMOND, VA.

Manufactured in the United States of America

CONTENTS

CHAPTER EIGHT · COMMENTS ON THE PRECEDING ANALYSES

PUBLIC DEBT AND FUTURE GENERATIONS

Chapter One

INTRODUCTION

BY *James M. Ferguson*

I

Most economists in recent decades have agreed that society as a whole composed of a fixed population bears no burden in future periods of any public expenditure financed internally by public debt (or taxes) which occurs in the current period. The real cost or burden of the project is the real resources withdrawn from the private sector in the period of the expenditure. There is no way that debt financing enables real resources to be transferred from the future to the present. Some citizens in future periods may pay taxes and some receive interest payments but these are transfer payments involving no real burden, because no real resources are used up in the process.

Economists started in 1958 to attack the relevancy and importance of this concept of burden or cost and this concept of society. Using a full employment model, the dissenters have defined the burden of public expenditure in terms of reductions in private consumption and have distinguished between the burden on society as a whole and the burden on present and future generations of taxpayers. The withdrawal of resources at the time of the expenditure does not mean that this burden is borne immediately. Others have continued to hold the no-shifting position and to argue that the dissenters' concept of burden is meaningless. The first section of the introduction outlines the reasoning in support of the new concept of burden, how the burden is shifted to future generations, and why taxpayers shift more of the burden to future generations under debt finance compared to tax finance. It also includes the main arguments of those who continue to hold that the burden cannot be shifted. The second section summarizes the evolution of the debt.

The dissenters include Bowen, Davis, and Kopf (who contribute joint articles), Buchanan, Ferguson, Miller, Modigliani, Musgrave, Neisser, Shoup, Tullock, and Vickrey. For these economists, the objective cost or gross burden of a public expenditure is the reduction in taxpayers' consumption of private goods and services required by the withdrawal of resources from the private sector. These authors analyze the distribution of this burden over time and among generations of taxpayers under tax and debt finance. Differences in the distribution, but not the size, of the gross burden of a given public expenditure distinguish the burden of debt from the burden of taxation. Under debt finance less of the burden will be borne in the period of the government expenditure and/or by the generation of taxpayers present at the time of the expenditure.

All admit that the net burden depends on the productivity of the expenditure. However, the productivity is irrelevant in analyzing whether part of the required reduction in private consumption can be shifted to future periods or to later generations. It is also irrelevant in comparisons of the distribution of the reduction in private consumption under tax and debt finance. The purpose of the dissenters' analysis is to determine who bears the objective cost of government expenditures and when they bear this burden.

While the dissenters all agree that part of the burden of government expenditure is shifted to future generations under debt finance, two different concepts of generation and two different types of shifting process are used. For some of them, the statement "a burden of the debt is shifted to future generations" means that when public debt is issued and resources withdrawn from the private sector, part of the required reduction in taxpayers' private consumption is shifted or postponed to future periods. For others it means that part of this gross burden is postponed to future periods and then shifted to later generations of taxpayers.

Buchanan considers a society composed of a fixed population over time but distinguishes between citizens in their roles as bond purchasers and as taxpayers. In a democracy taxpayers legally bear the objective costs of government expenditure and the burden is borne when taxpayers reduce private consumption. When public debt is used instead of taxes in the period of the expenditure, the legal obligation on taxpayers to give up the resources for the project is shifted to future periods. In this situation the real resources for the project are given up voluntarily by bond-purchasers, who exchange current purchasing power for future purchasing power. Taxpayers implicitly borrow the real resources from bond purchasers in the initial period in exchange for giving them control over real resources in future periods. Any reduction in current consumption by bond-purchasers is not part of the burden of the expenditure, and it will be offset by increases in consumption in later periods. In this context, taxes levied in future periods to service and retire the debt are not merely transfer payments—they correspond to the bearing of the objective cost of the government expenditure by taxpayers who must reduce their private consumption when they transfer purchasing power to bondholders. As Buchanan points out in his paper [5] (references on page 229), the analysis can be even more complicated, since the taxpayer-borrower can convert the future burden into a current one by reducing his private consumption in the initial period and buying bonds yielding a return sufficient to meet the future taxes to service the debt. But if most taxpayers wanted to reduce consumption immediately, this could be achieved more easily by just adopting tax financing.

Modigliani also assumes a society composed of a fixed population but looks at the burden in terms of the private real income of society as a whole at different points in time. He argues that society bears no burden in the current period when public expenditures are financed out of private saving, because people invest only to consume in later periods. The cost or gross burden is borne in future periods when consumption of private goods and services is reduced. Taxpayers will primarily bear this reduction in consumption.

Bowen, Davis, and Kopf consider a society with a changing composition over time and define burden in terms of the lifetime consumption of different generations of taxpayers. Even if the government bonds are paid for entirely out of current consumption funds, the initial generation of taxpayers alive at the time of the public expenditure can use the bonds to redistribute ownership

claims to real resources in future periods and to shift part of the
required reduction in private consumption onto future generations
of taxpayers, who are present when taxes are levied to service and
retire the debt. Selling the bonds to later generations, consuming the
proceeds, and giving them the tax liability increases the lifetime
consumption of the first generation and reduces the lifetime consumption of later generations. Just as government bonds together

with the taxing process provide a means of transferring ownership
of resources among members of a given generation through time,
so also does it provide a means of transferring ownership of real
resources among different generations of people present at a given
point in time.

However, Shoup recognizes that at the time of the transfer
additional private capital is used up by the initial generation which
would otherwise have been given to the next generation. As a
result the stock of capital obtained by the next generation is reduced, so the burden which is actually shifted can be measured in
terms of reductions in private investment. In addition, this type of
shifting among generations of people depends on selling the bonds,
not giving them, to the next generation. If the lands are given to
the next generation, none of the required reduction in consumption
will be shifted. Shoup and Elliott question the empirical importance of such shifting given all of the other assets which the initial
generation can consume rather than leave for later generations. The
amount of such shifting among generations, when public debt is
used, will depend on the number of people in the initial generation
who would have left no estate under tax financing. Debt financing
of the expenditure will, in effect, make it possible for these people
to leave a negative estate.

The participants also extensively compare taxpayers' reactions
under debt and tax finance. In the main they argue that taxpayers
will shift more of the burden to future periods under debt finance.
They offer three main factors which might cause less reduction
in current consumption in the initial period under debt finance.
Almost all of the writers refer to a public debt illusion which is a
collective term including all the factors which cause people to treat
the bonds as assets but to underestimate their liability as taxpayers
to pay additional taxes in future periods to service and retire the
debt. Uncertainty concerning future taxes (tax rates, number of
taxpayers, general economic conditions) and limited time horizons

can produce underestimation of future taxes. Treating the bonds to some extent as assets need not involve irrational behavior. When taxpayers in future periods include new members of society not present at the time of the expenditure, they may shoulder part of the burden of the expenditure and the initial generation's lifetime consumption can be higher than in the tax case. Finally, some members of the community, especially poorer ones, facing a current tax may have no alternative but to reduce current consumption, because of very high private loan rates. The interest rate on government bonds may be much lower than the private interest rate. The taxpayer who is legally obligated to pay for all government expenditures is able to postpone reducing consumption under debt finance as he implicitly borrows the resources for the project from bond-purchasers. In other words debt finance makes available to all taxpayers at equal rates the opportunity of postponing the required reduction in consumption. The lower rate to the poorer borrowers will, according to Mishan, lead them to postpone more of the required reduction in consumption.[1] All of these factors can cause taxpayers' current consumption to fall less and current private investment to fall more under debt finance compared to tax finance.

Notice that these arguments refer only to citizens' decisions as taxpayers. People save for other than tax reasons, such as to achieve an optimal temporal distribution of lifetime consumption. If one considers aggregate private investment under debt finance, then the taxpayers' decline in saving may be offset to some extent by an increase in investors' saving if interest rates increase when government bonds are issued. However, if the rate of saving is not perfectly inelastic with respect to the interest rate and interest rates rise when public debt is issued, the decrease in aggregate private investment will be *less* than the amount of the required reduction in taxpayers' private consumption shifted to future periods. Taxpayers' reduction in private consumption will be greater than this amount because bond purchasers' future consumption will be greater to compensate those who responded to the rise in interest rates for their additional sacrifice of current consumption. The decision by taxpayers to postpone a reduction in consumption is not the only decision which determines aggregate saving. Decreases in

1. Mishan is not a dissenter. He rejects the notion of a gross burden of public expenditure and denies there is any burden connected with the use of public debt. He mentions this argument while criticizing Buchanan.

aggregate private investment accurately measure the burden of the expenditure shifted to future periods by taxpayers only if the rate of saving does not vary with changes in the interest rate.

The defenders of the no-shifting view include Mishan, Scitovsky, Elliott, Lerner, and Wiseman. They reject the dissenters' concepts of burden and continue to assert that society as a whole must bear the burden or real resource cost of the public project in the period of the expenditure. These economists do not distinguish between different members of society nor allow the taxpayer group to change over time. For them the Bowen-Davis-Kopf type of shifting amounts to mere transfers among members of society. Society composed of a fixed population through time will suffer a burden of reduced total real consumption if the government project is less productive than the sacrificed alternative, *but this loss is due to wasteful expenditure and cannot be attributed to the use of deficit financing*. Mishan admits that the reduction in real consumption will be borne by taxpayers, but when the reduction occurs is of no concern to him. He objects to saying that a burden is shifted to future periods if current private investment is reduced because *total* current investment, private and public, may have been increased. In such cases future periods' real income will be higher than it would have been in the absence of the expenditure. Some government projects which are as productive as the sacrificed alternatives may result in a flow of goods and services only in the current period. Even if decreases in private investment may occur, such projects still ought to be undertaken. Bringing into the analysis such concepts of burden can only hamper selection of worthwhile government expenditures.

II

This volume contains all of the articles which have appeared in leading economic journals during the period 1958-63 on the question of the shifting of a burden of public debt onto future generations.[2] The essays are presented in this volume in roughly the temporal order in which they have appeared. This section of the

2. It contains only excerpts from the review articles of Buchanan's book, from the 1948 article by Lerner, and from books by Buchanan and Musgrave. Otherwise it includes the complete text of all the items listed in the bibliography except the recently translated piece by Maffezzoni.

At least three comments on Mishan's article by Buchanan, Modigliani, and Hause, and a reply by Mishan, will appear in a late 1964 issue of *The Journal of Political Economy*, too late for inclusion in this volume.

introduction demarcates the main lines of battle through which the discussion has evolved and identifies the main positions of the participants.

The no-shifting view held by most economists in the 1930's, 1940's, and 1950's is most clearly presented in the first item, which is composed of several excerpts from a 1948 article by Lerner. The second paper, written by Meade in 1958, is important because it represents a transition from the old to the new. Meade accepts the then current no-shifting view but goes on to discuss the adverse consequences on economic incentives of a large existing public debt and the taxes necessary to finance the interest payments, many of which are also discussed by Lerner. But such discussions suggest that all of the costs of debt-financed public expenditures may not be borne in the period the expenditure is made. Meade argues that the removal of deadweight government debt—debt not covered by any real assets—would permit lower taxes and as a result would improve economic incentives to work, to save, and to take risks.[3]

Modigliani criticizes Meade for arguing that the burden of tax-friction is due to the unproductive government expenditure. Any reduction in debt, deadweight or otherwise, would reduce the necessary taxes and reduce tax-friction. Both Buchanan and Hansen criticize Meade's methodology saying that it is not meaningful to begin, as Meade does, by assuming two societies similar in every respect except that one society has and the other does not have a national debt. Because having faced similar events, such as wars, one chose to finance it by borrowing and the other by taxation—and the two methods will have different effects on the operation of the economy and the stock of real private assets.[4] Therefore, the two economies will not be identical in subsequent periods. Hansen [9] goes on to argue that Meade should have considered the impact of the process of debt creation upon the economy. "The origin of the debt and the impact of its creation upon the economy must be considered, not merely the fact that the debt *exists*" (p. 375).

The publication of Professor Buchanan's book, *Public Princi-*

3. As soon as the distinction between the real resource cost of the expenditure and the burden of the expenditure becomes recognized, the debate shifts to the distribution of this burden, and incentive factors become secondary effects.

4. However, if perfect foresight is assumed, Meade's model, comparing the effects of existing debt on two economies alike in all respects except that one has an internal debt and the other does not, would be legitimate.

ples of Public Debt, marks the beginning of the current controversy. Buchanan argues that the man-in-the-street is correct in
believing there is an important difference between tax and debt
financing of government expenditures. Buchanan rejects the notion
that the burden of government expenditure is borne by society as
a whole. In a democracy individuals as taxpayers legally bear the
costs of government expenditures, but they bear this burden at
different times under the two methods of finance. When debt is
issued, the legal obligation on taxpayers is shifted to future periods,
and the burden of the expenditure on taxpayers can also be shifted
to future periods. Within the context of a full employment model,
he attacks the then prevailing argument that future generations
bear no burden of any public expenditure financed by debt which
is incurred in the current period because the interest-receivers and
the taxpayers are members of the same generation.

In this book, Buchanan defines burden in terms of reductions in
individual utility. He assumes utility is a function of current consumption and current net worth. If debt finance is used and the
taxpayers correctly anticipate the future taxes to service and retire
the debt, then they will count them as a liability, reduce net
worth, and bear the reduction in utility, the burden of the expenditure, immediately. They bear no burden in later periods when they
actually pay the taxes. The later reduction in consumption cannot
be counted as a burden because it is merely the objective counterpart
of the earlier reduction in utility. In this analysis, postponing or shifting the burden to future periods requires a public debt illusion (uncertainty concerning future taxes) which causes taxpayers to underestimate future taxes to service and repay the debt. As a result,
at least part of the reduction in utility is shifted to future periods.

Buchanan, in his later paper written for this volume, rejects
this concept of burden, because it confuses the two costs connected with every decision—the subjective opportunity cost borne
at the moment of decision and the objective cost which results
from decision. He now defines the burden or objective cost of
public expenditure to be the reduction in taxpayers' consumption
of private goods and services. Buchanan's emphasis consistently
remains on the difference in the position of the taxpayer under the
two methods of finance. Individuals as citizen-taxpayers vote for
the government project and the method of finance. They will select
taxation if they wish to bear the objective cost or burden im-

mediately. They will select debt finance if they wish to postpone the reduction in consumption. When debt is issued, taxes levied in future periods to service and retire the debt are not merely transfer payments. In paying the taxes, taxpayers bear the objective cost of the government expenditure and reduce private consumption. They transfer purchasing power to bondholders to compensate the latter group for giving up the resources for the project in the initial period.

As other economists perceived the distinction between real resource withdrawal from the private sector and the burden of public expenditure, debate developed on the definition of burden, the timing of the burden, and who bears the burden. Vickrey, Modigliani, Musgrave, and Neisser argue that whether the real resources for the public project come out of current consumption or current investment will affect the level of private real income in future periods. Under conditions of full employment, the choice between loan finance and tax finance will determine whether the resource withdrawal comes largely from private capital formation or largely from private consumption. These authors define the burden of the expenditure to be the decrease in consumption of private goods and services required by the withdrawal of resources from the private sector. They proceed to argue that reductions in private investment in the period of the government expenditure place a burden of reduced private consumption on those living in future periods, and this constitutes the burden of the government expenditure shifted to the future. Some burden is shifted to future periods even if the expenditure is financed by current taxation to the extent that the taxes are paid out of investment funds. The "burden of the debt" for this group is the amount of the decrease in current private investment (reduction in future periods' private consumption) when debt is issued *over and above* the decrease which would occur if current taxes were levied to finance a given public expenditure. Their analysis concentrates on the private real income of society as a whole in each period of time under the two methods of finance, although some of them suggest that the required reductions in private consumption in future periods will be borne by taxpayers. Differences in the temporal distribution of the burden occur because the current generation's choices between current consumption and current investment differ under the two methods of finance.

The third stage of the debate involves dissents to the view of the second group that the only way a burden can be shifted to future generations is through reductions in private investment by the initial generation. Bowen, Davis, and Kopf, who contribute joint articles, use a different concept of generation. Society at any point in time is composed of several generations of people. The gross burden of a public expenditure is the reduction in the lifetime consumption of each generation of taxpayers. Under debt finance, but not taxation, the initial generation, meaning all taxpayers alive at the time of the government expenditure, can shift part of the required reduction in consumption onto future generations, meaning taxpayers not alive at the time of the government expenditure but who are present in future periods when taxes are levied to service (and retire) the debt. This shifting can occur even if there is no reduction in private investment in the period of the expenditure. By selling the later generations the government bonds, consuming the proceeds, and giving them the tax liability to service and retire the debt, the initial generation can redistribute ownership claims to real resources in future periods. This redistribution will increase the lifetime consumption of the initial generation and reduce the lifetime consumption of later generations. The next generation in buying the bonds gives up purchasing power which it never recoups if it is taxed to retire the bonds. The first generation does have to forego consumption in the initial period until the period in which they sell the bonds to the next generation, but their total lifetime consumption can be the same as it would have been in the absence of the project.

Tullock advances an imaginative gold machine example to illustrate Buchanan's point that taxpayers need not bear the cost of the project at the time the resources are withdrawn from the private sector for the government project. Musgrave, although he agrees that in general the burden of the expenditure is shifted via reductions in private investment, offers an example of municipal finance in which debt finance distributes the cost of the project (reduction in income and consumption) among several generations of citizens without regard to changes in investment by the initial generation. The example illustrates, according to Musgrave, the use of pay-as-you-use finance for durable public facilities yielding services over a period of years. The pay-as-you-use principle states that public debt issued for such purposes should be repaid as the benefits from the initial expenditure are being exhausted. Musgrave then considers a public project yielding services over three periods and assumes that loans advanced by any one generation must be repaid within its life span (the period it resides in the locality). Each generation resides for three periods in the community—three different generations being present in any period. Using loan finance to secure funds to construct the facility and charging taxes (and retiring debt) in each period equal to the services provided results in an accurate division of cost among generations which could not be obtained using tax finance. But Shoup comments that this result depends on the assumption that each generation consumes its assets while still present with no private property transfers among generations. Obviously this condition is most applicable to cases of local finance with extensive turnover of people in the community.

Miller combines the gross and net concepts of burden when he suggests that a burden may be shifted to future periods under debt financing when people are led to form expectations concerning the future real purchasing power of assets which are not later realized. This is due partly to underestimation of future taxes to service the debt including inflation (which is a form of taxation under full employment). As a result people find that the real purchasing power of their assets in later periods is less than they had anticipated. How much of the frustrated-expectations burden would have also occurred under tax financing is not discussed by Miller. Needless to say the extra taxes and the reduced purchasing power of the bonds represent distinct burdens. However the latter may essentially be due to the fact that the government projects were wasteful—they did not result in a flow of consumer goods and services which could be purchased with funds obtained by selling the bonds.

Finally, Wiseman and Mishan argue that we should forget the notion of a burden of the debt. Wiseman's view is that the concept of burden of the debt is useless and misleading and has distorted policy discussion. There are many forms of public debt and varied economic conditions in which debt can be issued. Instead of a general discussion of burden, he suggests that it would be more fruitful to study particular situations in which debt financing is one means of achieving desired goals.

Mishan also rejects the whole notion of a burden of public debt.

If the public investment is successful, then it will yield services which can be sold to pay the interest so no future taxes need be levied. And total consumption (of private and public goods combined) can be as high in future periods as total consumption (of private goods) would have been in the absence of the project. Mishan agrees with Scitovsky that to the extent the project is wasteful (the return on the government use of resources is less than the foregone alternative investment) there will be a burden of reduced income and consumption. But this is not a burden of the debt, because it is not connected with the method of finance but rather with the productivity of the project. Mishan calls it nonsense to term reductions in private investment a burden on future generations, because in that context the decision not to reduce current investment imposes a similar burden on the current generation. A term which has all these meanings has no relevance for policy and the use of the term can only mislead politicians into believing that debt finance has undesirable costs or effects which taxation does not have.

Shoup comments on the various positions. Many of Shoup's cogent remarks have already been mentioned. He supports the shifting-via-reductions-in-private-investment approach. Ferguson argues that while Buchanan in his initial analysis paid too little attention to real flows, the analysis has now shifted too much toward only real flows to the neglect of individuals' utility streams. With a new utility function including only flow items, Ferguson proceeds to argue that there is no fixed size to the burden because a future sacrifice of consumption will impose a current loss of utility due to anticipation of the sacrifice in addition to the loss in the future when the sacrifice occurs.

Ferguson, defining burden in turns of utility, also suggests that there is a burden of the debt method of financing—attributable to the method of financing not to the government expenditure per se. The additional burden or loss of utility borne by taxpayers under debt financing relative to the burden under tax financing is due to factors inherent in the institution of public debt, which are described by the term "public debt illusion." The existence of a public debt illusion causes taxpayers to allocate their lifetime consumption in a non-optimal pattern—one which is different from the pattern which they would have chosen in the absence of the illusion. As a result of the distortion in their consumption pattern, taxpayers' lifetime utility under debt financing may be less than under tax financing.

Ferguson proceeds to use this result to answer Vickrey and Mishan who ask whether on welfare grounds debt financing is always preferable to tax financing because it allows individuals a wider range of alternatives. A negative answer can be given if the loss of utility from the distortions in the timing of taxpayers' consumption under debt financing is greater than the gain in utility from the wider range of choice.

Chapter Two

THE NEW ORTHODOXY

A/ THE BURDEN OF THE NATIONAL DEBT*

BY *Abba P. Lerner*

Millions of people are now taking time off from worrying about the prospects of atomic warfare to do some worrying on account of the burden of a growing national debt. But there are many quite different concepts of the nature of this burden. The purpose of this article is to examine the most important of these worries and to see to what extent they are justified and to what extent they are about imaginary burdens which only confuse the real issues.

I. Imaginary Effects of National Debt

1. By far the most common concern about the national debt comes from considering it as exactly the same kind of thing as a private debt which one individual owes to others. Every dollar of an individual's indebtedness must be subtracted from his assets in arriving at a measure of his net wealth. Indebtedness is impoverishment. It places the debtor in the hands of the creditor and threatens him with hardship and ruin. To avoid indebtedness as far as possible is undoubtedly an eminently well-established rule of private prudence.

The simple transferability of this rule to national debt is denied by nearly all economists. But nearly everybody who has ever

* Reprinted by permission from Lloyd A. Metzler and others, *Income, Employment, and Public Policy: Essays in Honor of Alvin H. Hansen.* Copyright 1948 by W. W. Norton & Company, Inc., New York.

suffered the oppressions of private indebtedness is tempted to apply the analogy directly, and the primary orthodoxy of the editorial writers, the dogma that sound government finance means balancing the budget, has no other basis.

One of the most effective ways of clearing up this most serious of all semantic confusions is to point out that private debt differs from national debt in being *external*. It is owed by one person to *others*. That is what makes it burdensome. Because it is *interpersonal* the proper analogy is not to national debt but to *international* debt. A nation owing money to other nations (or to the citizens of other nations) *is* impoverished or burdened in the same kind of way as a man who owes money to other men. But this does not hold for national debt which is owed by the nation to citizens of the *same* nation. There is then no external creditor. "We owe it to ourselves."

This refutation of the validity of the analogy from *external* to *internal* debt must not be interpreted as a denial that any significant problems can be raised by internal national debt. When economists are sufficiently irritated by the illegitimate analogy they are liable to say that the national debt does not matter at all. But this must be understood in the same sense as when a man who finds that rumor has converted a twisted ankle into a broken neck tells his friends that he is perfectly all right.

2. A variant of the false analogy is the declaration that national debt puts an unfair burden on our children, who are thereby made to pay for our extravagances. Very few economists need to be reminded that if our children or grandchildren repay some of the national debt these payments will be made *to* our children or grandchildren and to nobody else. Taking them altogether they will no more be impoverished by making the repayments than they will be enriched by receiving them.

Unfortunately the first few times people see this argument destroyed they feel tricked rather than convinced. But the resistance to conceding the painlessness of repaying national debt can be diminished by pointing out that it only corresponds to the relative uselessness of incurring it. An *external* loan enables an individual or a nation to get things from others without having to give anything in return, for the time being. The borrower is enabled to consume more than he is producing. And when he repays the external debt he has to consume less than he is producing. But this is not true for *internal* borrowing. However useful an internal loan may be for the health of the economy, it does *not* enable the nation to consume more than it produces. It should therefore not be so surprising that the repayment of internal debt does not necessitate a tightening of the belt. The internal borrowing did not permit the belt to be loosened in the first place.

3. Many who recognize that national debt is no subtraction from national wealth are nevertheless deeply concerned about the interest payments on the national debt. They call this the *interest burden* almost as if the interest payments constituted subtractions from the national income.

This involves exactly the same error. The interest payments are no more a subtraction from the national income than the national debt itself is a subtraction from the national wealth. This can be shown most clearly by pointing out how easy it is, by simply borrowing the money needed to make the interest payments, to convert the "interest burden" into some additional national debt. The interest need therefore never be more onerous than the additional principal of the debt into which it can painlessly be transformed.

Borrowing money to make the interest payments sounds much worse than simply getting into debt in the first place. Popular feeling on this score seems so strong that economists who are themselves quite free from the erroneous analogy have felt themselves constrained by the power of the prejudice to assume that the interest payments on national debt are never borrowed but raised by taxes.[1]

The strict application of such a secondary orthodoxy would mean much more than these economists intend to concede to the popular prejudice. It would mean nothing less than the prohibition of all borrowing, and a meticulous adherence to the primary orthodoxy of balancing the budget at all times. For as soon as there is any national debt at all on which any interest has to be paid, *any* further government borrowing is indistinguishable from borrowing to pay the interest—unless we are taken in by bookkeeping

---

1. E.g., Evsey D. Domar, "The Burden of the Debt and the National Income," *The American Economic Review*, XXXIV (December, 1944), 799. "This assumption (that all funds for payment of interest charges are to be raised by taxation) is made both to simplify the argument and to protect the reader from a shock. To many, government investment financed by borrowing sounds so bad that the thought of borrowing to pay the interest is simply unbearable." (Reprinted by permission.)

fictions of financial earmarking which say that the money borrowed goes for other purposes so that the particular dollars used to pay the interest come from taxation.[2]

. . . .

7. In attempts to discredit the argument that we owe the national debt to ourselves it is often pointed out that the "we" does not consist of the same people as the "ourselves." The benefits from interest payments on the national debt do not accrue to every individual in exactly the same degree as the damage done to him by the additional taxes made necessary. That is why it is not possible to repudiate the whole national debt without hurting anybody.

While this is undoubtedly true, all it means is that some people will be better off and some people will be worse off. Such a redistribution of wealth is involved in every significant happening in our closely interrelated economy, in every invention or discovery or act of enterprise. If there is some good general reason for incurring debt, the redistribution can be ignored because we have no more reason for supposing that the new distribution is worse than the old one than for assuming the opposite. That the distribution will be *different* is no more an argument against national debt than it is an argument in favor of it.

2. If we did permit ourselves to indulge in such make-believe, the secondary orthodoxy would be reduced to declaring that everything is all right as long as the interest paid on the national debt does not exceed the total tax revenue. It could then be declared that the interest payments all come out of taxes even if all other expenditures are financed by borrowing!

B/ IS THE NATIONAL DEBT A BURDEN?*

BY *J. E. Meade*

I

The view is sometimes expressed that a domestic national debt means merely that citizens as potential taxpayers are indebted to themselves as holders of government debt, and that it can, therefore,

* Reprinted by permission from *Oxford Economic Papers*, X (June, 1958).

have little effect upon the economy, except insofar as it may lead to a redistribution of income and wealth between taxpayers and owners of property. It is my purpose to refute this argument; to show that, quite apart from any distributional effects, a domestic debt may have far-reaching effects upon incentives to work, to save, and to take risks; and to examine the nature of these effects.

I shall say very little about the distribution of income and property. My thesis is that if the national debt could be removed in such a way as to leave the distribution of real income totally unchanged, then in certain specified ways it would improve economic incentives. In economic policy there is very frequently a conflict between the objectives of efficiency and of equality. Measures which improve incentives often increase inequalities; and measures which increase equality often blunt economic incentives. If it can be shown that the removal of the national debt in a way which did not affect the distribution of income would improve economic incentives, then it would not be difficult to show that the removal of the national debt in a way which did not affect incentives could be used to improve distribution.

This paper is concerned only with domestic debt. It is well known that an external debt is a burden on a community, since there must be a transfer of real goods and services from the debtor to the creditor country in payment of interest and sinking fund on the debt. A domestic debt, on the other hand, means merely a transfer from citizens as taxpayers to citizens as property-owners, so that there is no direct loss of real goods and services to the citizens as a whole.

But one must not conclude from this that a domestic debt has no adverse economic effects.[1] In order to examine these effects, a comparison will be made between two societies which are in

---

1. Some excellent articles have been written to remove fears about the evils to be expected from an ever-growing debt. For example, Professor A. P. Lerner ("The Burden of the Debt" in *Income, Employment, and Public Policy*) shows that there is no reason to believe that the debt will grow without limit, even if a debt is always created to finance a budget deficit so long as total demand is deficient; for when the debt has grown to a certain size its "Pigou-effect" (see p. 23 below) will serve to raise demand without further growth of debt. Professor Domar ("The Burden of the Debt and the National Income," *The American Economic Review*, XXXIV, 1944) has shown that even if debt grows without limit, the rate of tax necessary to service it may not grow beyond a certain limit, if the national income is also growing. But these articles show only that the debt is unlikely to grow without limit relatively to the national income. They do not show that a given debt has no adverse effects.

every respect similar except that the one has a large domestic
national debt and the other has no debt. This idea is a useful
analytical device to isolate certain factors at work in society; but
the concept is an artificial one and needs careful definition in particular in respect to the effect of the presence or absence of a national
debt upon the distribution of income and property.

We can apply this concept by supposing that we move by means
of a capital levy from a society with a national debt to a society
without a national debt. But this capital levy is a purely analytical
device.[2] We are really imagining two different societies, otherwise the same, except that history has left one with and the other
without a national debt; and this is put in terms of assimilating the
position of the former to that of the latter by means of a capital
levy merely as a way of explaining in what sense they are otherwise the same.

Let us then consider a society with a large national debt. We will
make one and only one simplifying assumption about distribution,
namely that all citizens in any one given income bracket have the
same ratio of income from work to income from property. The
rich man may have a higher ratio than the poor man of unearned
to earned income, but each rich man has the same ratio as every
other rich man and each poor man has the same ratio as every
other poor man. Suppose then that there is a capital levy of any
degree of progression, the total levy being on a scale sufficient
to redeem the whole debt. After the levy any citizen in any one
income bracket will have a lower gross income according to the
amount of income from property in that bracket and according to
the progressiveness of the levy on property. Let us suppose that
the scale of taxation on income is then so adjusted that each citizen
in each income bracket gains in reduced taxation on income exactly
what he loses in income from property.[3] Each citizen's net tax-free

2. For the reasons given below (p. 40) I would not personally advocate an
actual capital levy.
3. This involves the assumption that each citizen is paying sufficient in income
taxation for it to be possible to offset by a remission of such tax his loss of
income from property resulting from the levy on his capital. But this assumption can be safely made in conditions in which (i) income taxation accounts
for a large proportion of government revenue and debt interest for a small
proportion of government expenditure, so that much revenue from income tax
is needed even after the capital levy; and (ii) income taxation and the capital
levy are both progressive and people with large incomes hold large amounts of
property, so that the people who lose income from property are also the main
payers of income taxation.

income remains exactly the same as before, so that the capital levy has left the distribution of personal incomes unchanged. If the capital levy was a proportionate one, it would also have left the distribution of property unchanged, in the sense that it would have reduced all personal properties in the same proportion. If the capital levy was a progressive one, it would *pro tanto* have diminished the inequality of ownership of property.

There is, of course, a relationship between the degree of progression of the levy and the modification of the progressiveness of the existing taxation on income which is necessary to leave each citizen's net income unchanged.[4] But for our present purpose we can be content to conclude that on our assumptions in the society without the national debt (i) every citizen will own a

---

4. Let $e+pr$ be an individual's gross income, where e is income from work, p the value of property, and r the rate of interest on property. Let i be the rate of tax on his income before the capital levy, c the rate of levy on his capital, and i' the rate of tax on his income after the levy. For his net income to remain unchanged we have

$$(e+pr)(1-i) = \{e+(1-c)pr\}(1-i'),$$

or $\dfrac{1-i'}{1-i} = \dfrac{1}{1-ck}$ where $k = \dfrac{pr}{e+pr}$ or the proportion of his income which is unearned. Consider now an individual with a large total income denoted by subscript $_1$ and an individual with a small total income denoted by subscript $_2$.

Then $\dfrac{1-i_1'}{1-i_1}$ is $> \dfrac{1-i_2'}{1-i_2}$ if $c_1k_1 > c_2k_2$. The modification in the degree of progression of the income tax is thus seen to depend on the progressiveness of the capital levy (c_1 and c_2), and on the factors determining k_1 and k_2 which are the distribution of income from work (e_1 and e_2), the distribution of property (p_1 and p_2), and the yield of income from property (r). Now if the rich man has a higher ratio of unearned to earned income ($k_1 > k_2$) and the capital levy is progressive ($c_1 > c_2$), then $c_1k_1 > c_2k_2$. In this case taxation of income must be so adjusted that the tax-free proportion of gross income goes up in a greater proportion for the rich than for the poor $\left(\text{i.e. } \dfrac{1-i_1'}{1-i_1} > \dfrac{1-i_2'}{1-i_2}\right)$. In this sense the taxation of income must become less progressive; and its degree of progression will be reduced the more, the more progressive *ceteris paribus* is the capital levy, i.e. the greater is c_1/c_2. But the mere fact that the rich man has a greater *absolute* amount of property than the poor man (even if the capital levy remains progressive) is not sufficient to cause the post-levy taxation of income to become less progressive in the sense defined above. A man with a large income may have a larger absolute income from property and yet a smaller proportion of his income coming from property than in the case of a poor man, i.e. k_2 can be greater than k_1. If the capital levy is only slightly progressive (c_1 only slightly $> c_2$), it is possible that $c_1k_1 < c_2k_2$.

smaller amount of property, (ii) every citizen's gross income will be lower, (iii) every citizen's average rate of taxation on income will be lower, but (iv) every citizen's net income will be unchanged.

II

What would be the effects of these changes on the citizen's behavior? The first and foremost effect, but a strangely neglected effect, is the increased incentive to save which would be caused by the fact that each citizen's net income was unchanged while the value of his property had been reduced. Imagine the same individual in two situations; in both situations he has a tax-free income of £1,000 to spend or save; but in situation 1 he has £10,000 worth of property and in situation 2 he has only £5,000 worth of property against a rainy day, or for his old age, or to leave to his family, or to supplement his present consumption by living on his capital. The amount which he would spend on goods and services would almost certainly be considerably greater in situation 1 than in situation 2; or, to put the same thing another way, a man's net savings will be higher or his net dissavings lower, the lower is the ratio of his capital to his tax-free income. He may call this the Pigou-effect.[5]

Professor Hicks[6] has estimated that in 1947-49 the domestic indebtedness of the government which was uncovered by any real assets (which I will call the "deadweight debt") represented no less than 43 per cent of all privately owned property. The removal of the deadweight debt could thus be considered as capable in those circumstances of reducing the representative citizen's property by 43 per cent without reducing his tax-free income. This is what might be called a gigantic Pigou-effect and would clearly raise the incentive to save very greatly.[7]

This increase in the incentive to save is almost certain to repre-

---

5. See Pigou, "Economic Progress in a Stable Environment," *Economica*, XIV (1947).

6. See J. R. Hicks, *The Social Framework*, 2nd ed., p. 109.

7. We are not, of course, considering the effects of an actual capital levy, which might have other psychological repercussions upon the incentive to save, particularly if it were thought that the levy might be repeated. We are considering only how incentives in this country might differ from what they are if the past history of the country had been such as to leave it now with its present real income and real resources but without the deadweight debt.

sent an improvement from the point of view of society. If a reduction in the demand for consumption goods is desired either to
reduce an inflationary pressure or to release resources so that investment can be raised in the interests of economic growth, the
advantage is obvious. But even if no change in expenditure on consumption goods is desired, the increased incentive to save can be
made to have advantageous indirect effects. For in this case, rates
of taxation can be reduced so as to raise the citizens' tax-free incomes to the extent necessary to restore their demand for consumption goods; and these reductions in rates of tax will improve
incentives for work and enterprise.[8]

Moreover, the fact that the removal of the deadweight debt
would cause all personal properties to be smaller than before is
likely to improve incentives for work and enterprise as well as for
saving. Greater effort of every kind is likely to be made to be in a
position to build up private fortunes when these are not already
inflated by a deadweight debt.[9]

III

The second major effect of the disappearance of the deadweight
debt is the familiar one most usually discussed in this connection,
namely the improvement to incentives to save, to work, and to
risk brought about by the reduction in rates of taxation which it
would make possible directly as a result of the saving of interest
payments on the budget. The argument is in principle a very
simple one. The redemption of the deadweight debt would mean
a saving in budgetary expenditure on interest on the debt. This
would make it possible to reduce rates of tax; and this would
improve incentives to earn larger incomes by more effort and
enterprise.

That there would be some incentive to more work and enterprise and that this would mark an improvement in economic arrangements is almost certain. We are assuming that when the deadweight debt disappears each citizen experiences a reduction in the
rate of tax on his remaining income which exactly offsets his loss

8. It should be noted that these reductions of tax rates made possible by the
Pigou-effect are quite separate from, and additional to, any reductions in tax
rates made possible through a saving of interest payments from the State budget,
which are the subject matter of the next section.
9. Mr. N. K. Kaldor has suggested this point to me. I shall refer to it as the
Kaldor-extension of the Pigou-effect.

of income from property. So far he is in exactly the same real position with the same real income—neither better nor worse off. The only change is that if he earns an additional unit of income he will keep more of it. He will then take steps to earn more because he starts with the same real income and can get another unit of income more easily than before. And this change must be an improvement from his point of view because he could, had he so wished, have made no change in his income or leisure; and, so long as any positive rate of tax remains on income, he is likely by further effort to add more to the wealth of society than he takes from society after payment of tax on his additional earnings.

But how important are these effects of reduced rates of taxation on income likely to be? It has often been argued that they will be quantitatively very small if (i) the market rate of interest is low, (ii) the progressiveness of existing rates of taxation on income are high, (iii) there is a high correlation between large incomes and large properties, and (iv) the progressiveness of the capital levy is also high.[10] In these conditions a large redemption of debt is likely to lead only to a very small net saving of expenditure on the budget and so to make room for only a very small reduction of rates of taxation. If the rate of interest is low, a given redemption of debt will cause only a small gross saving of interest payment in the budget, if the levy on capital is progressive, if large properties are held mainly by people with large incomes, and if the marginal rates of tax on these incomes are very high, then most of this small gross saving of interest will itself be absorbed by a loss of revenue from the taxation of income. The net saving to the budget and so the consequential reduction in tax rates and so the consequential improvement in incentives to be expected from a redemption of debt will be very small.

The conditions which I have just enumerated existed in this

10. We are using the capital levy merely as an analytical device for comparing two otherwise similar societies, whose histories have differed in one way or another so that in one a large national debt has been contracted and in the other no debt has been contracted. Since a national debt involves the inflation of the total amount of privately owned property, the histories of our two societies must have differed in such a way that over the past years in one of them private citizens have been able to accumulate more savings than in the other. The assumption that the capital levy is progressive corresponds, therefore, to a difference in the past histories of our two societies such that it is those who were able to accumulate the largest sums in the one society who were most denied the opportunity to accumulate in the other.

country in the years immediately after the war; and for these reasons the existence of a very large national debt was not considered to have any seriously adverse effects on incentives. But, quite apart from the very important Pigou-effect, there are at least three reasons why the deadweight debt has been a more serious impediment to economic incentives than was generally recognized.

In the first place, the rate of interest was kept at a low level in large measure because of the existence of the national debt. These were years of heavy inflationary pressure. Reluctance to use monetary policy as one of the instruments to restrain inflation was greatly increased by the fact that an all-round rise in interest rates would immediately increase the budgetary burden of expenditure of interest on treasury bills and other short-term debt and would gradually lead to a rise in expenditure on longer-dated debt as it fell due for repayment.[11] With low interest rates a removal of the debt might cause only a small gross saving on debt interest; but it would mean that a rise of interest rates as an anti-inflationary device would no longer be open to the objection that it would seriously increase the budgetary problem. The removal of the national debt would thus have made it much easier to use the instrument of monetary policy flexibly for the control of inflation and deflation. Now that, for better or worse, interest rates have been raised to really high levels the argument can, of course, be put once more in its direct form. Rates of interest being high the redemption of national debt would mean a large saving of interest on national debt.

Our attitude to a deadweight debt must be much influenced by the surrounding economic climate. In times of economic stagnation like the 1930's, low interest rates and cheap money were most desirable in themselves to stimulate investment; this had the incidental result that a given national debt did not involve very high

---

11. It is not certain that a rise in interest rates increases the net burden of a given national debt. This depends greatly on the structure of the debt. If the debt consisted solely of short-term bills it would not affect the capital value of the debt but would add to the interest payments and so raise the rates of tax needed to service the debt. If the debt consisted solely of irredeemable bonds it would reduce the capital value of the debt without raising interest payments. In the former case there would be an unfavorable effect on tax rates with no favorable Pigou-effect; in the latter case there would be a favorable Pigou-effect with no adverse effects on tax rates.

rates of tax for its service and, at the same time, the Pigou-effect of a high capital sum of the debt in discouraging savings was positively beneficial. But in the present (and so much more desirable) world climate of economic development and buoyancy, high interest rates may be desired as a means of discouraging the least productive investment projects, and the Pigou-effect of the debt in discouraging savings is most undesirable. A deadweight debt may have been a blessing in the 1930's, but it is a curse in the 1950's.

Secondly, the fact that a progressive capital levy combined with a progressive system of taxation of income means that there is little scope for subsequent reduction in the existing schedules of taxation on income does not mean that it gives no increased incentive at the margin for greater work and enterprise. A capital levy reduces the property-owner's gross income; with a progressive system of taxation of income the reduction in the amount of his gross income by putting him into a lower income bracket causes the rate of tax on his income to be reduced. For this reason, even if there were no reduction whatsoever in the schedules of taxation of income after the capital levy, there would nevertheless be an improvement in marginal incentive. Because he was now in a lower gross-income bracket the representative taxpayer could keep a larger proportion of each additional £1 which he earned.

Thirdly, there is some reason to believe that a given reduction in the marginal rate of tax will be more important from the point of view of economic incentives when tax rates are high than when they are low. Consider two situations which are otherwise the same. In situation 1 the rate of income tax is 19s. 6d. in the pound because the cold war is on and there is a great deal of government expenditure on armaments to finance in addition to interest on the national debt. In situation 2 real peace has broken out and the rate of income tax is only 2s. in the pound because there is little government expenditure on armaments, though expenditure on interest on debt remains unchanged. Now in situation 1 remove just sufficient national debt to make possible a reduction of 6d. in the pound in the income tax while leaving every citizen with the same real income as before because his loss of interest on debt is just compensated by the fall in the rate of income tax. Then in situation 2 make a similar change; that is to say, remove that amount of debt which in situation 2 will permit a reduction of 6d. in the pound while leaving every citizen with the same real income. In situation 1 out of every additional £100 which he now earns a citizen can keep £5 instead of only £2. 10s. In situation 2 out of every additional £100 which he now earns he can keep £92. 10s. instead of only £90. The same reduction of tax of 6d. in the pound has in both situations left the taxpayer's spendable income unchanged; but it has raised his *marginal* reward by 100 per cent in situation 1 and by under 3 per cent in situation 2. Since in the "cold war" situation our taxpayer is so much worse off than in the "real-peace" situation we cannot say for certain that a 100 per cent increase in his marginal reward without any change in his total reward will have a greater effect on the amount of work which he does in situation 1 than a 3 per cent increase in his marginal reward without any change in his total reward in situation 2. But there is a strong presumption that he will increase his effort more in situation 1 than in situation 2.[12]

But even if he increased the amount of work which he did by the same amount in situation 1 when his marginal reward was doubled as in situation 2 when his marginal reward was increased by only 3 per cent, the reduction in tax would be much more important in situation 1 than in situation 2. In both cases his wage before tax measures the value of his marginal product, while his wage after tax measures the marginal disutility of effort to him. In situation 1 our citizen is working to a margin at which the value of his marginal product is no less than 40 times as great as the cost of his marginal effort (£100 ÷ £2. 10s. = 40). In situation 2 the value of his marginal product is only $1\frac{1}{9}$ times as great as the cost of his marginal effort (£100 ÷ £90 = $1\frac{1}{9}$). In the former case society as a whole stands to gain much more from additional work than it does in the latter case.

12. If his elasticity of demand for income in terms of effort is equal to unity, then he is supplying the same amount of work in situation 1 as in situation 2. The outbreak of the cold war and the consequent increase in the rate of tax from 2s. to 19s. 6d. in the pound will have raised the marginal utility of money income to him (by reducing his tax-free income) in exactly the same proportion as it has lowered his tax-free wage in terms of money. Since he is doing the same amount of work, the marginal disutility of work is in this case the same to him in situation 1 as in situation 2. In both cases when debt is removed and the tax rate is lowered by 6d. the marginal utility of income is unchanged (because he loses in interest as much as he gains by paying his tax); but in situation 1 his net reward for doing more work is doubled and in situation 2 it is raised by less than 3 per cent. He will be certain in this case to increase his supply of work more in situation 1 than in situation 2.

Thus it is certainly true that if the initial taxation of income is high and progressive, then a progressive capital levy will lead to only a small budgetary saving of interest on debt and will therefore permit only a small reduction in tax rates. But it is precisely when marginal rates of tax on income are high that a small reduction in tax rates may do much good.

IV

Up to this point the existence of death duties has been neglected. A removal of the deadweight debt would reduce the size of the average private holding of property; it would thus reduce the size of the average estate passing at death; and so with any given schedule of death duties it would reduce the annual revenue from such duties. This additional automatic loss of revenue, so it may be argued, still further weakens the case for a removal of the deadweight debt as a means of making possible a reduction of tax rates and so an improvement in incentives.

That one must be careful about this argument is forcibly demonstrated by the following consideration. If the rate of interest is sufficiently low, if the taxation of income is sufficiently high and progressive, if the capital levy itself is sufficiently progressive, if estates pass frequently enough by death from one owner to another, and if the rates of death duty are sufficiently high and progressive, then the removal of the deadweight debt may at existing tax rates cause budgetary revenue to fall by more than budgetary expenditure. The loss of death duties because of the reduction in the capital sum of personal properties may be greater than the small saving of interest after payment of income tax. To preserve the budgetary balance tax rates must be raised after the removal of the debt. The greater the national debt, the better the budgetary situation.

It is quite probable that in the years immediately after the war conditions were of this kind, so that the disappearance of the debt would have reduced budgetary expenditures less than budgetary revenue. Yet common sense rightly rebels against the conclusion that the great growth of debt during the war could have improved the budgetary situation in any basic sense. Where has the argument gone astray?

The answer is, of course, that there is no reason to believe that the balance between revenue and expenditure ought to remain unchanged when the deadweight debt is removed. In the modern

economy the basic purpose of taxation is to restrain the demands
of private citizens in order to release real resources from the production of goods and services for private consumption to the extent
that they are needed to meet the demands of current government
services and of the program of capital development that, with
given policies and institutions, the State and private enterprise plan
to carry out. As a first approximation we should judge the extent
to which tax rates can be reduced after the removal of the deadweight debt not by the criterion that the balance between budgetary revenue and expenditure should be unaffected, but by the
criterion that the demand of private citizens for goods and services
for private consumption should be unchanged. If this criterion is
applied, there can be no doubt that the removal of the deadweight
debt will permit some reduction of tax rates even in the extreme
conditions which we have been envisaging, in which, because of
the incidence of death duties, it will at unchanged rates of tax
worsen the balance between budgetary revenue and expenditure.

This can be demonstrated by the following example. In both
the pre-levy and the post-levy situations a representative citizen has
a net tax-free income of £1,000, but in the former situation he
possesses a property of £10,000 and in the latter he possesses only
£5,000 of property. His consumption will be greater in the first than
in the second case simply because he has so much property; and
if death duties are high and progressive, his consumption in the
first situation may be higher still because he is allowed to consume
all his property during his lifetime but cannot hand much of it
on to his heirs. But in the first situation the State will be enjoying
a large revenue from death duties (since some citizens will be
dying each year and handing on their considerable properties),
whereas in the second situation the State will receive much less
revenue from death duties because there is only half as much
private property to hand on at death. Now, since *ex hypothesi*
our citizen has the same tax-free income in both situations, the
State has already reduced rates of taxation of income between the
first and second situation sufficiently to leave him with the same net
tax-free income, even though he has lost half his income from
property. This in itself will have left the balance of revenue and
expenditure in the budget unchanged, since the State has lost in
tax payments by him exactly as much as it has reduced its interest
payment to him. But the State will also have lost a large part of its
revenue from death duties since there is now only half as much

private property to pass at death. Nevertheless, because of the Pigou-effect the reduction in our citizen's property will have reduced his expenditure on consumption and tax rates must be reduced still further if private consumption expenditure is to be maintained. In other words, when the deadweight debt is removed not merely should the loss of revenue from death duties be totally disregarded, but in addition rates of taxation on income can properly be reduced by more than would be sufficient to maintain the previous balance between revenue and expenditure even if there had been no fall in revenue from death duties.

V

The disappearance of the deadweight debt would also have a revolutionary effect in the capital and money markets through changes in the amount and the structure of capital assets available to be held by the banks and the rest of the private sector of the economy, and this would have some marked effects upon economic incentives which we must now examine.[13]

Let us divide the assets available to be held by the private sector of our community into four categories, namely: Money, Bills, Bonds, and Equities. Money includes coin, notes, and bank deposits, on all of which no interest is paid but all of which are fixed in money value and can be transferred at a moment's notice with negligible cost. Bills, of which the three-months' treasury bill is the pure example, are reliable promises to pay a fixed sum of money in a short time; their capital value when that time comes will be certain, but there is some possibility of moderate variations in their value with variations in the rate of interest before they reach maturity. Bonds, of which 2½ per cent Consols are the pure example, are reliable promises to pay a fixed annual money income with no obligation to repay the capital sum; income from them is certain but their future capital value may vary widely with variations in the rate of interest. Equities include ordinary shares and real assets like machines; the income from them is uncertain and the rate of interest at which that income should be capitilized is also uncertain; their future capital value is subject to a double risk.

We will for the moment make two simplifying assumptions,

13. See E. Nevin, *The Problem of the National Debt*, for a stimulating description and discussion of the effect of the debt upon the assets held by the various sectors of the United Kingdom economy.

both of which we shall in due course modify. First, let us assume that the disappearance of the deadweight debt does not disturb the banking system and that the total amount of coins, notes, and deposits made available by the banking system to the rest of the private sector of the economy remains unchanged. Second, let us assume that there is no attempt to keep the balance of revenue and expenditure in the budget unchanged, but rather that tax rates are reduced sufficiently to keep the total demand for private consumption goods at its previous level. In this case, since the market for finished goods is undisturbed, we can assume that there is no change in the absolute level of earnings expected on Equities.

There are two main ways in which the disappearance of the national debt might in these circumstances affect the incentive to invest, the first operating directly through the change in the amount of Bills-and-Bonds existing in the market and the second operating through the consequential changes in the prices of Bills, Bonds, and Equities.

The Kaldor-extension of the Pigou effect suggests that people might make all sorts of efforts to rebuild their private fortunes if they had been diminished by the disappearance of the deadweight debt. Such efforts might include greater activity on the part of business men, involving an increased incentive to invest in capital equipment. But there is an important influence operating in the opposite direction. The disappearance of the deadweight debt means that the entrepreneur (whether he be a private business-man or be taken to represent the managing body of a joint-stock company) will have at his command a much smaller amount of assets—and precisely of assets like government Bills-and-Bonds on the security of which, or through the sale of which, it is especially easy to raise funds for the finance of capital development. Both because the ratio of his total assets to liabilities will be lower and because the ratio of his readily realizable assets to other assets will be lower, the typical entrepreneur will be less able to finance projects of capital development, and the risks involved in doing so will be greater. Thus the incentive to invest may be increased, but the ability to finance investment is likely to be reduced, simply by the changes in the quantity of assets.[14]

14. The argument in this paragraph was suggested to me in discussion by Mr. N. Kaldor.

VI

But the disappearance of the deadweight debt will affect the prices as well as the amounts of various assets; and these changes in price may also affect the level of investment. The disappearance of the deadweight debt represents, on the one side, a reduction by that amount in the total capital wealth of the private sector of the community and, on the other hand, an equal reduction in the Bills-and-Bonds available to be held by the private sector, the amounts of Money and of Equities available in the market, and the level of earnings expected on Equities being unchanged. But when a private citizen has £5,000 less capital to hold with asset prices and expectations unchanged, he is unlikely to choose to hold £5,000 less Bills-and-Bonds; although his reduction in holdings of Money, Bills, Bonds, and Equities will not necessarily all be in the same proportion, he is likely to want at current asset prices to hold somewhat less of each type of asset.[15] In other words the disappearance of the deadweight debt will cause a scarcity of Bills-and-Bonds relatively to Money and relatively to Equities; in an otherwise unchanged market situation, the price of Bills-and-Bonds will probably rise in terms of Money and in terms of Equities.

The rise of the price of Bills-and-Bonds in terms of Money represents a fall in the rate of interest. The rise in the price of Bills-and-Bonds relatively to that of Equities represents a rise in the risk-premium. The margin between the rate of yield on Equities, on the one hand, and on Bills-and-Bonds, on the other hand, will be increased. It will be easier to borrow for capital development by the issue of fixed interest debentures than by the issue of ordinary shares. There will be a premium on capital development of a safe kind.

It would, of course, always be possible for the government to offset this change in asset prices by itself supplying risk-bearing. This it could do by issuing Bills-and-Bonds and investing the proceeds in Equities, so that, while the deadweight debt was eliminated, there remained a considerable governmental liability in the form of government Bills-and-Bonds balanced by an equal asset in the form of governmental investments in private industry.[16]

---

15. He will presumably wish to reduce his holding of foreign assets as well as of domestic assets. In this way a reduction of domestic deadweight debt might cause some easement on the capital account of a country's balance of payments.

16. In terms of our analytical capital levy this result would be brought about

But suppose that the government took no such action. Then, as we have seen, there will be some rise in the price of Bills-and-Bonds in terms of Money; this will represent a fall in the pure rate of interest; and a lower pure rate of interest is a price change which may help to stimulate some extra investment in safe, long-term projects such as house-building.

But a change in the price of Equities (which represents the market valuation placed on machines and other real assets in industry) is more likely to affect investment than is a change in the price of Bills-and-Bonds. Bills-and-Bonds go up in terms of Money and in terms of Equities. But will Equities go up or down in terms of Money?

The outcome will depend upon whether Bills-and-Bonds are better substitutes for Money than for Equities or whether, on the contrary, they are better substitutes for Equities than for Money. When the government Bills-and-Bonds disappear, the amounts of Money and of Equities remaining unchanged, the representative private citizen has got to increase by a given amount the proportion of his assets which he holds in Money and by another given amount the proportion of his assets which he holds in Equities. If Bills-and-Bonds are a good substitute for Money, then only a small rise will be needed in the money price of Bills-and-Bonds to persuade the representative citizen to make the needful shift into Money; and if Bills-and-Bonds are a bad substitute for Equities, a large rise in the price of Bills-and-Bonds will be necessary in terms of Equities to bring about the needed shift into Equities. In these conditions there will be only a small rise in the money price of Bills-and-Bonds, i.e., only a small fall in the pure rate of interest; and the increase in the risk premium will be large and will be brought about by a fall in the price of Equities. Similarly, in the opposite conditions where Bills-and-Bonds are a bad substitute for Money but a good substitute for Equities, the price of Bills-and-Bonds will rise a lot and the rate of interest will fall a lot in order to cause the necessary shift to Money; but the risk premium will

---

and all asset prices would remain unchanged if those liable to the capital levy were allowed at their choice to pay in Money, Bills, Bonds, or Equities, and if the government, after canceling any government Bills-and-Bonds which the payers of the levy surrendered, itself held on to the other private assets handed over to it, leaving outstanding in private ownership any government Bills-and-Bonds which had not been surrendered to it in payment of the levy.

have to rise only a little to cause the necessary shift to Equities, so that the money price of Equities will rise almost as much as the money price of Bills-and-Bonds.

Which of these two things is likely to happen in fact? We must distinguish between Bills-and-Bonds. Bills are more like Money than are Bonds, and Bonds are more like Equities than are Bills. When the private citizen loses his Bills he is likely to go for Money. But in fact most government short-term debt is held by the banks. As long as we are assuming that the banks are not disturbed by the change but supply an unchanged amount of money, the effect of the disappearance of the national debt on the private sector's structure of assets will be mainly a loss of Bonds. When property-owners are starved of Bonds will they shift to Money or to Equities?

There is, I think, no simple answer to this question. One can imagine circumstances in a mature economy with a tendency to secular stagnation in which exceedingly low rates of interest are necessary to prevent deflation, so that a further fall in interest rates is almost out of the question. In this case an increased risk margin will show itself in a fall in the money price of Equities rather than in a rise in the money price of Bonds. The disappearance of the deadweight debt will have made an already deflationary situation still more deflationary. On the other hand, one can imagine a buoyant situation in which interest rates are very high and in which it is the scarcity of capital rather than of risk bearing and of profitable opportunities for investment which holds back further development. In these circumstances a scarcity of Bonds might well cause a substantial fall in the rate of interest which might carry upwards the money price of Equities; and in this case, insofar as price effects in the capital market are concerned, the disappearance of the national debt would have made an inflationary situation still more inflationary.

But the analysis in the last paragraph has not allowed for the fact that substantial deflations or inflations of the general level of prices may be in progress and may be expected to continue. The capital value of Bills and the interest payable on Bonds are fixed in terms of Money; in the case of Equities, neither capital value nor yield is fixed. For this reason in times of rapidly changing money prices Bills-and-Bonds are likely to be better substitutes for Money than for Equities. This is an added reason why the disappearance of the national debt is likely to exert a deflationary influence on the price of Equities.

VII

We have still to modify our two assumptions that the disappearance of the deadweight debt does nothing in itself to affect either the absolute level of earnings expected on Equities or the total supply of Money. In fact in both these respects also it might exert a strong deflationary force.

For the reasons developed in Section II above, the disappearance of the deadweight debt would be likely to increase the propensity to save. The effects of this we have so far assumed to be offset by a reduction of tax rates by the government sufficient to restore private expenditure to its previous level. But, of course, tax rates might not be reduced in this way. The increase in savings and decrease in expenditure on consumption goods caused by the disappearance of the deadweight debt might be acceptable to the government if there was initially a strong inflationary pressure which it was desired to counteract. Or the reduction in the demand for consumption goods might be acceptable even in the absence of any inflationary pressure, if it was thought that too much of the community's resources was being devoted to consumption and too little to investment. In this case the reduced expenditure on consumption, by causing a fall in the absolute level of earnings expected on Equities would cause an undesirable deflationary pressure. In order that this should not cause an actual deflation of total demand, it would then be necessary for there to be an increase in total investment expenditure equal to the reduction in expenditure on consumption goods. To engineer an increased expenditure on capital development, when the market for finished consumption goods was actually being contracted, might require a very large increase in monetary liquidity and fall in interest rates or risk premium. In such circumstances the disappearance of the deadweight debt might well be deflationary unless the total supply of Money were considerably increased.

But how would the supply of Money react to the disappearance of the deadweight debt? At present the supply of Money depends upon the liquidity of the banking system which depends upon the issue of a sufficient amount of liquid treasury bills to be shuffled about between the Bank of England, the Discount Houses, and the

Clearing Banks. If these higher banking mysteries remain unchanged, then the disappearance of the deadweight debt including the disappearance of all government Bills would make the banking system highly illiquid and would cause a reduction in the supply of Money.[17] This deflationary effect could be offset if the government, while its net debt was zero, issued Bills to the banks and invested the money so borrowed in private Bonds or Equities. The government would buy private Bonds-and-Equities with government Bills in order that the banks might buy Bills with Money, unless there were a change in banking arrangements so that the banks themselves in these conditions bought Bonds-and-Equities with Money.

VIII

Whether the net effect of the disappearance of the deadweight debt would be inflationary or deflationary rests upon a complex balance of forces. The outstanding deflationary possibility would be its effect upon the banking system. If all treasury bills disappeared there would in present conditions be a catastrophic monetary deflation. Let us leave this on one side and assume that some alternative method is found for controlling the supply of Money. This is a *sine qua non* for the removal of the deadweight debt.

There would remain a number of conflicting forces at work.

(i) Because of the Pigou-effect people are likely to spend less on consumption and to save more, which in itself will be a deflationary force.

(ii) Because of the Kaldor-extension of the Pigou-effect and because of reductions in marginal rates of tax people are likely to produce more goods and services. Since producers are likely to increase their expenditures by less than their incomes (particularly when rates of taxation on incomes are high and progressive), this is likely to increase supplies relatively to demand and to exert a deflationary influence.

(iii) Entrepreneurs will have a smaller amount of easily re-

17. If the national debt consisted entirely of Bills held partly by the banks and partly by private owners and if, as is probable, Bills are a good substitute for Money, then the disappearance of the national debt would cause a large reduction of Money-and-Bills with an unchanged stock of privately issued Bonds-and-Equities. In this case the money prices of Bonds and of Equities would fall. In other words, the pure rate of interest would rise because the change would be essentially one of reduced liquidity.

alizable assets in their ownership and this will make the finance of investment more difficult.

(iv) If Bonds are a good substitute for Money and a poor substitute for Equities, then the disappearance of government Bonds is likely to cause only a small rise in the price of Bonds but a large fall in the price of Equities. This would probably exercise a deflationary effect upon investment. If, on the other hand, Bonds were a bad substitute for Money and a good substitute for Equities, the prices of Bonds and Equities would both rise with a consequential inflationary effect upon investment. But, as we have seen, in periods of rapid fluctuations in commodity prices, Bonds are unlikely to be a good substitute for Equities, and the inflationary effect upon Equity prices is not very probable in such circumstances.

(v) The desire to rebuild private fortunes which have been reduced by the disappearance of government debt might stimulate business men to greater risk-bearing and enterprise and thus to a higher level of expenditure on investment programs.

On balance it would appear probable that, even apart from any effects on the supply of Money through the banking system, the disappearance of the deadweight debt would exert a significant deflationary influence. But, provided always that the government has a firm grip upon monetary institutions and policies and is prepared so to control its monetary and fiscal policies as to stabilize the total demand for goods and services, this in present-day conditions must be counted a great advantage of the removal of the debt. In present-day conditions of economic expansion and buoyancy interest rates and rates of taxation have to be kept at otherwise undesirably high levels in order to avoid the threat of inflation. The disappearance of the deadweight debt could provide just the occasion for an otherwise desirable relaxation of monetary and fiscal conditions.

The danger might, however, remain that through the increased difficulty of finding finance for risky investment projects and through an increase in the risk premium on Equities, there would be a special deterrent to innovation and to the application of new and risky techniques. To counteract such a tendency it might be necessary for the government to relax its monetary and fiscal policies in ways which specially favored innovation and enterprise (e.g., by tax allowances for new investment), and to introduce new arrangements for the provision of risk capital through public or semi-public institutions. But, given this, the disappearance of the deadweight debt could be made the occasion for a great improvement in economic incentives.

IX

This paper has been devoted to the question whether an internal national debt is an economic burden or not. The method of analysis of this problem has been to remove the debt by means of an imaginary capital levy to see what difference this would make to economic incentives, if everything also remained unchanged. Our analysis has suggested that in certain important respects the existence of a large deadweight debt seriously blunts economic incentives. But before we rush to rebuild society with a zero deadweight debt there are two further questions which would require extensive investigation. In this paper they can only be briefly mentioned.

The first remaining problem is this. Granted that a positive deadweight debt is a burden, it does not follow that the optimum size for the deadweight debt is zero. Perhaps a negative debt would be still better. Or in terms of our national capital levy, why should the total levy be just equal to the deadweight debt? Might there not be advantages if it were still bigger and left the State a net creditor instead of a net debtor to the private sector of the economy? The argument for such a development runs as follows. The government has expenditures to finance on defense, justice, police, education, health, and social security. For this it has to impose taxes. Rates of tax cause divergences between efforts and rewards and thus interfere with economic incentives. If the State were a net owner of property which it itself used productively or hired out to the private sector of the economy, it would itself obtain a net income from rents, interest, and profits which it could use to finance part of its expenditures so that rates of tax could be further reduced. Provided that the State's property was devoted to uses where the marginal social return on it was at least as high as it would have been if it had been left in private ownership, the reduction in tax rates would represent a further net improvement in economic incentives; and there would, of course, be a still greater Pigou-effect stimulating private savings.

There would remain the question of the kind of assets which

the State should hold. Some assets, like roads, schools, and the equipment of nationalized industries are obvious candidates. But for the rest should the State invest in private Bonds or in private Equities? If it invested its funds in fixed charges like ground rents, mortgages, and debentures, it would still further usurp the function of the private *rentier*. The private-property-owner would willy-nilly be forced to become more and more of a private risk bearer, if not an actual entrepreneur. If, on the other hand, this would reduce the supply of risk-bearing too seriously, the State would have to hold private Equities rather than private Bonds; and an arrangement which was devised in the first place to give the State an income from property would have the indirect effect of forcing the State into participation in the management of private industry.

But with the present gigantic deadweight debt these problems are all ones for a still far distant Utopia. We should be happy enough to see a substantial reduction in the debt without demanding even its total elimination, much less its replacement by a net ownership of property by the State. Even so, there remains the great practical question: how is the reduction to be effected? The fact that the deadweight debt is a serious and real economic burden does not itself prove that it should be removed or even reduced. It might be a good thing if it had never existed; but it does exist and the best cure might be worse than the disease.

The first possibility is to use the capital levy not merely as a tool of economic analysis, but also as a practical means of debt redemption. I have been persuaded that we should not.[18] We have to face the following dilemma. A levy can be successful only if it is not expected that it will be repeated, since the expectation of a further levy would destroy all incentives to save. A successful levy will lead to the expectation that it will be repeated unless it is on such a scale that there remains no case for a repeat. But a levy on this scale would present such problems of administration and valuation, would so disturb the structure of the capital market, and would involve such vast changes in personal wealth that it really lies outside the range of what is practicable or suitable in our evolutionary methods of social and economic reform.

But alternative and less revolutionary methods are available to

18. The argument is exceedingly well put by Mr. C. A. R. Crosland in pp. 311–18 of his *The Future of Socialism*.

reduce the burden of the national debt. We may perhaps take the ratio of deadweight debt to total privately owned property as an index of the relative size of the debt. There remain three ways of reducing this proportion, namely: inflation, private savings, and public savings through budget surpluses.

First, it can be very effectively reduced by inflation. This has in fact been happening since the war. In the nine years since 1947-49 the general level of money prices of fixed assets in this country has risen by some 45 per cent. In 1947-49, 43 per cent of private property was deadweight debt.[19] If this 43 per cent remains fixed in money values and the other 57 per cent rises by 45 per cent in money values, then the deadweight debt represents only 34 per cent instead of 43 per cent of total private property.[20]

Second, the relative importance of the deadweight debt can be reduced by the accumulation of private savings.[21] Such savings, matched by an expansion of the community's real capital assets, represent a growth of total privately owned property, so that any given amount of deadweight debt will represent a smaller proportion of total privately owned property. In the nine years, 1948-57, total private savings reckoned at 1948 prices amounted to about £6,100 million, which represents an addition of some 15 per cent to the £40,500 million of total privately owned property which was estimated to exist in 1947-49.[22] Such an increase would reduce the proportion of deadweight debt to total privately owned property from 43 per cent to 38 per cent.

Third, there is the old-fashioned method of debt reduction through an annual surplus of revenue over expenditure in the State budget. Such public savings have a double effect in reducing the proportion of total privately owned property which takes the form

19. J. R. Hicks, *The Social Framework.*
20. I would like to thank Mr. J. Longden of the Faculty of Economics and Politics, University of Cambridge, for help in the preparation of the estimates in this and the following paragraphs.
21. For this and the following paragraph the total savings of the community have been divided between private and public savings. Private savings include the surpluses of public corporations as well as the undistributed profits of ordinary companies. The realization of assets for the payment of death duties has been treated as a reduction of private savings and accordingly the receipt of death duties has been allowed to swell the budget surplus. The current revenue of the public authorities, and so their savings also, includes the receipts of foreign aid. Public savings include the surpluses of local authorities as well as of the central government.
22. J. R. Hicks, *The Social Framework.*

of deadweight debt. Suppose that the government has an excess of revenue over current expenditure of £1 million. If the government invests this sum in new public works like schools, then £1 million of existing government debt ceases to be uncovered by real assets. Privately owned property remains unchanged in total, but it consists of £1 million less of deadweight debt and £1 million more of claims backed by real assets. If the government uses its surplus of £1 million to redeem outstanding national debt, then private owners must hold £1 million less of government debt and they must invest this sum in £1 million worth of additional private real assets. The ratio of the former to the latter has fallen both because the former has decreased and also because the latter has increased. During the nine years 1948-56 public savings amounted at 1948 prices to some £3,100 million. If we subtract this figure from the £17,500 million of deadweight debt outstanding in 1947-49 and add it to the £23,000 million of other privately owned property, outstanding at that time,[23] the ratio of deadweight debt to total privately owned property is reduced from 43 per cent to 36 per cent.

Nowadays, the desirability of a budget surplus is often argued on one or both of two grounds: first, that high levels of taxation and low levels of governmental expenditure are desirable in order to exert a disinflationary pressure in an inflationary situation and, second, that public savings through a budget surplus are a desirable supplement to private savings in order that, in the interest of economic growth, more resources may be devoted to capital development at the expense of immediate consumption. I would like to restore a third old-fashioned argument for a budget surplus, namely, that it will help to reduce the national debt and thereby improve economic incentives in the future.

Additional taxation even if it were paid wholly out of savings (i.e., even if it caused no reduction at all in private consumption and therefore served no useful purpose in fighting inflation or promoting economic growth) would nevertheless serve a useful purpose in debt redemption. It would reduce the amount of national debt held by individuals even though it caused no net increase in their holding of other assets. Of course, taxes imposed for this purpose as for all others should have as little adverse effect as possible upon current incentives for work and enterprise; the

23. J. R. Hicks, *The Social Framework*.

point is only that if taxes are imposed for debt redemption, they are not to be ruled out because they are paid out of private savings. Death duties and annual taxes assessed not on income but on the value of privately owned property may fall into this category. Such taxes may have the smallest adverse effects upon work and enterprise (though it would be rash to claim that they have no such effects), but they are likely to be paid wholly or in large part out of private savings. It might be wise to build up a considerable budget surplus financed out of these taxes and to use it for the redemption of the national debt.[24]

A budget surplus can also be achieved by a reduction in budgetary expenditure insofar as this is not offset by a reduction in rates of taxation. If expenditure is reduced for the purpose of debt redemption, the future advantages of a lower national debt are gained at the expense of the present restriction of government expenditure below the level which would otherwise be considered desirable.

Indeed we are faced as so often in economic policy, with a dilemma. There would be great future advantages in improved economic incentives if the debt were reduced. But the methods of doing this are likely to worsen economic conditions in the immediate present. Inflation is the great debt-reducer, but has many other bad marks to be set against it. Private savings may be stimulated, but after a point only by means of systems of taxation which involve a reduction in public savings or are undesirable on distributional or similar grounds.[25] A budget surplus can be achieved only by further increases in tax rates or by a reduction

24. Taxes of this sort (and in particular death duties) are not of the kind whose rates can appropriately be frequently varied. Insofar as variations in tax rates are needed to control total expenditure in order to avoid inflations and deflations of demand, alterations in rates of taxation on income or on purchases are more appropriate. But if, over and above such rates, there is a considerable and fairly stable revenue from death duties and other taxes which are paid out of savings, it should be possible normally to run a considerable budget surplus. Any reductions in other taxes which may then at any time be needed to offset the threat of a general deflation will involve the reduction of a budget surplus rather than the incurring of an actual deficit. Revenue from taxes paid out of savings thus allows fiscal measures to be used for reflationary purposes without a budget deficit and thus without building up once more a deadweight debt.

25. I would exempt from this criticism any shift from a progressive tax on income to an equally progressive tax on expenditure which, if administratively practicable, should greatly stimulate savings without other seriously adverse effects.

in other budgetary expenditures—when it is a main purpose of debt reduction to enable a given level of other budgetary expenditures to be maintained without the disincentive effects of high taxation. The purpose of this paper is the limited one of showing in what ways the existence of a large national debt blunts economic incentives; it has not attempted to assess the balance between the immediate costs and the ultimate gains of different methods of debt reduction.

C/ IS THE NATIONAL DEBT A BURDEN? A CORRECTION*

BY *J. E. Meade*

In my article in the *Oxford Economic Papers* for June, 1958, I made a serious mistake.[1] The point which I overlooked is one which would tend to raise the money price of privately held assets after their quantity had been reduced by the capital levy. The total value of the remaining capital assets would thus be greater than I allowed in my article; but, as I argue in this note, the rise in their price would not normally be great enough to restore the total value of privately held assets to their pre-levy value. Some element of the Pigou-effect (discussed in Section II of my article) would remain.

My blunder was as follows. In section VI of my article I argued as if the functional relationship expressing the demands for Money, Bills, Bonds, and Equities in terms of the total Money value of assets to be held and of the Money prices of Bills, Bonds, and Equities would be the same before and after the levy. But this is not so because of the lower rate of tax on interest and dividends after the levy. The gross (or *cum* tax) and net (or *ex* tax) yield on Money is always zero; with a gross yield on Bonds of 4 per cent, the net yield is 2 per cent with a rate of tax of 10s. in the

* Reprinted by permission from *Oxford Economic Papers*, XI (June, 1959).

1. This mistake has come to light as a result of a correspondence with Mr. John Spraos, to whom I would like to acknowledge my indebtedness.

£ and 3 per cent with a rate of tax of 5s. in the £. This means that, after the levy, income-yielding assets become so much the more attractive at any given price in terms of Money. This will cause their price to be driven up (i.e., their gross yield or the rate of interest to be driven down) not only because they are now scarce relatively to Money (the point which I made) but also because their net yield is now higher while that on Money remains zero (the point which I overlooked in my article).

Nevertheless, I think that there remains a presumption that the price of income-yielding assets (Bills, Bonds, and Equities) will not rise to the extent necessary to restore the total value of such assets to the pre-levy total. The argument may be put in the form of a *reductio ad absurdum.* Suppose that the rate of interest did fall to the extent necessary to restore the pre-levy total value of all assets. Then there are two reasons why it would rise again.

First, the net rate of yield on such assets would now be *lower* than in the pre-levy situation and this would cause people to desert income-yielding assets for Money, i.e., would cause some rise in the rate of interest. The reason for this is that, while the loss of interest on the national debt is exactly counterbalanced by a reduction of income tax (assuming income tax to be the only form of tax and a balanced budget to be maintained), the loss of interest on debt is wholly a loss of income from property but the gain through lower tax is spread over earned and unearned income. Thus the tax-free income from property is lower post-levy than pre-levy, so that if the total market value of property is to be the same post-levy as pre-levy the net rate of return on income-yielding property must be lower post-levy than pre-levy. If the tax remission were confined to the remission of tax on income from property, it might be argued that the first presumption in the capital market is that the total value of income-yielding assets will be exactly restored by a fall in the rate of interest; for in this case the amount of Money, the value of other assets, and the net yield on other assets would all remain unchanged; but insofar as some of the tax remission is on earned income the net yield on income-yielding assets is reduced and their value will tend to fall.

Second, suppose that the tax remission were confined to taxation of income from property so that the above considerations would not prevent the value of assets being restored to their pre-levy level. There would now be no Pigou-effect to cause a rise in savings and so a deflation in the demand for consumption goods, and for exactly the same reason there would be no deflationary influence damping down investment of the kind which I mentioned in my article. But insofar as the rate of interest affects investment, there would now be an inflationary demand for investment goods because it is the *gross* and not the *net* rate of yield which affects investment incentives. So far nothing would have happened to make people expect a lower gross rate of profit on any given new investment, but the gross rate of interest would have fallen so as to keep the net tax-free rate of yield unchanged. The fall in the rate of interest would cause an inflation; and if monetary policy and not budgetary policy were used to prevent this the amount of Money would have to be reduced and the rate of interest raised again somewhat, so that the total value of assets would fall. Indeed, if on these grounds monetary policy was so devised as to keep the gross rate of interest at its pre-levy level, there would be a completely unmitigated Pigou-effect; the total value of privately held assets would fall by the amount of the levy.

The net effect of this correction is, therefore, to suggest that, while there would still be a Pigou-effect, it might be less marked than I supposed it to be in my article.

Chapter Three

THE CHALLENGE TO THE
NEW ORTHODOXY

═══════════════════════════════════════

A/ THE ITALIAN TRADITION IN FISCAL THEORY*

BY *James M. Buchanan*

The theory of public debt has been a central issue in Italian fiscal theory, and the contributions of Italian scholars are sufficiently unique, both in approach and analysis, to warrant a special discussion. The issue, in effect the debate, has been drawn almost exclusively in terms of the basic Ricardian proposition concerning the fundamental equivalence between extraordinary taxes and public loans.

The Ricardian thesis was elaborated and extended by De Viti De Marco.[1] Ricardo argued that the fully rational individual should be indifferent as between paying an extraordinary tax of $2,000 once-and-for-all and paying an annual tax of $100 in perpetuity, assuming an interest rate of 5 per cent. He extended this analysis to apply to all individuals, and concluded that if the government borrows $2,000 and commits taxpayers to finance interest pay-

---

* Reprinted by permission from James M. Buchanan, *Fiscal Theory and Political Economy: Selected Essays* (Chapel Hill: The University of North Carolina Press, 1960). The Italian discussion contains many of the arguments which appear in the following articles.

1. Antonio De Viti De Marco, "La pressione tributaria dell' imposta e del prestito," *Giornale degli economisti* (1893) I, 38-67, 216-31. Essentially the same analysis is contained in *First Principles of Public Finance*, tr. E. P. Marget (New York: 1936), pp. 377-98.

ments of $100 annually, the individual living in a future income period would find himself in an identical position with that which he would have enjoyed had the government chosen to impose the extraordinary tax of $2,000. The individual will fully capitalize the future tax payments when the debt is created, and he will write down the capital value of the income-earning assets which he owns by the present value of these future tax payments.

The limited life span of the individual does not affect the analysis. If an individual pays the once-and-for-all extraordinary tax, his heirs will receive capital assets reduced in value by this amount. If, on the other hand, the debt is created, his heirs will receive capital assets yielding a higher gross income. But when the interest charge is deducted, the net income stream is identical with that received in the tax situation.

The analysis would, at first glance, appear to apply only for those individuals possessing patrimony or capital. Its extension to individuals, members of professional or laboring groups, who own no income-earning assets is not initially evident. But Ricardo, and De Viti De Marco, anticipated this and made this extension. The individual who possesses no capital assets which he can sell to raise funds to meet his extraordinary tax obligation must of necessity borrow privately, thereby obligating himself to meet future interest charges on a private debt. In this case, provided only that the interest rates on the public and the private debts are the same, the individual owes an equivalent interest charge in each future period. The effect of the government's replacing the extraordinary tax with the public loan is nothing more than the replacement of a whole set of private loan arrangements with the public loan.[2]

It is at this point that Ricardo as well as De Viti De Marco became confused. Accepting the restrictive assumptions necessary for the analysis to be valid, how does this analysis affect the question as to whether the burden of the debt is shifted forward in time? Both Ricardo and De Viti suggested that the full burden of the debt must rest on individuals living at the time of debt creation.

But how may the "burden" of the debt be defined? In one sense we may define it as the sacrifice of goods and services which

2. The most complete statement of Ricardo's position is to be found in: *Principles of Political Economy and Taxation, Works and Correspondence* (London: Royal Economic Society, 1951), I, 244-46.

could have been consumed if the public expenditure which the debt financed had not been undertaken. It is clear that burden in this sense must rest on individuals living in future generations. They are the individuals who must sacrifice a portion of their income for debt service which they otherwise could have consumed. And the fact that bondholders receive the interest payments on internal debt does not modify this conclusion. If, however, the burden of the debt is defined in this manner, how can individuals living in future time periods be in equivalent positions in the two situations, with the debt and with the extraordinary tax. The answer can only be that individuals living in future time periods *must also bear the real burden of the extraordinary tax under the narrowly restrictive Ricardian-De Vitian assumptions.* It is true that, under these assumptions, the effects of the loan and the extraordinary tax are equivalent, but the correct inference is that the real burden of both is passed on to future time periods, not that this burden is borne in both cases by the individuals living during the initial period.

This rather paradoxical conclusion may be readily seen when the nature of the extraordinary tax required to make the Ricardian proposition hold is examined. Both Ricardo and De Viti assumed that such a tax would either be drawn wholly from privately-held capital assets, that is to say, that individuals would sell off capital holdings sufficiently to finance the tax obligation, or they would create private debts (incur capital liabilities) to the full amount of the individual share of the tax. In other words, the extraordinary tax was to be a capital levy *in fact,* regardless of the form which the fiscal authority chooses. If the full amount of the tax is financed from capital, then it becomes clear that the current generation does not suffer any real income reduction. The current generation essentially "draws on capital" in the form of the public project undertaken.

The failure to grasp this point appears to have been fundamental, but the reason for this is not difficult to find. The individuals who are coercively forced to give up resources, whether these are drawn from consumption or investment uses, are normally considered to "bear" the costs of the project financed. Taxes, of any sort, are held to impose a sacrifice on individuals during the period when the tax obligations must be met. This becomes a reasonable, and correct, inference when it is recognized that the ownership of capital assets itself provides some utility to the individual. This being the case, we can say that regardless of the source of the funds paid out in taxes, the individual undergoes a "sacrifice" of utility. It may also be claimed that, if individuals fully discount future tax obligations, the creation of future interest payments on a debt reduces the present value of an expected utility stream. Thus, both the extraordinary tax and the public debt of like amount must be "paid" by individuals during the time of the original transaction.

Thus, we have reached diametrically opposing conclusions; first we stated that the burden of both the extraordinary tax and the public loan rests, under the Ricardian-De Vitian assumptions, exclusively on individuals living in future time periods. This conclusion holds when we consider burden in terms of sacrificed real goods and services. Secondly, we stated that the burden of both the extraordinary tax and the public loan rests, under the full Ricardian-De Vitian assumptions, on the individuals living during the initial period. This conclusion holds when we try to measure sacrifice or burden in terms of the change in present value of an expected or anticipated utility stream, and when we attribute some positive utility to the holding of income-earning assets.

The confusion of these two concepts becomes especially likely when it is recognized that the actual form of any conceivable tax levy, either extraordinary or normal, must differ from the Ricardian model in the direction which adds to the confusion. The Ricardian model overlooks the essential difference between the coercive levy of taxes and the voluntary subscription to public loans. Any coercive imposition of a tax seems certain to reduce both current consumption spending and investment spending. The assumption that only the latter is affected, that is, only private capital formation is reduced (private liability formation increased), is clearly incorrect. If we make the assumption that an individual attempts at any point in time to attain some marginal equalization between the present value of expected future enjoyments of income and the present value of current enjoyments of income, then any tax imposition will cause him to adjust both types of outlay downward. Some portion of any tax must come from current consumption spending, whatever the form that this tax takes. This being the case, some share of the extraordinary tax comes to rest on individuals living in the initial period, even if we consider only the real aspects and ignore the utility aspects altogether. On the other hand, the public loan operates through voluntary subscription. Individuals are likely to reduce current consumption outlay only insofar as the interest rate encourages an increased rate of saving, a questionable relationship. The major share of funds going into the purchase of government securities does come from private capital formation. The generation of individuals currently living sacrifices nothing in utility and little, if anything, in real goods and services in creating the loan. Therefore, in the real sense, there is a differential effect between the extraordinary tax and the public loan.

This differential effect is further widened when it is recognized that the full Ricardian assumptions do not hold on the utility side either. Individuals do not fully discount future tax payments. If the Ricardian-De Vitian reasoning is accepted for all individuals owning capital assets and receiving sufficient income to allow them to borrow privately, there still may be other large groups of individuals. These comprise the bulk of the lower income or laboring classes. It is impossible to levy extraordinary taxes on these individuals. The extraordinary tax must be levied on the first two groups. But, if the public debt is created, some portion of the annual interest charges may be placed on the third group. The lower income classes in future time periods may bear a portion of the burden of the public loan whereas they must, by definition, escape fully the burden of the extraordinary tax. This is the objection which Griziotti raised to the De Viti elaboration of the Ricardian thesis.[3]

De Viti De Marco attempted to refute this objection, but he was not really successful. He tried to show that even the complete exemption of all non-propertied individuals from the extraordinary tax would not affect his conclusions. Here he introduced a long-run competitive model. He reasoned that such exemption would tend to increase the relative attractiveness of the professional nonpropertied occupations. This would, in turn, cause more people to enter these occupations and to turn away from those activities such as management and administration of property. In the long run, the lot of the non-propertied classes would tend to be identical

---

3. Benvenuto Griziotti, "La diversa pressione tributaria del prestito e dell' imposta," *Giornale degli economisti* (1917). Reprinted in *Studi di scienza delle finanze e diritto finanziario* (Milan: 1956), II, 193-261.

with that which they would enjoy even if they were taxed for the service of the public loan. As Griziotti suggested, this represents the stretching of the competitive model a bit too far.

Griziotti went further and argued that, even for individuals owning capital assets, discounting of future tax payments does not take place fully. Individuals do not act as if they live forever, and familial lines are not treated as being continuous. There is nothing sacred about maintaining capital intact, and individuals will not necessarily do so. The equivalence hypothesis requires continued abstinence from consuming capital on the part of those holding capital assets after public debt is created. Whereas the extraordinary tax effectively removes from an individual's possibilities the capital sum (once he has paid the tax he can no longer convert at least that portion of his capital into income), the disposition over this capital remains in his power in the public debt case. He may convert this capital into income at any time, without in any way removing the tax obligation on his heirs which is necessitated by the debt service.

Griziotti's claim that the creation of public debts does involve a shifting of the tax burden forward in time was not successful in overcoming the dominance of the De Viti De Marco elaboration of the Ricardian thesis in Italy. The prestige and apparent logical clarity of the De Vitian argument coupled with the changed conditions were successful in reducing the Griziotti influence. There have been isolated supporters of Griziotti,[4] but the De Viti formulation continues to dominate the Italian scene.

Additional elements of the De Viti De Marco conception of public debt may be mentioned since he anticipated much of the "new orthodoxy," which came to be adopted in the United States only after the Keynesian revolution. To anticipate erroneous ideas is, of course, no great contribution, but De Viti's arguments concerning the problem of debt repayment are surprisingly modern in this respect. Included in his discussion of the public debt is what he called the theory of automatic amortization. De Viti used this to demonstrate that debt should never be repaid. De Viti started from his interpretation of the Ricardian argument that public debt merely serves as a substitute for private debts. He

4. For example, see F. Maffezzoni, "Ancora della diversa pressione tributaria del prestito e dell' imposta," *Rivista di diritto finanziario e scienza delle finanze,* IX (1950), 341-75.

assumes a community of three individuals, only one of whom is a capitalist.[5] Now assume that the state requires a sum of 1,200,000 and levies an extraordinary tax, 400,000 on each individual. Individual 1 being the capitalist, individuals 2 and 3 will find it necessary to borrow from him in order to meet their tax obligations paying an assumed interest rate of 5 per cent. As these individuals save in future periods, they may amortize their debt to the capitalist.

Now assume that the government, instead of levying the tax, borrows the 1,200,000 directly from Individual 1. The annual interest charge will be 60,000, and it is assumed to collect 20,000 from each of the three citizens. As in the first case, as individuals 2 and 3 save they may utilize this savings to purchase the government securities, which are assumed to be marketable, from Individual 1. Their purchase of government securities in this case is identical in effect to their paying off private debts in the other case. Therefore, as the government securities are widely circulated among the population the real debt is more or less automatically amortized. Individuals in purchasing debt instruments acquire an asset to offset their tax liabilities. The weight of the debt is effectively destroyed; hence debt need never be repaid and there need be no fear that a country cannot bear the burden of public debts, however heavy these might appear to be.

This construction is both ingenious and misleading. Let us consider the private borrowing case carefully. Individuals 2 and 3, as they accumulate savings, increase their net worth, and they must also increase some item on the asset side, let us say, cash. When they accumulate sufficient cash to warrant paying off a portion of the private debt, the transaction is represented on their balance sheets as a drawing down of the cash item and a corresponding drawing down of their liability item. *Net worth does not change with debt repayment.*[6]

The construction is identical with the public loan. As individuals accumulate savings these must take some form, cash, savings accounts, etc. Net worth is increased along with whatever asset item the individual chooses to put his savings into. At one

5. This argument is developed in *First Principles of Public Finance*, pp. 390-93.
6. Cf. F. Maffezzoni, "Ancora della diversa pressione tributaria del prestito e dell' imposta," p. 348.

point we assume that the individual accumulates sufficient funds to purchase a debt instrument. In so doing, he reduces his cash item and increases another asset item, government securities. He has, in this particular transaction, merely transformed one asset into another. *His net worth is not modified.* Therefore, the weight of having to pay the annual tax upon the debt instrument is precisely as heavy after as before his acquisition of the security.

De Viti De Marco is correct, in the extremes of his model, in saying that this transaction is equivalent to the repayment of private loans. In this sense the public debt is said to be amortized. But his error lies in inferring from this that public debt should not be repaid in fact. This error is based upon a misunderstanding of private loans. Implicit in the De Viti formulation is the idea that the repayment of private loans is necessarily beneficial to the individual. De Viti assumed that such repayment increases private net worth, and thereby reduces the weight or "pressure" of the loan. He failed to see that the new savings which go into private debt repayment have alternative employments. Whether or not private debt repayment reduces "pressure" on the individual economy, depends solely upon the relative rates of return.

The same is true for public debt. Having demonstrated that the transfer of public debt instruments might be similar in some models to private debt repayment, De Viti inferred that this "amortization" reduces the pressure or weight of the public debt. This is not necessarily true at all. The weight of debt remains as it was before, and the purchase of government securities can modify this only insofar as the relative rates of yield on government securities and other assets place the individual in a more preferred position.

This demonstration that the De Viti argument does not show that public debt should not be repaid cannot be applied in reverse. By saying that De Viti De Marco was wrong in making this extension is not to say that public debt *should be repaid*.

B/ CONCERNING FUTURE GENERATIONS*

BY *James M. Buchanan*

The Analytical Framework

Initially I shall discuss public debt in what may be called its "classical" form. The existence of substantially full employment of resources is assumed. Secondly, I shall assume that the debt is to be created for real purposes, not to prevent or to promote inflation. The government desires to secure command over a larger share of economic resources in order to put such resources to use. This assumption suggests that debt instruments are purchased through a transfer of existing monetary units to the government. Thirdly, I shall assume that the public expenditure in question is of a reasonably limited size relative to both the total income and investment of the community, and, consequently, that the effects of the sale of government securities on the interest rate and the price structure are negligible. Fourthly, I shall assume that the funds used to purchase government securities are drawn wholly from private capital formation. I shall also assume that competitive conditions prevail throughout the economy. Finally, I shall make no specific assumption concerning the purpose of the expenditure financed. I shall show that this purpose is not relevant to the problem at this stage of the analysis.

These assumptions may appear at first glance to be unduly severe. They will, of course, be relaxed at later stages in the argument, but it is perhaps worthwhile to point out that these assumptions are largely applicable to the debt problem as it has been, and is being, faced in the 1950's. They apply, by and large, to the highway financing proposals advanced by the Clay Committee in early 1955. They apply, even more fully, to the debt problems facing state and local units of government, which alone borrowed more than five and one-half billions of dollars in 1956.

* Reprinted by permission from James M. Buchanan, *Public Principles of Public Debt*. Copyright 1958 by Richard D. Irwin, Inc., Homewood, Illinois.

By contrast, the assumptions do not accurately reflect the conditions under which the greater part of currently outstanding public debt has been created. This qualification may appear to reduce somewhat the generality of the conclusions reached. Such is, however, not the case. The initial restriction of the analysis to public debt in the "classical" form allows the characteristic features of real debt to be examined; other forms of public debt are less "pure," and it is appropriate that they be introduced only at a second stage of analysis. When this is done in later chapters, the conclusions reached from the initial analysis will be found generally applicable, and the apparently contradictory conclusions stemming from the new orthodoxy will be explained on the basis of the methodological confusion discussed in Chapter 3.

The first of the three basic propositions will now be examined in the light of the specific assumptions stated above.

The Shifting of the Burden to Future Generations

Before we can proceed to discuss the question of the possible shifting of the debt burden, we must first define "future generations." I shall define a "future generation" as any set of individuals living in any time period following that in which the debt is created. The actual length of the time periods may be arbitrarily designated, and the analysis may be conducted in terms of weeks, months, years, decades, or centuries. The length of the period per se is not relevant. If we choose an ordinary accounting period of one year and if we further call the year in which the borrowing operation takes place, t_0, then individuals living in any one of the years, $t_1, t_2, t_3, \ldots t_n$, are defined as living in future "generations." An individual living in the year, t_0, will normally be living in the year, t_1, but he is a different individual in the two time periods, and, for our purposes, he may be considered as such. In other words, I shall not be concerned as to whether a public debt burden is transferred to our children or grandchildren as such. I shall be concerned with whether or not the debt burden can be postponed. The real question involves the possible shiftability or nonshiftability of the debt burden in time, not among "future generations" in the literal sense. Since, however, the "future generation" terminology has been used widely in the various discussions of the subject, I shall continue to employ it, although the particular definition here given should be kept in mind.

What, specifically, do the advocates of the new approach mean when they suggest that none of the primary real burden of the public debt can be shifted to future generations? Perhaps the best clue is provided in a statement from Brownlee and Allen: "The public project is *paid for* while it is being constructed in the sense that other alternative uses for these resources must be sacrificed during this period."[1] (Italics mine.) The resources which are to be employed by the government must be withdrawn from private employments during the period, t_0, not during any subsequent period.

This last statement is obviously true, but the error lies in a misunderstanding of precisely what is implied. The mere shifting of resources from private to public employment does not carry with it any implication of sacrifice or payment. If the shift takes place through the voluntary actions of private people, it is meaningless to speak of any sacrifice having taken place. An elemental recognition of the mutuality of advantage from trade is sufficient to show this. If an individual freely chooses to purchase a government bond, he is, presumably, moving to a preferred position on his utility surface by so doing. He has improved, not worsened, his lot by the transaction. This must be true for each bond purchaser, the only individual who actually gives up a current command over economic resources. Other individuals in the economy are presumably unaffected, leaving aside for the moment the effects of the public spending. Therefore, it is impossible to add up a series of zeroes and/or positive values and arrive at a negative total. The economy, considered as the sum of the individual economic units within it, undergoes no *sacrifice* or *burden* when debt is created.

This simple point has surely been obvious to everyone. If so, in what sense has the idea of burden been normally employed? The answer might run as follows: To be sure no single individual undergoes any sacrifice of utility in the public borrowing process because he subscribes to a voluntary loan. But in terms of the whole economy, that is, in a macro-economic model, the resources are withdrawn from private employment in the period of debt creation, not at some subsequent time. Therefore, if this sort of model is to be used, the economy must be treated as a unit, and we may speak of a *sacrifice* of resources during the initial time period. In the macro-economic model we are not concerned with individual utilities, but with macro-economic variables.

It is perhaps not surprising to find this essentially organic concep-

---

1. O. H. Brownlee and E. D. Allen, *Economics of Public Finance* (2nd ed.; New York, 1954), p. 126. Also, see Henry C. Murphy, *The National Debt in War and Transition* (New York, 1950), p. 60.

tion of the economy or the state incorporated in the debt theory of Adolf Wagner,[2] but it is rather strange that it could have found its way so readily into the fiscal theory of those countries presumably embodying democratic governmental institutions and whose social philosophy lies in the individualistic and utilitarian tradition. The explanation arises, of course, out of the almost complete absence of political sophistication on the part of those scholars who have been concerned with fiscal problems. With rare exceptions, no attention at all has been given to the political structure and to the possibility of inconsistency between the policy implications of fiscal analysis and the political forms existent. Thus we find that, in explicit works of political theory, English-language scholars have consistently eschewed the image of the monolithic and organic state. At the same time, however, scholars working in fiscal analysis have developed constructions which become meaningful only upon some acceptance of an organic conception of the social group.[3]

In an individualistic society which governs itself through the use of democratic political forms, the idea of the "group" or the "whole" as a sentient being is contrary to the fundamental principle of social organization. The individual or the family is, and must be, the basic philosophical entity in this society. This being true, it is misleading to speak of group sacrifice or burden or payment or benefit unless such aggregates can be broken down into component parts which may be conceptually or actually imputed to the individual or family units in the group. This elemental and necessary step cannot be taken with respect to the primary real burden of the public debt. The fact that economic resources are given up when the public expenditure is made does not, in any way, demonstrate the existence of a *sacrifice* or *burden* on individual members of the social group.

The error which is made in attributing a *sacrifice* to the individual who purchases a security, be it publicly or privately issued, has time-honored status. One of its sources, for there must be several, may lie in the classical doctrine of pain cost. Nassau Senior is generally credited with having popularized, among economists, the notion of abstinence. This concept was introduced in order to provide some philosophical explanation and justification for profits or

2. *Finanzwissenschaft* (Leipzig, 1877), Vol. I, p. 122.
3. For a further discussion of this point, see my "The Pure Theory of Government Finance: A Suggested Approach," *The Journal of Political Economy*, LVII, (1949), 496-505.

returns to capital investment. The individual, in abstaining from consuming current income, undergoes the pain of abstinence which is comparable to that suffered by the laborer. Abstinence makes the receipt of profits, in an ethical sense, equally legitimate with wages in the distributive system of the late classical economists.

Traces of this real or pain-cost doctrine are still with us, notably in certain treatments of international trade theory, but neoclassical economic theory has, by and large, replaced this doctrine with the opportunity cost concept. Here the works of Wicksteed and Knight generally and of Ohlin in particular must be noted. In the neoclassical view, resources command a price not due to any pain suffered by their owners, but because these resources are able to produce alternative goods and services. Resources may be used in more than one line of endeavor. A price, that is, a payment to the resource owner, is necessary in order to secure the resource service. Its magnitude is determined by the marginal productivity of the resource in alternative uses.

This shift of emphasis from the real cost to the opportunity cost conception has profound implications, some of which have not yet been fully understood. The real cost doctrine suggests, for example, that a man is paid because he works, while the opportunity cost doctrine reverses this and suggests that a man works because he is paid. The emphasis is placed on the individual choice or decision, and the gain or benefit side of individual exchange is incorporated into the theory of market price. The classical economists did not clearly view the distributive share as a price and the distribution of real income as a pricing problem.[4] Neoclassical theory does interpret the distributive share as a price, and the factor market is subjected to standard supply and demand analysis. The mutuality of gain from trade becomes as real in this market as in any other.

It becomes irrelevant whether the individual undergoes "pain" as measured by some arbitrary calculus when he works. If he works voluntarily, he is revealing that his work, when coupled with its reward, enables him to move to a preferred position. The individual is in no sense considered to be *paying for* the output which he cooperates in producing, merely because his productive services enter

4. For the best discussion of all these points see F. H. Knight, "The Ricardian Theory of Production and Distribution," *Canadian Journal of Economics and Political Science*, 1935. Reprinted in F. H. Knight, *On the History and Method of Economics* (Chicago, 1956), pp. 37-88,

into its production. I am not, in my capacity as a member of the faculty of the University of Virginia, *paying for* the education of young men merely because my time is spent in classroom instruction, time which I could spend alternatively in other productive pursuits. Clearly the only meaningful *paying for* is done by those parents, donors, and taxpayers, who purchase my services as a teacher. What I am paying for when I teach is the income which I earn and by means of this the real goods and services which I subsequently purchase. Only if a part of my income so earned is devoted to expenditure for education can I be considered to be *paying for* education.

All of this is only too obvious when carefully considered. It is a very elementary discussion of the wheel of income which every sophomore in economics learns, or should learn, on the first day of class. If *sacrifice* or *payment* is to be used to refer both to the producer and the final consumer of goods and services, we are double counting in the grossest of ways; we are *paying* double for each unit of real income. We are denying the existence of the circular flow of real income in an organized market economy.

It is not difficult to see, however, that this error is precisely equivalent to that committed by those who claim that the real payment or sacrifice of resources must be made by those living in the period of public debt creation. The purchaser of a government security does not *sacrifice* resources *for* the public project; that is, he does not *pay for* the project any more than I pay for the education of young men in Virginia. He *pays for* real income in some future time period; he exchanges current command over resources for future command over resources. No payment or sacrifice is involved in any direct sense. The public project is *purchased*, and *paid for*, by those individuals who will be forced to give up resources *in the future* just as those who give up resources to pay my salary at the University of Virginia pay for education. It is not the bond purchaser who sacrifices any real economic resources anywhere in the process. He makes a presumably favorable exchange by shifting the time shape of his income stream. This is not one bit different from the ordinary individual who presumably makes favorable exchanges by shifting the structure of his real asset pattern within a single unit of time.

All of this may be made quite clear by asking the simple question: Who suffers if the public borrowing is unwise and the public expenditure wasteful? Surely if we can isolate the group who will be worse off in this case we shall have located the bearers of the primary real burden of the debt. But clearly the bondholder as such is not concerned as to the use of his funds once he has received the bond in exchange. He is guaranteed his income in the future, assuming of course that the government will not default on its obligations or impose differently high taxes upon him through currency inflation. The taxpayer in period t_0 does not sacrifice anything since he has paid no tax for the wasteful project. The burden must rest, therefore, on the taxpayer in future time periods and on no one else. He now must reduce his real income to transfer funds to the bondholder, and he has no productive asset in the form of a public project to offset his genuine *sacrifice*. Thus, the taxpayer in future time periods, that is, the future generation, bears the full primary real burden of the public debt. If the debt is created for productive public expenditure, the benefits to the future taxpayer must, of course, be compared with the burden so that, on balance, he may suffer a net benefit or a net burden. But a normal procedure is to separate the two sides of the account and to oppose a burden against a benefit, and this future taxpayer is the only one to whom such a burden may be attributed.

Widespread intellectual errors are hard to trace to their source. We have indicated that the pain cost doctrine may have been responsible for some of the confusion which has surrounded public debt theory. But there are other possible, and perhaps more likely, sources for the future burden error. One of the most important of these is the careless use of national income accounting which has grown up in the new economics. Attention is focused on the national or community balance sheet rather than on individual or family balance sheets. In relation to debt theory, this creates confusion when future time periods are taken into account. There is no net change in the aggregative totals which make up the national balance sheet because the group includes both bondholders and taxpayers. The debits match the credits, so no net burden in the primary sense is possible. "Future generations" cannot be forced to *pay for* the resources which have already been used in past periods.

This simple sort of reasoning makes two errors. First, the effect on the national balance sheet is operationally irrelevant. As pointed out above, the nation or community is not a sentient being, and decisions are not made in any superindividual or organic way. Individuals and families are the entities whose balance sheets must be examined if the effects on social decisions are to be determined. The presumed canceling out on the national balance sheet is important if, *and only if*, this is accompanied by a canceling out among the individual and family balance sheets.

A moment's consideration will suggest that genuine canceling in the latter sense does not take place. The balance sheet of the bondholder will include an estimated present value for the bond, a value which is calculated on the certain expectation that the interest payments will be made and the bond amortized when due. These interest payments represent the "future" income which the bondholder or his forbears *paid for* by the *sacrifice* of resources in the initial period of debt creation. These payments are the *quo* part of his *quid pro quo*. They are presumably met out of tax revenues, and taxpayers give up command over the use of resources. This sacrifice of income has no direct *quid pro quo* implication; it is a sacrifice imposed compulsorily on the taxpayer by the decision makers living at some time in the past. To be sure, as pointed out above, if the public expenditure is "productive" and is rationally made, the taxpayer may be better off with the debt than without it. His share of the differential real income generated by the public project may exceed his share of the tax. But the productivity or unproductivity of the project is unimportant in itself. In either case, the taxpayer is the one who *pays*, who *sacrifices* real resources. He is the final "purchaser" of the public goods and services whether he is a party to the decision or not. His is the only sacrifice which is offset, if at all, by the income yielded by the public investment of resources made possible by the debt.

From this analysis it is easy to see that much of the recent discussion on the burden of transfer misses the point entirely. One senses as he reads the discussion, notably that of Ratchford, that underlying the argument for the existence of a transfer burden there is an implicit recognition that the primary real burden does fall on taxpayers of future generations.[5] But the transfer burden advocates were unable to escape the real sirens of the new orthodoxy, the na-

5. Ratchford, Pt. IV. Abbott, in his work on debt management, appears also to recognize implicitly that the primary real burden of debt is borne by taxpayers of "future generations." He does not, however, discuss this aspect of the problem directly. See Charles C. Abbott, *Management of the Federal Debt* (New York, 1946).

tional balance sheet and the false analogy. Their deep and correct conviction that all was not happy in the conceptual underpinnings of the newly rediscovered edifice properly led them to re-examine the theory; but they accepted entirely too much before they started. They gave away their case, and their efforts resulted in little more than a slight modification of the theory. They did little more than to force a new emphasis on the secondary burden of making transfers.

The transfer burden analysis suffers the same methodological shortcomings as the more general approach of the new orthodoxy. If public debt issue is analyzed in terms of the whole set of relevant alternatives, in this case notably that of taxation, the burden associated with the making of an interest transfer cannot fail to be viewed as a primary one akin to that which is imposed through taxation. The failure to consider the position of the individual bondholder under each of the alternative situations led the "transfer burden" analysts to accept the fundamental premise of the new orthodoxy, that interest payments do, in a differential sense, represent a net "transfer" among individuals within the economy.

C/ EXCERPTS FROM REVIEWS OF PUBLIC PRINCIPLES OF PUBLIC DEBT

BY *James M. Ferguson*

This section contains brief comments on and brief excerpts from six reviews of Buchanan's book which appeared in leading economic journals. While each of the reviewers applauded many aspects of the book, only the major criticisms of his analysis of the shifting of a burden of the debt onto future generations are discussed. A number of the points made here are developed more fully in subsequent notes and articles on the shifting question.

Professor Alvin H. Hansen [9] (references on page 229) argues:

With respect to the matter of shifting the burden to future generations, the issue basically relates to the impact of the borrowing process and the resulting debt upon the real income of the future generation as a whole.

orrowing achieves a smoother shift of resources to the war
produces fuller and more efficient use of resources, then the
emerge from the war stronger and better equipped to go for-
There remains the incentive problem which we have already
nd the fact that future tax payers must pay more taxes to off-
ationary effects of the added money income received by the
bondo..... rs. . . . On the other hand, Professor Buchanan appears to
exclude altogether the matter of real sacrifices—harder work and re-
stricted consumption—and to limit himself too exclusively to financial
considerations. It is however the *real* factors that are important: in particular the impact of the borrowing upon the *real* income and *real* assets
of future generations [pp. 377-78].

Professor Abba P. Lerner declares that Buchanan is not attacking
the New Orthodoxy, which analyzes the burden due to the existence of internal debt, but rather straw men. Buchanan deals with
the effects of borrowing as compared with taxing and spending in
various situations and refuses, says Lerner, to consider the effects of
existing debt. And in discussing the effects of borrowing as compared with taxing in shifting a burden from the present to future
generations, Lerner [12] argues that Buchanan is not disputing the
New Orthodoxy view:

. . . that a closed society cannot shift any burden from the present into
the future by borrowing money from itself, but what he is really showing is that it is possible by borrowing instead of taxing to make the public at-large feel richer (in part because it is myopic about future taxes),
thus inducing it to consume more, so that less can be invested. This is
indeed a real burden on future generations. But the artificiality of saying
that it is *the debt* that constitutes this shift of burden from the present to
future generations can be brought out by noting that this burden would
in no way be mitigated by the repudiation of the debt at any time in the
future. The New Orthodoxist would merely say that investment enriches
future generations, and anything that reduces investment or induces dis-
investment puts this kind of burden on the future. He would deal with
such effects of debt or of borrowing under the heading of indirect or
secondary effects . . . [p. 205-6].

Professor Alan T. Peacock's criticisms center on the narrowness
and incompleteness of Buchanan's analysis. Buchanan's voluntary
theory of the state implies that taxpayers-cum borrowers freely
choose debt financing as they would in private expenditures, making
it possible to argue that such voluntary decisions imply no future
burden. Peacock objects to Buchanan's use of the term "burden of
the debt" to mean only the primary effects on individuals' net
worth. Buchanan excludes from this term the effects of government

borrowing on price levels, interest rates, and incentives. Peacock [21] concludes:

He is obviously right in insisting that the effects of debt increase must be compared with other methods of financing some given level of expenditure, but wrong to contend that *the consequences* of adopting public borrowing as the means of finance cannot be ascribed to the decision to borrow [p. 166].

Professor B. U. Ratchford declares that Buchanan sometimes fails to distinguish between the monetary and real aspects of the analysis. Ratchford makes an argument similar to that of Peacock when he notes that on the basis of the type of analysis Buchanan presents in the discussion of private debt creation, there is no more burden when the debt is paid off than when it is incurred. He refers to Buchanan's view that while a borrower sacrifices command over resources when he repays his debt, this is no different from the usual sacrifice involved in any expenditure. There does not appear to be any concept of burden other than opportunity cost, aside from the psychological burden connected with the coercive payment of taxes. Ratchford [23] states:

The economy is producing at capacity, and the total production gets distributed among the members of that generation in some fashion; what the taxpayers lose the bondholders gain. The difference in views here is probably based on psychological factors. As the author points out in several places, bondholders usually capitalize the future interest payments and thus discount them; they would receive such payments even if there were no public debt since they could have made private investments. Thus their receipt of interest is not dependent on the existence of the public debt. But taxpayers usually do not capitalize their future liabilities and discount future income accordingly and thus the payment of taxes is a greater psychological burden. But if there had been no public debt and no public project, the private investment funds would have gone into private projects and taxpayers would, as consumers, have paid interest on the investment embodied in the price of the goods produced in lieu of the public project. Taxes are more readily identified and thus psychologically more burdensome. Thus the major question is whether these differences in psychological behavior and financial practices constitute a real economic burden. In my opinion they do not [p. 215].

Professor A. R. Prest suggests that Buchanan means by the term "primary real burden of debt" that some people will suffer in any income-redistribution resulting from a debt issue. But Prest denies that future tax and interest payments can be sharply separated. Prest argues that Buchanan's reasoning appears to break down in a full-employment case where the government expenditure is as productive as the sacrificed alternative, in which case no additional taxes are necessary. Prest [22] concludes by questioning how important it is in practice to locate the debt burden:

> If we assume as a rough hypothesis that debt stays more or less constant in peace-time, then although the sins of the present generation rest on their descendants, they themselves are the legatees of the sins of their own ancestors. It might be plausibly argued on this sort of basis that there is no net handing down of burden from one generation to another generation—leaving war-time out as a different matter [p. 360].

Finally, Professor Earl R. Rolph, like Lerner, repeats that the resources must be surrendered immediately and the opportunity cost of these resources, the value of alternative products cannot be postponed. Rolph [24] also questions whether in practice you can locate who bears the burden:

> The accompanying question of what group in a society is to be identified as paying for the use of resources to produce for government account is a different one and may not even have an answer. . . . Who can say whether the dollars spent on planes that do not fly come from the tax on cigarettes, the income tax on people with taxable incomes in excess of $20,000, from the interest on the British loan, or from the sale of Treasury Bills? What is lost is the output, government or private, that could have been produced instead of the planes [p. 184].

He concludes by predicting that the success of Buchanan's book will depend upon the amount of controversy it provokes!

Chapter Four

SUPPORTERS OF BUCHANAN AND THEIR CRITICS

*A/ THE PUBLIC DEBT: A BURDEN ON FUTURE GEN-
ERATIONS?**

BY *William G. Bowen, Richard G. Davis, and David H. Kopf*

"Personally, I do not feel that any amount can be properly called a surplus as long as the nation is in debt. I prefer to think of such an item as a
reduction on our children's inherited mortgage."
—President Eisenhower, *State of the Union Message,* January 7, 1960.

Two things are certain. The first is that, whatever else this quota-
tion from President Eisenhower's State of the Union Message may
imply, the President appears convinced that the costs of debt-
financed public projects can be passed on to future generations. The
second is that the popular economics textbooks of our day are nearly
unanimous in their rejection of this "naïve" view of the public debt.
The purpose of this brief note is to suggest that in this instance it is
the President who is—in at least one highly important sense—right.[1]

* Reprinted by permission from *The American Economic Review,* L (September, 1960).

1. J. M. Buchanan [1] (references on page 74) is one of the few contempo-
rary economists to argue in favor of the proposition that the real burden of a
public debt *can* be shifted to future generations. It was Buchanan's stimulating
book that started the train of thought that has resulted in the argument contained in this paper. The reason for the present paper is that while Buchanan
has arrived at essentially the same conclusion, he has apparently not succeeded
in convincing very many people that he is right—at any rate, he has not convinced several reviewers of his book (see, for example, the reviews by Rolph

The basic question at issue seems simple indeed: Can the "real burden" of a public project financed by a privately held internal debt be shifted from one generation to another? The usual economics textbook answer to this question is that the burden can *not* be shifted to future generations because government spending must drain real resources from the community at the time the government project is undertaken (assuming full employment of resources) regardless of whether the project is financed by borrowing, taxes, or money creation. As Samuelson puts it: "To fight a war now, we must hurl present-day munitions at the enemy; not dollar bills, and not future goods and services."[2]

What is wrong with this by-now-standard argument? Absolutely nothing, if the real burden of the debt is defined as the total amount of private consumption goods given up by the community *at the moment of time the borrowed funds are spent.* Under this definition of real burden, the cost of the public project simply must be borne by the generations alive at the time the borrowing occurs.

There is, however, another definition of real burden which permits, under certain circumstances, present generations to shift the burden to future generations. And this definition, we submit, is a more accurate representation of the everyday notion of burden and is a more sensible concept for deciding if the real cost of a certain project can or cannot be postponed to future generations. Let us define the real burden of a public debt to a generation as the total consumption of private goods foregone *during the lifetime* of that generation as a consequence of government borrowing and attendant public spending. (For the moment, we are not taking into account

---

[5], Lerner [4], and Hansen [2]). Perhaps the reason these reviewers have not accepted Buchanan's conclusion on this point is that Buchanan: (1) does not always define "real burden" in a sufficiently clear manner; (2) defines "generation" in such a manner that the same person can be considered a member of many different generations [1, pp. 33-34]; and (3) relies on what Rolph [5, p. 184] has called a "proof by indirection." We have tried to avoid these pitfalls.

2. [6, p. 351]. Among the widely used elementary texts, C. L. Harriss' book [3, pp. 689-97] seems to come the closest to accepting the line of argument presented here. However, Harriss' exposition is badly impaired by an unclear distinction between "real costs" and "money costs." All writers seem to agree that the so-called "transfer payments" necessitated by a public debt involve real burdens in the sense that taxes used to meet interest payments may impair incentives to work and save. Neither this aspect of the debt problem nor the relationship between the public debt and economic stabilization are discussed in this paper.

the benefit that may result from the public expenditure, and so we are talking about a "gross burden.") Our preference for the lifetime of a generation as the unit of account is based on the proposition that people can and do forego consumption at a moment of time in order to be able to consume more later, and that to use the amount of consumption foregone at any one moment of time as some sort of index of the over-all sacrifices made by a generation is misleading.

Let us now consider the following situation. Assume a full-employment economy. Assume further that there is within the society an identifiable "generation" of people, all of whom are, let us say, 21 years old. Suppose that at a given moment of time the government sells bonds to the private sector of the economy in order to finance public project X^3 and that all of these bonds are voluntarily purchased by the group of 21-year-olds, whom we shall refer to as Generation I.

To determine the allocation of the burden of public project X between generations, consider a point of time 44 years later when all members of Generation I are 65 years old and the rest of the community is made up of a Generation II, whose members are all 21 years old. Suppose that at this moment of time all the members of Generation I who own the still outstanding government bonds sell these securities to members of Generation II and use the proceeds for the purchase of consumer goods during retirement.

In this case it is clear that the lifetime consumption of the members of Generation I has not been reduced even though the total subtraction from the production of private goods due to the carrying out of public project X took place during their lifetime. The reason is simply that the saving represented by Generation I's original purchase of the bonds has been matched by the dissaving resulting from the later sale of the bonds to Generation II and the subsequent spending of the proceeds. Conclusion: Generation I has not assumed any of the burden entailed in financing public project X by the issuance of government bonds. (For the time being, we ignore the interest charges on the debt.)

Let us now examine the situation of Generation II. If the government makes no effort to retire the debt during the lifetime of Generation II, and if Generation II sells its bonds to Generation III, then

3. At this juncture, the precise characteristics of the government project are best left unspecified. The relevance of the particular type of government project undertaken will be considered shortly.

Generation II also escapes the burden of paying for the public project, and so on. To make a potentially long story short, suppose, however, that during the lifetime of Generation II the government decides to retire the debt by levying a general tax in excess of current government spending and using the surplus to buy up the bonds that are now held by members of Generation II. The inevitable outcome of this decision is a reduction in the lifetime consumption of Generation II. The taxpayers of Generation II forego consumption in order to retire the debt and yet the bondholders of Generation II do not experience any net lifetime increase in their claims on consumption goods since they are simply reimbursed for the consumption foregone at the time when they (Generation II) bought the bonds from Generation I. Conclusion: the burden of public project X rests squarely on Generation II, and not on Generation I.

⌐   The skeleton of our argument is now complete: While the resources consumed by a debt-financed public project must entail a contemporaneous reduction in private consumption, the issuance of government bonds permits the generations alive at the time the public project is undertaken to be compensated in the future for their initial sacrifice. Generation I merely makes a loan of its reduced consumption, and the real reduction of consumption is borne by the generation(s) alive at the time this loan is extinguished. Consequently, even though the real private consumption of the community as a whole need not be altered by the growth of the public debt, it is still possible for the distribution of the community's private consumption *between generations* to depend on whether or not public projects are debt-financed.

One other form in which the general argument that no burden can be passed on to future generations often appears is the "we owe it to ourselves" or "assets equal liabilities" version:[4] No burden can be passed on because corresponding to every asset in the form of a government bond outstanding there is an equal liability in the form of liability for taxes to meet the interest charges and to repay the principal of the debt. Since there are always these two offsetting sides to the debt instrument, the argument proceeds, future generations cannot be handed any burden since when our taxpayer-children inherit the tax liability our bond-holder children will acquire an equal asset.

4. For a fuller exposition of this line of argument, with references to the literature, see [1, pp. 4-14, and *passim*].

The difficulty with this argument is simply that the asset and liability sides of the public debt are "passed on" in significantly different ways. Insofar as the government bonds are acquired by Generation II by purchase rather than bequest, the recipients of the bonds have only received a *quid pro quo*. On the other hand, the members of Generation II who are handed the tax liability are not reimbursed for accepting this liability. From the vantage point of Generation I, the bondholders in this generation received claims on consumption in exchange for the asset (bonds) which they sold to Generation II; at the same time, the members of Generation I as liability-holders passed on their tax liability to Generation II by the simple expedient of dying, and thus did not have to give up consumption goods to get rid of the liability. Consequently, unless Generation II can in turn pass its assets on to Generation III by sale while at the same time passing on its liability without making a compensating payment, the burden of the debt will be borne by Generation II.

We come now to the question: How about interest payments? We shall argue that the interest payments on the debt represent some burden on each and every generation that must pay taxes to make such payments.

To show why this is so it is necessary to reconsider the meaning of our definition of real burden—namely, "the total consumption of private goods foregone during the lifetime of a generation." Thus far we have implicitly assigned all amounts of consumption enjoyed during the generation's lifetime equal weights in arriving at total lifetime consumption, and have disregarded entirely the stage in a generation's lifetime at which various amounts of consumption were enjoyed. Consequently, we were able to argue that a generation which gave up a certain amount of consumption early in life to buy bonds and then was able, by selling the bonds later in life, to enjoy the same amount of consumption during retirement years had avoided all of the burden involved in the debt financing of project X. The difficulty with this treatment is obvious. So long as people have a positive rate of time preference (that is, prefer present consumption to future consumption), they will feel that they have made a sacrifice if they give up a certain amount of consumption in their youth and then receive back exactly the same amount of consumption in their old age.

If we assume that the interest rate on the government bonds

approximates the generation's rate of time preference, then the interest payments on the national debt serve to compensate the owners of the debt for their willingness to forego consumption early in life, and thus (along with the recapture of the principal late in life) serve to make the discounted value of the lifetime consumption of the bondholders the same as it would have been if project X had never been contemplated.

Turning now to the tax side of the interest transaction, it is clear that the tax payments needed to make interest payments represent a real reduction in the lifetime consumption of the people paying the taxes. Furthermore, since any given year's debt service is paid out of approximately contemporaneous tax payments, the same generation that receives the interest payments will be making a large part of the tax payments. The inescapable conclusion is that while the interest payments (along with the repayment of the principal) do not increase the discounted lifetime consumption of a generation, the tax payments do decrease lifetime consumption. Consequently, the discounted lifetime consumption of the generation is, on balance, reduced by the existence of debt service. This burden represents the real loss of welfare incurred by the generation as a consequence of the fact that it postponed its consumption but did not—because it received in interest payments only what it paid in taxes—receive any compensation for this distortion of its preferred consumption pattern.

The reason that in our discussion of interest payments we have spoken of "a" generation or "the" generation is that this burden (measured now in terms of the reduction in the discounted value of the generation's lifetime consumption is borne, of course, by each generation that pays a service charge on the debt. Consequently, even if the principal value of the debt is continually passed on, each generation bears a burden in the form of an uncompensated distortion of its preferred pattern of consumption.

So far we have avoided consideration of the type of government project financed by the initial borrowing. Actually, whether the government funds are spent wisely or foolishly is largely irrelevant to the question at issue here; for we are concerned solely with the allocation of the real *cost* of debt-financed government spending between generations and not with the allocation of the benefits of the government spending over time. Consequently, our conclusion that it is possible to shift at least a part of the cost to future generations does not imply that the absolute well-being of the future generations has been worsened by the combined borrowing and spending operation. If the borrowed funds were spent on a project whose benefit stream extends far into the future (for example, on fighting a "war-to-end-wars"), then the generation that assumes the main burden of the debt may still be much better off than if the debt had never been incurred. Our point is simply that the use of borrowing—as opposed to taxation or money creation—has improved the lot (measured in terms of lifetime consumption) of the first generation relative to the lot of succeeding generations.[5]

There is one final qualification to our argument. We have constructed a somewhat simplified case by assuming that all the bonds held by Generation I are sold to Generation II and that the proceeds are used entirely to increase consumption during the remaining years of Generation I's life. If, for example, all the members of Generation I were to will their bonds to Generation II, all real sacrifice of consumption would be borne by Generation I. Nevertheless, in spite of this simplification, the argument undoubtedly contains a large measure of relevance for the real situation. Purchasers of bonds, during a war for example, lose current consumption and receive marketable securities which surely are at least in part intended for conversion into spending on consumables in later years. The resulting claims upon consumer goods are realized at a time when they draw against the productivity of new members of the community who would otherwise enjoy a higher level of consumption. The existence of the marketable bonds undoubtedly makes possible at least some transfer of real income between generations.

Our conclusion that the real cost of debt-financed government spending can (at least in part) be transferred to future generations does not, of course, establish any prima facie case against deficit financing or in favor of the prompt retirement of the national debt.

5. There is a second, closely related reason for not tying the argument of this paper to a particular government expenditure, whether it be the construction of public schools or the giving of an enormous fireworks display. If, at the time public debt is issued, the government is spending money for many activities and financing these activities by taxes (and perhaps by money creation) as well as by borrowing, then it is hard to see how one can impute any specific project to any specific method of finance. The fact that we cannot solve this version of the imputation problem is irrelevant to the basic proposition that the cost of debt-financed government projects can be passed on to future generations, and thus cannot be used to disprove this proposition.

For one thing, to the extent that public projects undertaken today aid future generations, it may be fairer to let these future generations help pay the cost of these projects than to put the entire burden on present generations. Furthermore it is obvious that many considerations other than the location of the debt burden—such as the employment situation, the needs of the country for collective consumption, and the effect of taxes on incentives—are relevant in determining budget policy. However, at the present moment, there seems to be less danger that economists will forget the importance of these other considerations than that they will deny the possibility that the public debt can be used to shift a part of the real cost of public projects on to later generations.

References

1. Buchanan, J. M. *Public Principles of Public Debt.* Homewood, Illinois: Richard D. Irwin, Inc., 1958.
2. Hansen, A. H. "The Public Debt Reconsidered: A Review Article," *The Reviews of Economics and Statistics,* XLI (June, 1959), 377-78.
3. Harriss, C. L. *The American Economy.* 3rd ed. Homewood, Illinois: Richard D. Irwin, Inc., 1959.
4. Lerner, A. P. (Review of 1), *The Journal of Political Economy,* XLVII (April, 1959), 203-6.
5. Rolph, E. R. (Review of 1), *The American Economic Review,* XLIX (March, 1959), 183-85.
6. Samuelson, P. A. *Economics: An Introductory Analysis.* 4th ed. New York: McGraw-Hill Book Company, Inc., 1958.

B/ THE BURDEN OF THE PUBLIC DEBT: COMMENT*

BY *William Vickrey*

In a recent note Messrs. Bowen, Davis, and Kopf present a case for the classic view that deficit financing of public expenditures places a burden on future generations, as compared with pay-as-you-go financing [1] (references on page 81). The purpose of this comment is to suggest that they are right for reasons that are, if

* Reprinted by permission from *The American Economic Review,* LI (March, 1961).

not wrong, at least needlessly roundabout and largely irrelevant, and that former President Eisenhower was right, if at all, only under circumstances that are still far from being realized.

The authors of the note base their discussion on what would, in non-emergency times, be a rather unlikely reaction of individuals to the change in fiscal policy in question, namely the financing of bond purchases entirely by curtailing consumption, and trace the results through generations of individuals in a way that tends to obscure some of the fundamental repercussions on such matters as investment and the marginal productivity of labor. Their analysis may have some validity in a borrowing and rationing situation such as occurred during the second world war, but it seems inapplicable to periods where individuals are in fact free to expand their total consumption. The Eisenhower statement is less specific, but while its implications could be supported in a context where full employment was assured, this was so far from being the case in early 1960 that it must be considered at least ill-timed. The analysis that follows is equally irrelevant to the current situation, in that it attempts to trace the consequences of debt finance under full-employment conditions. However, it is based on assumptions about consumer behavior that might be more appropriate to an era characterized by a vigorous full-employment policy but without widespread direct controls such as rationing. Unlike Bowen, et al., no attempt is here made to separate out the generations in terms of age groups; for simplicity the population at a given epoch is considered as a whole, except as it may be appropriate to consider a subdivision into recipients of labor income and property income respectively.

The crux of the problem of the relative burden of debt finance and tax finance is that monetary and fiscal policy together provide two major degrees of freedom for over-all public policy by means of which control can be exercised, within limits, over two basic parameters of the economy: the aggregate level of activity and consequent output, on the one hand, and the way in which this aggregate output is apportioned between current consumption and capital formation, on the other. A firm commitment to the maintenance of a given level of activity and employment will use up one of these degrees of freedom; but within this commitment there remains one degree of freedom in the choice of suitable combinations of fiscal policy and monetary policy. If a combination of monetary and fiscal policy is chosen which offsets the greater inflationary effects of lower taxes and more borrowing with restrictive monetary policy and higher interest rates, this will lead to more consumption, less investment, and thus to a retardation of economic growth and a reduction in the heritage of accumulated resources to be handed on to future generations.

Where Bowen, Davis, and Kopf go wrong is in asserting that "resources consumed by a debt-financed public project must entail a contemporaneous reduction in private consumption" [1, p. 703]. If we assume full employment to be maintained whether the project is debt-financed, tax-financed, or not undertaken (and without this assumption the whole argument collapses), and if we assume a "public debt illusion" under which individuals pay no attention to their share in the liability represented by the public debt in determining how much of their income they will spend, we can expect consumer demand to be higher when the project is debt-financed than when it is tax-financed; if inflationary pressures are to be avoided, aggregate demand must be kept within the capacity of the economy by curtailing private investment demand, the increased demand for borrowed funds represented by the debt financing must be allowed to tighten the money market, and if necessary supplementary monetary measures must be adopted so as to lower liquidity, drive interest rates up and generally increase the difficulties of financing to the point where private investment is curtailed sufficiently to remove the inflationary pressure. Only if savings were highly interest-elastic and investment highly inelastic, or if the project financed were specifically such as to substitute directly for consumption expenditure could it be assumed that the resources used would be derived from a reduction in private consumption.

The shifting of the burden to the future that is produced by debt financing is then essentially the shifting of resources out of private investment and into consumption that is induced by the change in method of financing. The relationship, however, may not be dollar for dollar. On the one hand, the marginal propensity to consume may be less than 1, so that a reduction in taxes of $100 might cause an increase of spending by only $80. Further, the tightening of the money market may have repercussions on consumption, so that the actual amount of added consumption and added burden on the future is only $70. At this point, however, some caution is needed, for the main effects of monetary stringency are likely to be on expenditure for housing and durables, and a precise evaluation would have to consider changes in the residual value of consumer durables as part of the change in the heritage carried into the future, so that only repercussions on net current consumption would be relevant.

Actually, this analysis can show an element of future burden even where additional current public expenditures are financed out of current taxes. If we can assume that the added current public expenditures are not such as to change the consumption function expressed in terms of disposable income, then the financing of $100 of added outlays by $100 of taxes will reduce consumption by only say $80, and if $100 of resources are to be freed for the public purpose, an additional $20 will have to come out of private investment, whether through a tightening of the money market or, if the public expenditure is in some way less of a stimulus to private investment than is the consumer demand it replaces, through the acceleration effect of the decline in consumer demand. If the public expenditure is indeed of only transitory benefit, the heritage left for the future will then be decreased by $20. If the public expenditure of $100 is to be financed in such a way as not to diminish the heritage left for the future, it would be necessary to levy taxes of $125, so that individual consumption would be reduced by $100, and the $25 surplus would serve to replace in the capital market the vanished individual savings of $25.

In this analysis it makes no difference whether the heritage is regarded as being left to future generations considered as different individuals or merely to the later years of the same persons. There is, however, one further aspect of the future burden that is important. In the Bowen-Davis-Kopf representation, where the resources required by the project come from consumption, the productive capacity of the economy is unimpaired, and indeed if the interest payments are financed by further borrowing, the final apportionment of the "burden" is deferred until this accumulated debt is retired; if the economy is growing at a rate as great as the rate of interest, there is no essential reason why this cannot be put off indefinitely, so that no identifiable group is harmed, on balance, and the "burden" vanishes from sight. If there is any burden here, it lies in the impairment of the capacity of the future generations to pull this stunt themselves! This paradoxical situation may perhaps be taken as indication that a long-term interest rate lower than the growth rate represents an unstable situation. In any case, there exists an unavoidable "real" burden on future generations whenever the more tangible resources available to the future generations are impaired. If in the face of such an impairment of resources an attempt is made to avoid the burden on any particular generation by maintaining consumption at the level it would otherwise have reached, further impairment of capital will take place, with an ultimate day of reckoning.

In an epoch where we contemplate with increasing equanimity the possibility that the national debt might be allowed to grow indefinitely, at least in absolute terms if not as a fraction of national income, some allocation of the burden is needed other than in terms of the taxpayers who finance a retirement of the debt that may never occur. If debt financing results in a lower level of investment (as compared with tax financing of the same government outlays), so that some future generation finds itself with a lower endowment of real capital, who in particular are the losers? If at this point we invoke a strictly competitive economy with a classically homogeneous production function with diminishing returns to increments of each factor as one or more of the others is held constant, we find that interest rates and the marginal productivity of capital are higher than they would otherwise have been, while wage rates are lower than they would otherwise have been by an amount sufficient not only to absorb the entire reduction in output caused by the reduction in resources, but to allow for the increased rate of return on investment. All of which can be summed up by saying that, *given full employment,* shifting the fiscal policy-monetary policy mix in the direction of debt finance tends to place a burden on the future measured by a fraction of the debt increment somewhat smaller than the marginal propensity to consume; that in the absence of debt retirement or other compensatory action the primary burden of diminished future income will be felt by future wage earners, and that there will in addition be a tendency for the income distribution to shift in favor of property incomes.

While this analysis does depend on a public-debt illusion or its equivalent, elimination of this factor eliminates the shifting to the future entirely, and with it, indeed, the effectiveness of fiscal policy as an instrument of stabilization. It is perhaps paradoxical that it is precisely in the field of local finance where the debt burden is most clearly a charge against identifiable pieces of property and the public-debt illusion should be at its weakest that the virtues of "pay-as-you-go" have been most universally applauded. Indeed it is here that the property owner in a town that floats a debt instead of raising the property tax rates can maintain a financial status equivalent to that of his peer in the neighboring debtless community by taking his tax savings and stepping up his mortgage payments. The reduced mortgage balance will offset the decline in market value produced by the overlying public debt, so that his equity will remain unchanged. Aside from the gain he may realize by reason of the margin between the interest rate on his (taxable) mortgage and that incurred on the (tax-exempt) public debt, he cannot ultimately escape his share of the burden even by dying penniless, for in the sale of his property a rational market will have capitalized the future debt service burden allocable to it. To be sure, a rigorous analysis is complicated by the fact that new construction in a debt-burdened community will be discouraged by the consideration that improvement will increase the share of the debt burden borne by the property being improved. But by and large, assuming a fully rational market, local debt finance will not shift the burden to the future, though it may, if carried too far, cause further administrations to have financial headaches, particularly if they are hemmed in by statutory limits on tax rates and debt rates.

If the unrealistic assumption is adhered to that the resources are taken entirely from current consumption, then it is fair to say that it is not the undertaking of the expenditure on the basis of debt finance that has imposed a burden on future generations, but rather the decision of the present generation as individuals not to bequeath the bonds thus acquired to their heirs in the subsequent generation. If individuals of this generation have objections to imposing a burden on the future, it will always be open to them to avoid this result by increasing the amount they individually bequeath to the future generation by an amount sufficient to pay off the debt. Moreover, while this is always possible (and would not even be frustrated by the imposition of death duties, since the added revenues thus produced would also be available to retire part of the debt), the reverse option, *i.e.*, that of taking individual action, where the project is tax-financed, which would impose a burden on the future generations, is less completely available: it is often difficult to arrange to leave a negative estate when the estate was originally zero or very small. On this basis one could even argue that debt financing is the preferable policy in the abstract, in that it leaves a wider range for individual choice: if policy B gives individuals the freedom to choose actions which will bring about all of the results that are possible under policy A, whereas under policy A there are no available actions which would reproduce some of the results available under policy B, then B is necessarily to be preferred. The need to deny this proposition if pay-as-you-go financing is to be advocated may incidentally compel recognition that the "conservative" point of view in this case necessarily implies the acceptance of some kind of social as distinct from individualistic values.

Thus far the discussion has been largely in terms of relative interests of groups of individuals, in the individualistic tradition of classical economics. The more popular concern, nowadays, is with the promotion of economic growth. It is apparent from what has been said above that to the extent that growth is a result of capital formation, policies involving excessively large amounts of debt financing are inimical to growth. Indeed, if short-run stability were not in question, the maximum rate of growth compatible with a level price trend and a given pattern of government outlays would be obtained by having a maximum degree of monetary ease, the lowest possible interest rates, and a level of taxation sufficiently high to offset the resulting inflationary pressure, probably but not necessarily involving a substantial budgetary surplus.

Maintaining maximum growth under these circumstances involves abandoning monetary policy as a means of checking downward fluctuations, and having to rely solely on more cumbersome and slower acting tax or expenditure changes as a means of correcting deflationary developments. Moreover, in an open economy, the "growth" may take the form of foreign investment and the accumulation of claims to income from abroad, a development that may on the one hand involve risk of default or expropriation and on the other may forfeit whatever local benefits may derive from external economies.

If a more rapid rate of growth than this is desired, or if it is felt essential to maintain a larger reserve of potential monetary stimulus, this can only come about either through a larger scale of direct government investment, through shifts in tax policy from taxes on property and on corporate income and the like to taxes on personal income and consumption, through outright subsidy to private investment, or through the adoption of policies which will make inflation of the price level (not necessarily uncontrolled or accelerating) the normal expectation of investors generally [3]. In this last case we would have the paradox that while a large public debt is generally considered to be inflationary, deliberate inflation might be the means whereby full employment would be made compatible with a reduction in the real debt and an enhancement of the heritage being bequeathed to the future.

In any case the essential precondition is *given full employment*. The analysis is relevant only where it is assumed that some given level of employment is to be maintained. If variations in fiscal policy are undertaken without the proportionately vigorous correlative monetary measures needed to stabilize employment and prices, then a surplus, far from being "a reduction in our children's inherited mortgage" [2] can easily give rise to increased unemployment and a multiplied and fruitless burden on both the present and the future. In the context of January 7, 1960, the multiplied burden would seem to have been a more likely outcome than the reduction of the mortgage, and indeed we may yet be a shockingly long way from being able to count on that degree of coordination and vigor in the application of monetary and fiscal policy that would make the classical analysis of the debt burden once again relevant and the Eisenhower attitude regarding the virtues of a surplus an appropriate one.

References

1. Bowen, W. G., R. G. Davis, and D. H. Kopf. "The Public Debt: A Burden on Future Generations?" *The American Economic Review*, L (September, 1960), 701-6.
2. Eisenhower, President Dwight D. *State of the Union Message*, January 7, 1960.
3. Vickrey, William. "The Optimum Trend of Prices," *The Southern Economic Journal*, XXV (January, 1959), 315-26; "Stability Through Inflation," in *Post-Keynesian Economics*, ed. K. Kurihara. New Brunswick: Rutgers University Press, 1954, pp. 89-122.

C/ THE BURDEN OF THE PUBLIC DEBT: COMMENT*

BY *Tibor Scitovsky*

In "The Public Debt: A Burden on Future Generations?,"[1] Messrs. Bowen, Davis, and Kopf have failed to prove President Eisenhower right and the majority of professional economists wrong; but they have given us new insight into the problem by introducing, perhaps not quite deliberately, a useful distinction between social cost in the sense of resources diverted and subjective burden as experienced by individual citizens. We remain unconvinced that the social cost of a public project can, without an external debt, be shifted from the time when it is incurred; but the authors seem right in saying that its burden can be so shifted if by burden is meant what individuals consider a burden: the balance of private costs and private benefits, corrected for changes in disposable income occasioned by the public debt.[2]

If carried out at a time of full employment, a $1 billion public project, however financed, involves the *cost* of $1 billion worth of resources diverted from consumption and/or private capital formation; but it imposes no *burden* on the community if people voluntarily give up their command over these resources in exchange for government bonds. By buying the bonds, the public reveals its preference for the bonds over current consumption or private securities and incurs no more of a burden than if it had bought Ford stock or Ford automobiles instead.[3] A burden is imposed on the public only if *and at the time when* the promise written into the bonds is either formally broken or broken in

---

*Reprinted by permission from *The American Economic Review*, LI (March, 1961).

1. *The American Economic Review*, L (September, 1960), 701-6.

2. This correction is necessary because individuals in their economic calculations always assume their incomes to be fixed.

3. It might be argued, however, that the purchase of war-bonds under pressure of patriotic appeal does involve a burden; but is this more of a burden than that imposed on the buyer of a new car who acts under the influence of high-pressure salesmanship?

spirit. This happens, for example, when the public project financed by the bonds fails to raise the gross national product and the government pays interest on the bonds out of additional taxation. In such a case, the interest payments fail to add to disposable income and thus fool the public. This constitutes, in a sense, a breaking of the government's original promise, since the public sacrificed consumption and/or private capital formation in exchange for the promise of additional income (the interest on the bonds) which it is not getting. Bowen *et al.* are right in arguing that the burden so imposed is a genuine burden and that it is distributed over the entire lifetime of the bonds—as well as over the lifetime of all future bonds that may be issued for the sake of redeeming the original ones.[4]

I part company with the authors when they speak of yet another burden imposed by and at the time of the redemption of the bonds. They argue that when the government repays the debt, the additional taxation reduces disposable income and hence consumption, while the replacement of the public's holdings of bonds by cash has little or no effect on its market behavior, so that on balance consumption is reduced, which, they assert, is the main burden of the debt. This would be all right, except that the authors forget about the crucial assumption of full employment they made earlier. If full employment and stable prices obtain when the debt falls due for redemption and an unenlightened government raises taxes (or lowers public spending) in order to create the budgetary surplus needed to redeem the debt, then the redemption will lower GNP and inflict a burden on society—but the assumption of full employment has thus been abandoned half-way. If on the other hand the government successfully offsets the restrictive effects of its budgetary surplus by a monetary policy designed to encourage private investment, then the resulting rise in GNP will offset the effect of higher taxes on disposable income and no burden will be imposed on the public. Or again, if all this happens at a time of inflationary pressures and the government redeems the debt as part of its price-stabilization policy, then again no additional burden is imposed; for the additional taxes merely accomplish what in their absence the rise in prices would have done.

---

4. In the language of opportunity cost, this burden is the foregone fruit of growth sacrificed.

D/ THE BURDEN OF THE PUBLIC DEBT: COMMENT*

BY *James R. Elliott*

The Bowen-Davis-Kopf thesis presented in "The Public Debt: A Burden on Future Generations"[1] purports to show that, under certain circumstances, the burden of a portion of the national debt can be shifted to future generations. What Bowen *et al.* have succeeded in demonstrating is that a given generation (Generation I) *could* pass the burden of a deficit-financed project to a future generation (Generation II) by selling their bonds (to Generation II) and using the proceeds to raise their level of consumption.

The possibility of this eventuality, it should be noted, existed long before the days of multibillion-dollar deficit finance and existed even in the absence of deficit finance. The older members of any economy which incorporates the principles of private property and the right of transfer are always free to sell their creditor claims. The sale may be made to other members of Generation I or to those of Generation II. If, during the lifetime of Generation I, there had been no deficit finance, they would still be free to liquidate *other* forms of creditor claims—life insurance, industrial bonds, common stock, etc. As a general rule, however, Generation I does not sell its creditor claims (or savings) to Generation II—the transfer is made by bequest.

None of this denies the possibility of the Bowen-Davis-Kopf conclusion; it merely questions the plausibility. In special cases, as where, for example, substantial damage to the productive facilities of the economy, or to some factor, during the lifetime of Generation I result in a low level of living relative to previous levels, the bondholders would be tempted to liquidate their bonds in an attempt to maintain their standard of living. In such a case, the shift of burden would, of course, be more probable.

* Reprinted by permission from *The American Economic Review*, LI (March, 1961).
1. *The American Economic Review*, L (September, 1960), 701-6.

However, even if one assumes that Generation I does sell its bonds to Generation II, it does not necessarily follow that increased consumption by Generation I after the transfer has occurred will require decreased consumption by Generation II. Conceivably, if this bond transfer takes place during a period in which substantial quantities of economic resources are idle, Generation I's attempt to increase consumption may increase aggregate income and, in turn, lead to a general increase in consumption—including consumption by Generation II. Thus, the existence of unemployed resources at the time of Generation I's increase in consumption would dissolve "the burden of the debt."

Reflection upon the years following the second world war lends the above consideration additional importance. While we describe the period as one of full employment punctuated by mild recessions, in few of the years, if any, were resources utilized to the fullest extent. Certainly, in most of these years a net increase in real GNP could have been attained had consumer demand (or investor or government demand) been greater.

But if there are no idle resources, as Bowen *et al.* assume, then Generation II gets just what it bargained for—it exchanges current consumption claims for claims against future goods.

While these considerations confine the Bowen-Davis-Kopf thesis to a rare application, no challenge to the internal consistency of the thesis is intended. There is, however, a weak point in the Bowen-Davis-Kopf chain of logic: the implicit assumption that increased taxes necessarily reduce aggregate *real* consumption. They state:

. . . suppose . . . that during the lifetime of Generation II the government decides to retire the debt by levying a general tax in excess of current government spending and using the surplus to buy up the bonds that are now held by members of Generation II. The inevitable outcome of this decision is a reduction in the lifetime consumption of Generation II. The taxpayers of Generation II forego consumption in order to retire the debt and yet the bondholders of Generation II do not experience any net lifetime increase in their claims on consumption goods since they are simply reimbursed for the consumption foregone at the time when they (Generation II) bought the bonds from Generation I. Conclusion: the burden of public project X rests squarely on Generation II, and not on Generation I.

If, however, taxpayers reduce consumption in order to pay additional taxes, who will consume the goods made available? Surely not the bondholders whose bonds are retired. Had they wished to consume, they would have sold the bonds on the market or not bought them in the first place. The bond retirement will force the (former) bondholders to shift their savings into other forms—insurance, equity securities, industrial bonds, etc. Bowen *et al.* implicitly assume that the bondholders of Generation II, having been bought out, would use the proceeds for consumption. This is a completely unwarranted assumption. The bond retirement program simply changes the form of the assets of the (former) bondholders from bonds to deposits but does not increase their income or consumption.

As the government (of Generation II's lifetime) raises the tax surplus to retire the debt, one of two possibilities may occur: (1) aggregate *real* consumption does not decline (although aggregate dollar consumption does) in which case the bond retirement must have been effected during a period of inflationary pressure; or (2) aggregate real consumption does decline, forcing GNP and investment down, and possibly initiating a chain reaction.

In the first case there has been no burden whatever on Generation II. The real standard of living remains constant and the debt has been repaid from otherwise-inflationary purchasing power. In the second case (which is actually outside of the Bowen-Davis-Kopf frame of reference because they assume full employment), there is a very real burden but it follows from poor fiscal policy rather than from the repayment of debt.

Were prices free and flexible, a surplus in taxes and a concomitant reduction in dollar consumption would lead to lower prices—leaving the taxpayer with fewer dollars for consumption but with correspondingly lower prices. In this case, too, the repayment is burdenless. In an economy with sticky, administered prices, however, a surplus cannot be accumulated through taxation during a potentially deflationary period without serious consequences. But the consequences do not follow from the repayment of debt—rather from poorly conceived fiscal policy.

E/ THE BURDEN OF THE PUBLIC DEBT: REPLY*

BY *William G. Bowen, Richard G. Davis, and David H. Kopf*

We welcome the comments by Vickrey, Scitovsky, and Elliott. At the same time, however, we must insist that none of these comments alters our central point—that debt financing, by means of the intergeneration transfer process described in our original paper, can serve to shift the burden of government spending from present to future generations.

The main thing to be said about Vickrey's paper is that it represents a different approach to the debt burden problem. Whereas we chose to analyze the debt burden in terms of the distribution of lifetime consumption between generations, Vickrey has chosen to analyze the effects of debt finance on the future level of real income for society as a whole.

From this latter vantage point, Vickrey is certainly entitled to object to our assumption that bond purchases are financed entirely out of consumption.[1] In the real world an increase in the public debt will undoubtedly lead to a reduction in both consumption (C) and investment (I); and the secular growth in GNP will be slower the greater the reduction in I relative to C.

But this is by no means the only way in which debt financing can alter the *relative* economic position of different generations. Vickrey's line of reasoning is in no way inconsistent with the important point that, regardless of whether loan finance reduces C or I, loan finance can result in intergeneration transfers of burden. No matter what happens to C and I, Generation I (the present generation) is going to enjoy a higher level of lifetime consumption relative to the consumption of future generations if government expenditures are financed by issuance of debt instruments than if taxes are

---

* Reprinted by permission from *The American Economic Review*, LI (March, 1961).

1. There are several places in our original paper where it appears that we *assert*—rather than assume—that borrowing affects only consumption. This was unfortunate, and we apologize for any resulting confusion.

employed. Under the tax option, Generation I loses either immediate consumption or private claims against investment goods and receives no monetary asset in exchange; under the debt option, Generation I also sacrifices some combination of *C* and *I*, but in this case receives an asset (government bonds) in exchange, and thus enjoys the option of selling these bonds later in life to obtain either consumption goods or claims against private investment. Consequently, the assumption that loan finance reduces private consumption is in no way essential to the logic of our argument, and was used to highlight the otherwise unrecognized fact that even if loan finance fails to dampen private investment, the present generation can still shift at least a part of the burden of government spending to future generations.

Another way of making the same point is to note that even if the method of finance were to leave the investment-consumption mix unaltered, the loan-finance technique would make the members of Generation I better off relative to subsequent generations than would the tax-finance method. Since the loan-finance procedure does, in fact, alter the mix against private capital formation, Vickrey's argument should be regarded as supplemental to our own. Our major quarrel with Vickrey's paper is, therefore, that it does not make clear that his position complements—rather than competes with—the position stated in our original paper.

The papers by Scitovsky and Elliott do deal directly with our intergeneration transfer argument, and we are indebted to these authors for pointing out that higher tax collections *cum* debt retirement are going to have a fiscal effect that challenges our full-employment assumption. But, Scitovsky and Elliott are wrong if they mean to suggest that we must abandon our full-employment assumption if we are to prevent the debt-retirement phase of our argument from collapsing.

We are quite prepared to assume (as we have all along) that, by some method such as flexible monetary policy, full employment and price stability are maintained continuously. Now, if a tax surplus is used to retire debt, monetary policy will have to be used to restore full employment. If this is done, Scitovsky and Elliott argue, the reduction in consumption engendered by the tax surplus will be just offset by the rise in GNP brought about by compensatory stabilization policies, and so we shall be exactly where we would have been if no debt retirement had occurred, and therefore there will be no burden on generations alive at the time the debt is retired.

There are two related fallacies in this line of reasoning. First, Scitovsky and Elliott seem to have forgotten that our definition of burden runs in terms of reduced lifetime consumption, not income foregone at a moment of time. Second, Scitovsky and Elliott neglect the asset effect of the debt retirement operation. Taking account of both these considerations, the following picture emerges: Generation II gave up consumption to Generation I when it bought the bonds from Generation I; the bonds are, of course, the means whereby Generation II hopes to recapture, later in life, the consumption given up early in life. It is true that at the point of time when these bonds are retired, thanks to the compensatory stabilization policies, there need be no drop in the private spending of Generation II. What does happen, however, is that Generation II is stripped of its bonds, and thus loses the assets that it had hoped to use later in life to recoup the consumption foregone early in life. It is by destroying these claims against future consumption that debt retirement locates the burden of the public project on generations alive at the time the debt is retired. Consumption was transferred from Generation II to Generation I when bonds were purchased by Generation II, and now debt retirement has extinguished the possibility that an equivalent amount of consumption could later be transferred from Generation III to Generation II. Hence, on balance, over its lifetime, Generation II has suffered a reduction in consumption even though aggregate real consumption for society as a whole need never have been affected by the whole operation.

We must also be careful not to make the mistake of saying that the public has been given additional money in place of bonds and so has suffered no net reduction in its assets. The money paid to bondholders is nothing but the money given up by taxpayers. Therefore, the aggregate stock of money in the hands of the public is unchanged by the government's fiscal operation, while the public's bondholdings are reduced—hence Generation II suffers a net reduction in its assets. And, as a consequence, Generation II has fewer assets to carry into the future as a means of competing with Generation III for consumption goods produced in later years than would have been the case if debt retirement had not occurred.

Finally, it is important to note that the above logic is unaffected if compensatory monetary policy (as is likely) fills the largest part of the deflationary gap created by the tax-induced reduction in consumption, not with new consumption, but with new investment. In this case the new claims against investment goods of course represent claims against future consumption. These claims can be considered either as a substitute for the immediate loss of consumption attributable to the debt-retiring taxes or as a substitute for the former claims against future consumption (*i.e.*, the government bonds which have now been retired). But, these new claims against private investment cannot *simultaneously* be considered a substitute for both. Consequently, the creation and retirement of public debt can lead to a redistribution of lifetime real income between generations, given conditions of full employment, regardless of differential effects on consumption and investment.[2]

2. Five very brief comments are in order, although these do not cover all of the points we would like to discuss if space permitted: (1) For simplicity of exposition we have assumed that all taxes levied to retire the debt fall on Generation II; if Generation III is also old enough to share in the tax payments, then Generation III will also share in the burden since their net assets (claims against future consumption) will also be reduced by the combined tax-collection and debt-retirement operation. (2) Throughout this discussion we have been considering debt retirement only in the strict sense of bonds retired through a tax surplus, and have not considered the case where the government "monetizes" the debt. This monetization might be deliberate, or it might arise if the government, faced with falling national income because of its debt-retirement policy, created (and spent) new money. (3) The existence of inflationary pressures at the time of debt retirement does not (as Scitovsky and Elliott argue) vitiate our argument. Here again, higher taxation *cum* debt retirement will not affect real incomes, but will reduce net assets and thus extinguish the claims against future consumption that Generation II received in exchange for its earlier transfer of consumption to Generation I. (4) Nor does consideration of the liability side of the public debt invalidate the conclusions stated above. Whereas government bonds are clearly an asset to the individual and influence his financial planning, individuals do not normally consider their full share of the public debt as a personal liability in calculating their own net worth. And, this is not merely an "illusion," since the taxpayer knows that his death will extinguish his responsibility for this obligation. (5) The reader who would like to see, in a somewhat different context, an arithmetical example of the way debt financing can be used to affect the relative economic positions of different generations is referred to R. A. Musgrave, *The Theory of Public Finance*, New York, 1959, pp. 562-65. Musgrave also discusses Vickrey's topic (the effects of debt finance on consumption versus investment) in considerable detail.

F/ THE BURDEN OF DEBT*

BY *Abba P. Lerner*

"But look," the Rabbi's wife remonstrated, "when one party to the dispute presented their case to you you said 'you are quite right' and then when the other party presented their case you again said 'you are quite right,' surely they cannot both be right?" To which the Rabbi answered, "My dear, you are quite right!"

Messrs. Bowen, Davis, and Kopf have shown[1] that the real burden of a project using up resources in the present can be shifted to future generations by internal borrowing, providing one defines "generation" in a particular way. It is just as easy to prove that all politicians are economists or that all economists are dunces, provided one defines "economist" in a particular way. But even if I call the tail of a sheep a leg that will not turn sheep into quintapeds. The issue is of course terminological rather than substantive. It is nevertheless one of the utmost importance because the conclusion reached by Bowen *et al.*, although not incorrect on their own definitions, is bound to be misinterpreted as meaning what it seems to be saying in English and as indeed implying that most politicians understand economics better than the economists—most, if not all, of whom are dunces.

Bowen, Davis, and Kopf are absolutely right when they agree that there is "absolutely nothing" wrong with the standard argument of modern economists that the real burden of a debt can *not* be shifted to future generations if it is defined as "the total amount of private consumption goods given up by the community *at the moment of time the borrowed funds are spent.*" But President Eisenhower "appears convinced that the costs of debt-financed

---

* Reprinted by permission of the publishers from *The Review of Economics and Statistics*, XLIII (May, 1961).

1. W. G. Bowen, R. G. Davis, and D. H. Kopf, "The Public Debt: A Burden on Future Generations?" *The American Economic Review*, L (September, 1960), 701-6.

public projects can be passed on to future generations." Like the
Rabbi in the story, Bowen *et al.* want to say that he too is right,
but in their enthusiasm they even say that the purpose of their
note "is to suggest that in this instance it is the President who is—
in at least one highly important sense—right," thus clearly implying
that the economists are wrong.

To make the President appear right, Bowen *et al.* redefine "present generation" to mean the people who lend the money to finance
the project, and they redefine "future generation" to mean the people
who pay the taxes that are used to repay the principal and the interest on the loans. The perversity of the redefinitions is obscured
by supposing that the lenders ("this generation"), are all 21 years
old at the time of the execution of the project when they lend
the money and by supposing that they are repaid 44 years later, on
their 65th birthday, with funds obtained at that time from 21-year-
old taxpayers ("the next generation"). The burden is thereby
shifted from "this generation" to "the next generation."

What has been proved, if we obstinately insist in expressing the
conclusion in English, is that it is possible to shift the burden from
the Lenders to the Taxpayers or, we might say, from the Lowells
to the Thomases. The Lowells are better off and the Thomases
are worse off than if the Lowells had been taxed to raise the money
for the project in the first place.

The "red herring" nature of having the Lowells lend the money
now (so that we can call them the present generation) and having
the Thomases pay the taxes in the future (so that they can be called
the future generation) jumps to the eye if we note that the
shifting of the real burden of the project from the Lowells to the
Thomases (or indeed of any other burden) could take place just
as well at the time of the project (or at any other time) by simply
taxing the Thomases instead of the Lowells.

No economist, so far as I am aware, has ever denied the possibility of borrowing or of lending or of taxing some people instead of
others, or of any combinations of such operations. And if we redefine Mr. Eisenhower's words so that they mean only that such operations are possible, then indeed the words used by the President
constitute a true statement. But there is no reason for supposing
that the President was trying to use any language other than English, and what the President said is simply wrong (in English), unless indeed all the economists (including Bowen *et al.*, as well as

J. M. Buchanan, who plays similar linguistic tricks[2]) are absolutely wrong.

The real issue, and it is an important one, between the economists and Mr. Eisenhower is not whether it is possible to shift a burden (either in the present or in the future) from some people to other people, but whether it is possible by *internal borrowing* to shift a real burden from the present generation, in the sense of the present economy as a whole, onto a future generation, in the sense of the future economy as a whole. What is important for economists is to teach the President that the latter is impossible because a project that uses up resources needs the resources *at the time that it uses them up*, and not before or after.

This basic proposition is true of all projects that use up resources. The question is traditionally posed in terms of the burden of a *public* project financed by *privately* held internal debt; but the proposition is quite independent of whether the project is public or private as well as of whether the debt is private or public. The proposition holds as long as the project is financed *internally*, so that there are no outsiders to take over the current burden by providing the resources and to hand back the burden in the future by asking for the return of the resources.

It is necessary for economists to keep repeating this basic proposition because one of their main duties is to keep warning people against the fallacy of composition. To anyone who sees only a part of the economy it does seem possible to borrow from the future because he tends to assume that what is true of the part is true of the whole. It *is* possible for the Lowells to borrow from the Thomases, and what this borrowing does is to shift a burden from the Lowells to the Thomases in the present, and then to shift an equal burden from the Thomases to the Lowells in the future when the loan is repaid. To the Lowells (and to anyone else who sees only the Lowells) the combination of these two shifts looks like the shifting of a burden from the present into the future or the shifting of resources from the future into the present. To the Thomases, of course, the transactions will look like the opposite, namely, the shifting of a burden from the future into the present or the shifting of resources from the present into the future. But the borrowing and the repayment do not make a Time Machine. There is no shift of resources or of burdens between different points in

2. In his *Public Principles of Public Debt* (Homewood, Illinois, 1958).

time. It is possible for a *part* of the economy (the Lowells) to shift *its* burden into the future only as long as *another part* of the present economy (the Thomases) is ready to take it over for the intervening period. It is not possible for *the whole* of the present generation to shift a burden into the future because there are no Thomases left to play the magician's assistant in the illusion.

This is not to say that there is no way at all in which the present generation can shift a burden onto future generations. Our proposition is only that this is not done by internal borrowing. We can impoverish the future by cutting down on our investment in capital resources (or by using up or destroying natural resources) that would have enabled future generations to produce and enjoy higher standards of living. There is even a possible connection between internal debt financing and this way of really impoverishing future generations. If full employment (or some other level of employment) is somehow being maintained, and if the conditions of the borrowing and the kinds of people from whom the borrowing is done are such that they reduce consumption by less than consumption would have been reduced if the money had been raised instead by taxes, then there will be more consumption and there will therefore have to be less investment. The borrowing will then have reduced the real resources inherited by future generations.

But there is no *necessary* connection. It would almost certainly not work this way in the conditions of 1960. Whether the borrowing increases or decreases consumption depends on the nature and on the conditions of the borrowing on the one hand and of the alternative—the taxation—on the other hand. Furthermore, at the present time, when we have considerable unemployment and unused capacity, an increase in consumption is more likely to lead to *more* investment (out of unutilized resources) and therefore to an *increase* in productive resources inherited by future generations. And it is quite certainly not these complicated considerations that are responsible for the President's belief that internal borrowing increases and repayment reduces "our children's inherited mortgage." In any case even the *possibility* of a genuine impoverishment of future generations by an induced reduction in investment is *explicitly* ruled out by Bowen *et al.* when they say that the resources consumed by the project "*must* entail a contemporaneous reduction in private consumption."[3]

Any genuine impoverishment of future generations must be the

3. Bowen, Davis, and Kopf, "The Public Debt," p. 703, my italics.

result of *not* reducing private consumption by the full amount of the resources used up in the project so that some of these resources must come out of alternative investment (if we rule out the use of unemployed resources). It is only the curtailed alternative investment outside of the project that can tend to impoverish future generations (although this might be more than made up for them by the benefits that these same future generations will derive from the project in question).

We can also impoverish the future by using up in the production of armaments too much of the resources that would have gone into investment; and we can equally impoverish the future by an over-economy in armaments, or by skimping in our contribution to the building of a healthy world, so that we invite aggression or foster resentments and revolutions. But both of these possibilities are completely independent of whether we borrow or tax.

Semantic playfulness like that of Bowen *et al.* seriously sabotages economists in their important task in educating the public to the appreciation of an important truth. By their ingenious redefinition of "generations" they have made it more difficult to point out just where the fallacy of composition is perpetrated. It is perpetrated when a part of the economy (as in their definition of this or that generation) is taken for the whole (as in the usual meaning of a generation as *all* the people living at a certain date); and this is exactly what Bowen *et al.* do when they say that President Eisenhower (speaking English) is right.

They have taken a true proposition—i.e., that some poeple can shift a burden into the future by borrowing from other people—and rewritten it in such a manner that almost everyone will read in it the false proposition that the nation as a whole can filch resources from the future by internal borrowing (public or private), thereby impoverishing future generations. It is unfortunately the false proposition that is implied in the statement by the President, and believed by many people in positions to make vital decisions. The false belief may well contribute to a failure of the free nations to take the steps necessary to maintain and extend freedom in the world. There is even a clear and present danger that because of a baseless fear of impoverishing future generations by leaving them with a larger internal debt (which they will owe to themselves), we may fail to protect them from nuclear war and/or totalitarian domination; the confusion sown by Bowen *et al.* tends to increase that danger. It is to be hoped that these authors will tell the

President that they were using a special language of their own and did not mean what they seemed to be saying when they seemed to be denying a proposition with which, as they themselves declare, there is "absolutely nothing" wrong.

G/ THE DISTRIBUTION OF THE DEBT BURDEN: A REPLY*

BY *William G. Bowen, Richard G. Davis, and David H. Kopf*

It is almost a pleasure to be denounced in prose as delightful as that employed by Lerner in his critique of our public debt article— even in view of his somewhat alarming suggestion that the publication of our paper has increased the danger of nuclear war.[1] However, our pleasure would have been less mixed if he had not misunderstood the point of our argument and confused some of the basic issues. In an effort to clarify the situation, we offer the following comments.

First, no amount of "linguistic playfulness" on the part of anybody should be allowed to obscure the substantive point of our argument: that debt finance can be used to alter the lifetime distribution of claims against consumption goods between people alive at the time borrowing takes place and people not yet born. The basis for this argument is spelled out in our first paper on this subject and amplified in a subsequent rejoinder.[2] Since Lerner offers no substantive criticism of this argument, there is no need to repeat it here.

The word "generation," which causes Lerner so much anxiety, has been omitted altogether from the above summary statement to emphasize that *this is not a terminological dispute*, as Lerner im-

---

* Reprinted by permission of the publishers from *The Review of Economics and Statistics*, XLIV (February, 1962).
1. A. P. Lerner. "The Burden of the Debt," *The Review of Economics and Statistics*, XLIII (May, 1961), 139-41.
2. W. G. Bowen, R. G. Davis, and D. H. Kopf, "The Public Debt: A Burden on Future Generations?" *The American Economic Review*, L (September, 1960), and "The Burden of the Public Debt: Reply," LI March, 1961), 141-43.

plies. The essence of Lerner's criticism seems to run as follows: Bowen, Davis, and Kopf obtain their result by using a trick definition of "generation" so as to make what is in fact simply a redistribution of burden among existing taxpayers look like a shift in burden over time. We deny the validity of this criticism.

With regard to our definition of "generation," we are willing to agree that this word, like so many other words, can be used in a variety of ways. Nevertheless, we thought that it was clear from the whole context of our original article that the essential point of our definition of generation was to distinguish between different groups of people born at different times, so as to enable us to trace through the effects of a given fiscal action on the *lifetime* consumption of groups of people born at different points of time. We still fail to see anything "perverse" in this use of words.

However, we are more interested in making sure that the substance of our argument is clear than in arguing for any particular terminological trappings. Consequently, we are glad to have this opportunity to try to remove any vestiges of semantic confusion. In this connection, it may be helpful to refer to all persons alive at the particular moment of time when the borrowing occurs (t_0) simply as "Set I."[3] As each year passes, the total size of Set I will diminish steadily as more and more Set I persons die and are replaced in the population by persons born after t_0. As this change in the composition of the population takes place over the years, the Set I persons who bought bonds at t_0 will sell at least some of these bonds to the newcomers. Some bonds will also, no doubt, be exchanged among Set I persons, but transactions of this sort are of no lasting significance in the context of this discussion. Eventually, of course, we shall reach the year in which not a single member of old Set I is still alive; by this time we can be sure that all of the bonds originally purchased by Set I will have been sold (ignoring bequests, which modify the problem quantitatively, but not qualitatively) to persons born after t_0. Our proposition is that the use of debt finance permits, by the process described in our original paper, a relative improvement in the lifetime economic position

3. How the bonds are distributed among different age-groups within this Set is of no consequence from the standpoint of the question to which our analysis is addressed. In our original paper we assumed that all bonds were sold to persons 21 years old at the time of the borrowing. This artifice was designed solely to simplify the exposition; we could just as well have assumed that the bonds were sold to all persons alive at t_0, regardless of age.

of Set I persons vis-à-vis a situation in which taxation was employed at t_0.

It must be emphasized that the lifetimes of persons born in different years do overlap at points in time, and that recognition of this basic fact of life is essential to an understanding of the logic of our argument. Any transfer of real resources must take place at some point in time and obviously can take place only between persons alive at the same point in time. Indeed, this is just the process by which the burden is transferred from persons alive at t_0 to persons born later. But this transfer of real resources does not take place at the time the debt is issued; nor is it true, as Lerner suggests, that what is gained at one point of time must be lost in the future. ("It is possible for the Lowells to borrow from the Thomases, and what this borrowing does is to shift the burden from the Lowells to the Thomases in the present, and then to shift an equal burden from the Thomases to the Lowells in the future when the loan is repaid."[4]) To use Lerner's terminology, the Thomases will end up with the burden, or they may pass it on to the Lowells' children, but they will obviously be unable to pass it back to the Lowells if the Lowells have all died by the time the debt is repaid.

In short, Lerner misleads the reader when he suggests that the redistribution of burden we are talking about is nothing more than a redistribution among taxpayers alive at the time the borrowing occurs. A redistribution of lifetime real income between people alive at the time the borrowing occurs and people born later can take place even if all people alive at the time the borrowing occurs buy bonds in amounts exactly equivalent to their taxpayer liabilities for the public debt. Regardless of the distribution of bond holdings among the working population alive at the time of World War I, there is little doubt but that some part of the goods and services foregone by these persons during World War I was recouped as the bond-holders subsequently exchanged their bonds for claims against consumption goods produced in later periods— goods produced in part by individuals not alive at the time the original debt was incurred. And this process is still going on. It seems clear that had World War I been financed entirely by taxes, the lifetime consumption of the 1917-18 population would have

4. Lerner, "The Burden of the Debt," p. 140.

been lower, apart from any effects of debt finance on the consumption-investment mix.

We wish to stress that we are not suggesting that World War I was fought with shells still being produced. In our analysis it is individuals, with their claims against consumption goods, who move through time, not real resources. Our analysis is concerned with the effects of debt finance on the *distribution* of lifetime consumption between persons alive at the time the borrowing occurred and persons yet to come, not on the level of output of the economy as a whole at different points in time.

Lerner, on the other hand, seems unwilling to speak of the "burden of the debt" in terms of any measure other than induced changes in the level of national income. This is the way in which economists have become accustomed to defining the burden of the debt, it is *one* useful way of looking at the effects of debt finance, and we of course agree with Lerner that debt-financing produces a burden in this sense only if there are effects on the investment-consumption mix. We submit, however, that it is also meaningful to ask if the use of debt finance alters the distribution of lifetime consumption between persons alive when a debt is incurred and persons born later. The answer to this question is "yes," and in this sense debt finance does improve the relative economic position of the "present" populace vis-à-vis the future populace. Given these two ways of looking at the effects of debt finance, Lerner's rabbi was, after all, a very wise man.[5]

Finally, we wish to re-emphasize a point made (we thought) very clearly in our original article but ignored by Lerner. There are many considerations relevant to the choice among alternative methods of financing government expenditures in any given situation. Under many (probably most) circumstances, such issues as effects on employment, effects on price stability, and effects on incentives will outweigh any consideration of equity in the intergeneration distribution of income. Our only concern is that many economists have explicitly or implicitly denied the very

5. It may be noted in passing that the effect of debt finance on the investment/consumption mix (and thus on the relationship between present and future levels of national income enjoyed by society as a whole) and on the distribution of lifetime income between persons born at different times are not, however, completely unrelated. To the extent that debt finance makes the populace alive at the time of the borrowing better off, it is reasonable to expect some derived effects on the volume of saving, consumption, and investment.

existence of such a consideration. In so doing, they have been in error.

H/ PUBLIC DEBT—WHO BEARS THE BURDEN?*

BY *Gordon Tullock*

A few years ago almost all economists, at least in the Anglo-Saxon countries, agreed that the real burden of a domestically held public debt was represented by the withdrawal of private goods and services from the community made necessary when the borrowed funds were spent. The line of reasoning upon which this view was based depended critically upon the apparent fact that the total amount of goods and services available to the economy was not changed[1] by government bond issues. Thus, if the government built an aircraft carrier the private share of the total national product was reduced and the government share increased, regardless of whether the money to pay for the carrier was raised by taxation or by borrowing.

Economists five or six years ago not only were generally agreed on this view of the burden, they also normally were quite proud of the difference between the professional viewpoint and that of the common man. The "orthodox" opinion of the economically unsophisticated common men, of course, held that public borrowing was just like private borrowing. It resulted in obtaining funds now in return for agreeing to repay them with interest in the future. In other words, it shifted the costs of the aircraft carrier onto future taxpayers. Dwight Eisenhower was merely expressing this common opinion when he warned against governmental borrowing as placing a burden on posterity.

* Reprinted by permission from *Rivista di dirrito finanziario e scienza delle finanze*, XXII (June, 1963).

1. For the purposes of the discussion the countercyclical possibilities of deficit financing were assumed away. This was not through ignorance; indeed the bulk of the economists who were advocates of countercyclical policies held the view we are discussing. The argument was that the burden of "real" borrowing was felt at the time the money was spent. Countercyclical borrowing, with its effect on the money supply raised quite different issues.

In 1958, Professor James Buchanan published a book[2] contending that almost all economists[3] had been wrong and that President Eisenhower was fundamentally right. The startling nature of this thesis, together with the cogency of the arguments offered for it, created a small crisis for many economists. The idea that the common man was more sophisticated on a rather important point than the economics profession was not only intellectually, but emotionally disturbing. The consequence has been a continuing debate in which a group of young "radicals" defending Buchanan have been opposed by older and more conservative scholars in the field of public finance. The debate has surely generated more heat than light, but it has served to illuminate a number of dark corners.[4]

In the course of this debate, however, there has been some shift away from the issues raised by Buchanan and toward a discussion of other problems. Vickrey and Modigliani[5] have agreed that debt financing of governmental expenditures may reduce the income of future generations, but through a completely different mechanism than that suggested by Buchanan. Although they seem not to realize it, their position does not contradict, but supplements that of Buchanan. Briefly, Vickrey and Modigliani argue that most of the money raised by government bond sales would other-

2. *Public Principles of Public Debt* (Homewood, Illinois).

3. Including, alas, the author of this note.

4. The student interested in getting the general tenor of the conflict can do so by examining one battle. Bowen, Davis, and Kopf published "The Public Debt: A Burden on Future Generations?" in *The American Economic Review*, September, 1960, pp. 701-6. This attracted no less than three critical comments by William Vickrey, Tibor Scitovsky, and James Elliott which were published in the March, 1961, issue of the *Review*, pp. 132-41. Bowen, Davis, and Kopf replied briefly in the same issue, pp. 141-43. Abba Lerner then published "The Burden of the Debt" in the May, 1961, issue of *The Review of Economics and Statistics*, pp. 139-41, and Bowen, Davis, and Kopf replied with "The Distribution of the Debt: A Reply," in the February, 1962, issue, pp. 98-100. In this particular case the difference between the ages of the proponents and opponents of Buchanan's view is particularly striking.

The following other discussions of the problem may also be of interest: Abba Lerner, *The Journal of Political Economy*, XLVII (April, 1959), 203-6; Earl Rolph, *The American Economic Review*, XLIX (March, 1959), 183-85; Alvin Hansen, *The Review of Economics and Statistics*, XLI (June, 1959), 377-78.

5. Vickrey's views are contained in his criticism of Bowen, Davis, and Kopf cited in the previous footnote. Modigliani's may be found in "Long-Run Implications of Alternative Fiscal Policies and the Burden of the National Debt." *The Economic Journal*, LXXI (December, 1961), 730-55.

wise have been invested in the private sector. Most of the money raised by taxation on the other hand, would probably have been spent on consumption. Government borrowing, therefore, results in the total capital supply of the society being less than if the same funds were raised by taxation, and hence results in future incomes being smaller.

No one doubts the correctness of this position of Vickrey and Modigliani, but it neither contradicts nor proves Buchanan's basic point, and hence serves to divert attention from the original problem. The same may be said about discussions of the "Fiscal Illusion." That this is an important problem, and a difficult one has been clear since the time of Ricardo. The controversy set off by Buchanan has served to shed some light in this rather murky area, but this should be thought of as a by-product, not as a direct part of the debate.

When Bowen, Davis, and Kopf published their article in 1961, they made no claim to theoretical originality, they simply said Buchanan's position had been widely misunderstood, and they proposed to introduce a new model to clarify his position.[6] Since the debate has continued to be confused, and since Buchanan's position is still not clear to many scholars in the field, I intend in this article to follow their example. For this purpose I also will introduce a simplified model in the hopes of making the situation clearer. I will make use of a little science fiction, but my model will be no less realistic than many other economic models.[7]

Suppose that a scientist has invented a remarkable machine. It will, on a strictly temporary basis, create gold bars. If it is set properly, gold bars in unlimited quantities will pour out of the machine. There is, however, a limitation on the use of this machine. The gold must be returned to the machine within twenty years or certain conservation laws will be violated, and there will be an unimaginable catastrophe. If 100 gold bars are produced by the machine, 100 gold bars must be put back in. The bars returned to the machine simply disappear. The machine is already in existence in the scientist's laboratory and its operation is costless.

6. In view of this fact it is notable that none of the older economists who attacked the article referred to Buchanan's book. Two of them, Scitovsky and Elliott, credit the three young men with contributions which clearly originated with Buchanan.

7. As a safeguard against the possibility that it is I who misunderstood Buchanan, I have discussed the model with him and have his agreement that it does represent his position.

The scientist, being patriotic, offers the government exclusive use of this device for purposes of governmental finance. After the death by apoplexy of several senators, the scientist's proposal is accepted. A bill is passed providing that a certain quantity of gold bars is to be temporarily produced and sold to the public, the proceeds to be used to cover various governmental expenditures. The bill also obligates the government twenty years in the future to buy back the gold and return it to the machine. Who bears the burden of the governmental expenditures?

Clearly, no one is in any way injured at the time the expenditure is made.[8] There is, then, no burden at that time. Twenty years later, however, it will be necessary to tax people for this purpose and hence there will be a burden. What has happened is that the total wealth of the nation has been temporarily increased by the machine. Later, when the gold bars are returned to the machine, the national wealth will be reduced and the only burden felt by anyone is the result of this decrease.

It would be inconvenient, however, for the gold bar salesmen to carry around large stocks of heavy gold bars. Suppose then that when an individual purchases a gold bar from a government representative, he is given a receipt. The government undertakes when the receipt is presented at the laboratory, to turn on the machine, produce a gold bar, and give it to the receipt holder. Different people, of course, would present their receipts at different times. It would be absurd, however, to assume that this changed things particularly. Mr. A pays a salesman and receives his receipt. He promptly rushes to the laboratory and gets his gold bar. Lazy Mr. B, on the other hand, pays a salesman on the same day as Mr. A, but puts off his visit to the laboratory until the following week when he will be in that part of town on another errand. Suppose that the government spends the money that it has received from Mr. A and Mr. B during the interval. Does this make any difference? Surely, it would be absurd to say that a burden is imposed on the "present generation" when the government spends the money Mr. B has paid in but not when it spends that paid in by Mr. A. Further, this would require assuming that the burden somehow vanished when Mr. B actually got his gold to reappear twenty years later.

Having a bar of gold around the house is, in some ways, incon-

8. Any change in purchasing patterns does affect some producers, but I follow the usual custom in ignoring both injuries and benefits from this source. Presumably, also, there would be some changes in investment patterns.

venient. It might be that some of the buyers of gold would decide to simply keep their receipt until such time as they actually needed the gold for some purpose. Clearly, since they consciously choose to hold the receipt instead of converting it into gold, they are in no way disadvantaged by the fact that they have no gold. To say that their choice in this matter somehow imposes a burden on their "generation" which would not have existed had they decided to exchange their receipt for gold seems ridiculous. Surely, the only person affected by the choice would be the chooser, and he cannot be assumed to be "burdened" by the results of his free choice.

The same conclusion would apply if some purchaser chose to keep his receipt for the full twenty years, with the consequence that the gold bar never even came into existence. Still, it is clear that no one suffers any burden when the government makes its sale and spends the proceeds. There is, however, a real burden on the taxpayers when the gold or certificates are repurchased. If the government chose to pay a small sum each year to people who kept their certificates instead of converting them into gold,[9] this also would not change the situation. No person would bear any burden at the time the government expenditure was made, but there would be a burden when the certificates had to be bought back. The interest charges, also, would impose a burden on the taxpayer. But here we clearly have a simple sale of government bonds, and it does shift the burden forward in time.

We can make the resemblance to government bonds even plainer by a few additional assumptions. Suppose the government produces the gold, but keeps it in its own vaults, selling only warehouse receipts on it to the public. If it were necessary to return the identical gold bars to the machine this might well be a sensible precaution. If the government paid small amounts each year to the holders of the warehouse receipts, then they would differ hardly at all from bonds. The same thing would be true, of course, if the government contracted with a bank to store the gold instead of keeping it in its own vaults. Another alternative would be to sell the gold bars, but subject to the restriction that the purchaser, or his assigns, must preserve the individual bars and resell those specific bars to the gov-

9. Motivated, perhaps, by a slight distrust of the scientist's calculations. The model can be extended by assuming that the "gold-maker" actually will not work, so that there is no real possibility of creating the gold bars.

ernment in twenty years. Since the purchaser would be providing storage for the gold, regular payments to him for this service would be sensible, thus the gold bars themselves would have a remarkable economic resemblance to bonds.

We can make a still further change. One of the advantages of an imaginary machine is that we can easily make changes in its design. Suppose, then, that the gold produced by the machine is rather peculiar in its nature. The process of making the gold has an after-effect which leads the gold bars to expand at the rate of 4 per cent per year for the full twenty years that they can continue to exist. The government could sell these bars to the public, and would then be completely free of any obligation for twenty years. The expansion of the bars, however, would give the holders a net return from the mere act of keeping them. At the end of the twenty year period, of course, the government would have to buy back all the gold, including that which had grown from the original bars, and this would be the equivalent of the discounted cost of paying 4 per cent interest over the period. This would appear a particularly clear case of shifting burdens to the future. Present taxpayers would pay nothing for the benefits they derive from the government expenditure, while the taxpayers of twenty years in the future, quite a different group of people, would pay a whopping fee for which they received nothing. Its economic effect on both individuals and the government, on the other hand, would be substantially identical with that of twenty year government bonds similar to the "E Bonds" which were so important in the financing of the American participation in World War II.

All of this may seem simply playing with an unreal system, but it does serve to clarify the situation. None of the assumed sets of circumstances raises any problem for the economists who assume that borrowing money rather than raising the same sum through taxation transfers the burden of the expediture to the shoulders of future taxpayers. The economist who believes that such transfers do not take place, on the other hand, has great difficulty in dealing with these cases. Since some of the assumed sets of circumstances are economically identical with bond issues, this would seem to demonstrate that the "shifting" hypothesis is the correct one.

In order to make the point absolutely clear, let us introduce one final bit of science fiction. Suppose that eighteen years after the original machine is put in operation another scientist discovers another machine. This machine makes it unnecessary to return the gold bars to the first scientist's machine. Thus the burden of the original expenditures disappears. If the burden were transferred twenty years into the future, then it is still two years in the future at the time this machine is developed, and no problems are raised. If, however, the burden were borne by the economy when the gold bars were first produced, then it is eliminated retroactively, which is absurd.

Chapter Five

THE AGGREGATE
INVESTMENT APPROACH

A/ LONG-RUN IMPLICATIONS OF ALTERNATIVE FIS-CAL POLICIES AND THE BURDEN OF THE NATIONAL DEBT*

BY *Franco Modigliani*

I. Introduction

The time-honored controversy over the burden of the National Debt has flared up once more.[1] The view, almost unchallenged a few years back, that the National Debt is no burden on the economy and that the real cost of government expenditure, no matter how financed, cannot be shifted to "future generations" has been on the retreat under a powerful counterattack spearheaded by the contributions of J. M. Buchanan,[2] J. E. Meade,[3] and R. A.

* Reprinted by permission from *The Economic Journal*, LXXI (December, 1961).

1. A number of colleagues at Massachusetts Institute of Technology and other institutions have greatly helped me with their comments on a preliminary draft of this paper. I wish particularly to acknowledge the many useful suggestions of Ralph Beals, James Buchanan, Sukhamoy Chakravarty, Margaret Hall, and Merton Miller.

2. J. M. Buchanan, *Public Principles of Public Debt* (Homewood, Illinois: Richard D. Irwin, 1958).

3. J. E. Meade, "Is the National Debt a Burden?" *Oxford Economic Papers*, X (June, 1958), 163-83, and "Is the National Debt a Burden: A Correction," *ibid.*, XI (February, 1959), 109-10.

Musgrave.[4] These authors, while relying to a considerable extent on older arguments, have significantly enriched the analysis by blending the traditional approach with the new insights provided by the Keynesian revolution. But even these most recent contributions have failed, in our view, to provide an altogether adequate framework—a failure resulting at least in part from the Keynesian tendency to emphasise flows while paying inadequate attention to stocks. It is the purpose of this paper to propose a fresh approach to this problem, and to show that, unlike its predecessors, it leads to a consistent and yet straightforward answer to all relevant questions.

Unless otherwise noted, the National Debt will be defined here as consisting of: (1) all claims against the Government held by the private sector of the economy, or by foreigners, whether interest bearing or not (and including therefore bank-held debt and government currency, if any); less (2) any claims held by the Government against the private sector and foreigners.[5]

From a methodological point of view, the central contention of our analysis is that to grasp fully the economic effects of alternative fiscal policies and of the National Debt, we must pay proper attention to stocks as well as to the usual flow variables and to the long-run as well as to the impact effects. Among the substantive implications of this line of approach, the following may be mentioned here by way of a rough summary: (1) Given the government purchase of goods and services, an increase of the (real) National Debt, whether internal or external, is generally advantageous to those present at the time of the increase (or to some subset

---

4. R. A. Musgrave, *The Theory of Public Finance* (McGraw-Hill, 1959), especially Chapter 23. Other recent contributions include: the reviews of Buchanan's book by A. P. Lerner, *The Journal of Political Economy*, XLVII (April, 1959), 203-6; E. R. Rolph, *The American Economic Reviews*, XLIX (March, 1959), 183-5, and A. H. Hansen, *The Review of Economics and Statistics*, XLI (June, 1959), 377-8; also "The Public Debt: A Burden on Future Generations?" by W. G. Bowen, R. G. Davis, and D. H. Kopf, *The American Economic Review*, L (September, 1960), 701-6; and the forthcoming note by A. P. Lerner, "The Burden of Debt," *The Review of Economics and Statistics*, LIV (May, 1961).

Since the completion of this paper, three comments on the Bowen, Davis, and Kopf communication by W. Vickrey, T. Scitovsky, and J. R. Elliott, and a reply by the authors have also appeared in the March, 1961, issue of *The American Economic Review*, pp. 132-43.

5. This definition implies that the National Debt could in principle be negative. Even in this case we shall refer to it by the same name, although its magnitude will be expressed by a negative number. Similarly, we refer to an operation that reduces the algebraic value of the National Debt as a "reduction," even if the debt was initially zero or negative.

thereof). (2) Such an increase will generally place a "gross burden" on those living beyond that time through a reduction in the aggregate stock of private capital, which, as long as the (net) marginal productivity of capital is positive, will in turn cause a reduction in the flow of goods and services. Furthermore, this loss (as well as the gain under (1) above) will tend to occur even when lack of effective private demand would prevent the maintenance of full employment in the absence of the deficit, though the relative size of gain and losses may be quite different in these circumstances. (3) These conclusions hold in reverse in the case of a reduction in the real National Debt. That is, such a decline is burdensome on those present at the time of the reduction and tends to generate a gross gain for those living beyond. (4) *If* the rate of interest at which the Government borrows can be taken as a good approximation to the marginal productivity of private capital, then the gross burden (or gain) to "future generations" referred to under (2) and (3) can be *measured* by the interest charges on the National Debt. (5) The gross burden may be offset in part or *in toto*, or may be even more than offset, in so far as the increase in the debt is accompanied by government expenditure which contributes to the real income of future generations, *e.g.*, through productive public capital formation.[6]

This summary is very rough indeed and is subject to numerous qualifications and amendments, many of which will be noted below. In any event, I should like to emphasise that the stress of this paper is on developing a method of analysis rather than on presenting a body of doctrines. For this reason I will try to relate my analysis to earlier points of view whenever this seems helpful in clarifying the issues involved. At the same time I will endeavor to stay clear of many traditional but somewhat sterile controversies, such as whether the analogy between private and public debt is true or false.

II. A Bird's Eye View of the Classical and Post-Keynesian No-transfer and No-burden Argument

We begin by reviewing the very persuasive arguments supporting the doctrine that the cost of the current government use of resources

6. The difference between the increase in the National Debt in a given interval and the Government expenditure contributing to future income corresponds roughly to the net increase in what Professor Meade has called the "deadweight" debt.

cannot be transferred to future generations and that the National Debt is no burden on them. Since these arguments have been presented many times in the last couple of centuries and have been extensively restated in recent years, we can afford to recapitulate them very briefly in terms of the three propositions presented below—at the cost of glossing over some of the fine points and of foregoing the pleasure of citing "chapter and verse."[7]

(1) Individuals or sub-groups within an economic system can, by means of borrowing, increase the current flow of goods available to them and pay for this increase out of future output. But they can do so only because their borrowing is "external," *i.e.*, matched by a lender who yields current goods in exchange for later output. But a closed community cannot dispose of more goods and services than it is currently producing. It certainly cannot increase this flow by paying with future output, for there is no way "we can dispose to-day of to-morrow's output." Hence the goods and services acquired by the Government must always be "paid for" by those present at the time in the form of a reduction in the flow of goods available to them for private use, and cannot possibly be paid for by later generations, whether the acquisition is financed by taxes or by internal borrowing. Only through external borrowing is it possible to benefit the current generation and to impose a burden on the future.

(2) Although internal borrowing will leave in its wake an obligation for future tax-payers to pay the interest on the National Debt and, possibly, to repay the principal, this obligation is not a net burden on the community as a whole, because these payments are but transfers of income between future members of the community. The loss of the tax-payers is offset in the aggregate by the gain of the beneficiary of the payment. These transfers may, of course, occur between people of different ages and hence of different "generations," and in this sense internal borrowing may cause "inter-generations transfers," but it will not cause a net loss to society.

The above two arguments, or some reasonable variant thereof, have provided the cornerstone of the no-transfer, no-burden argument over the last two centuries or so. It was left for Keynesian

---

7. The reader interested in establishing just who said what will find much useful material in Buchanan, *Public Principles of Public Debt*, especially Chapters 2 and 8, and in B. Griziotti, "La diversa pressione tributaria del prestito e dell'imposta" in *Studi di scienza delle finanze e diritto finanziario* (Milano: Giuffre, 1956), II, 193-273.

analysis to provide a third argument, removing thereby a potentially troublesome objection to the first two. If the cost of government expenditure always falls on the current generation, no matter how financed, why not forego altogether the painful activity of levying taxes? Yet our common sense rebels at this conclusion. A partial answer to this puzzle was provided by recognizing that taxes, even when paid back in the form of transfers, generate some "frictional loss," because most if not all feasible methods of raising tax revenue tend to interfere with the optimum allocation of resources.[8] Presumably the ever-increasing level of the National Debt resulting from full deficit financing of current expenditure would require raising through taxes an ever-growing revenue to pay the interest on the debt. Eventually the ratio of such taxes to national income plus transfers would exceed the ratio of government expenditure to national product, giving rise to frictional tax losses which could have been avoided through a balanced budget. While these considerations do provide a *prima facie* case for a balanced-budget policy, the case is not tight, for could not the interest itself be met by further borrowing?

However, we need not follow these fancy possibilities, for the Keynesian analysis has provided a much more cogent argument to support the need for an "appropriate" amount of taxation, although not necessarily for a balanced budget. This argument, which reaches its most elegant formulation in the so-called principle of "functional finance" enunciated by Lerner,[9] can be roughly summarized as follows.

(3) Given the full employment output, say $\overline{X}$, and given the share of this output which it is appropriate to allocate for government use, say $\overline{G}$, there is a maximum amount of output that is left available for the private sector, say $\overline{P} = \overline{X} - \overline{G}$. Now the private sector demand for output, say P, is a function of income and taxes, say $P = P(X, T)$, with $\dfrac{\delta P}{\delta T} < 0$. Taxes are then to be set at that level, say $\overline{T}$, which satisfies the equation $P(X, T) = \overline{P}$. A higher

8. See, *e.g.*, J. E. Meade, "Mr. Lerner on 'The Economics of Control,' " *The Economic Journal*, LV (April, 1945), 47-70.

9. See, *e.g.*, "Functional Finance and the Public Debt," *Social Research*, X, No. 1, and "The Burden of the National Debt," in *Income Employment and Public Policy* (New York: W. W. Norton & Company, 1948).

level of taxes would generate unemployment and a lower level would generate inflation, both evils which it is the task of the Government to avoid. T may turn out to be larger than $\overline{G}$, calling for a surplus, or smaller than $\overline{G}$, or even perchance just equal to $\overline{G}$, implying a balanced budget. But in any event, the purpose of taxes is not to make the current members of the community pay for the government use of goods, which they will do in any event; the real reason we need to put up with the unpleasantness of taxes is to prevent the greater social evil of inflation.

III. A Bird's Eye View of the Classical and Post-Keynesian Transfer and Burden Argument

The basic contention of this school of thought, which itself has a long tradition, is that in general—though possibly with some exceptions—a debt-financed public expenditure will place no burden at all on those present at the very moment in which the expenditure takes place, and will instead place a burden on all tax-payers living thereafter. This burden may fall in part on those present at the time of the expenditure, but only insofar as they are present thereafter. The arguments which support this position have also been repeatedly stated and have been thoroughly reviewed quite recently by Buchanan. It will therefore again be sufficient to summarize them very briefly in the following two propositions:

(1) The cost of a tax-financed expenditure is borne currently, for the resources obtained by the Government come from a forcible reduction in the resources of current tax-payers. But an expenditure financed by debt, whether internal or external, as a rule places no burden on those present at the time of the expenditure in that, and insofar as, the resources acquired by the Government are surrendered in a voluntary exchange by the savers, who thereby acquire government bonds (in lieu of some other asset).

(2) The burden is imposed instead on all future tax-payers, who will have to pay taxes to service the debt. These taxes are *not* a mere transfer of income, but a net burden on society, for, in the absence of the debt-financed expenditure, the taxes would not have been levied, while the investors in bonds would have received the income just the same, directly or indirectly, from the return on the physical assets in which their savings would have been invested. This argument *does not* imply that a debt-financed expenditure will neces-

sarily affect future generations unfavorably. In order to assess the "net outcome," we must subtract from the gross burden represented by the extra taxes benefits, if any, resulting from the expenditure. Thus the net outcome might even be positive if the expenditure undertaken produced greater benefits than the private capital formation which it replaces. But the argument does imply that, through deficit financing, the expenditure of the Government is being "paid for" by future generations.

A careful application of the *reasoning* underlying (1) and (2) will reveal circumstances in which the above conclusions do not hold and the allocation of the burden may be independent of the form of financing used. There are in particular two important cases which are treated at some length by Buchanan and which bring to light the contribution of Keynesian analysis also to this side of the argument. The first is the case of debt-financed expenditure in deep depressions, when private capital formation could not, in any event, provide an adequate offset to full-employment saving. Here, according to Buchanan, not even a gross burden need result to future taxpayers, for the expenditure could in principle be financed by interest-free issuance of currency. The second exception discussed by Buchanan is that of a major war. Unfortunately, the chapter on war financing is one of the least convincing in his book, and what follows may represent more nearly my application of his framework than a faithful summary of his argument. Suppose the war effort is sufficiently severe so that the allocation of resources to various uses, and to capital formation in particular, is completely determined by war necessities. In such a situation the way in which the Government finances its expenditure cannot affect private consumption or capital formation. It would seem therefore that the burden of reduced consumption must be borne by the current generation, even if the reduction is achieved not through taxes but through a combination of rationing and voluntary increases in saving and the unspent disposable income is invested in claims against the Government. Similarly, the burden of the reduction in useful capital formation is borne by those living after the war, again independently of financing. In this case, as well as in the case of depression financing, the taxes levied to pay the interest on the increased debt would indeed seem to result in a pure transfer, for the income associated with the bonds would *not* have come to exist had the Government decided respectively to tax, or to print money, instead of borrowing.

J. E. Meade has also lately associated himself with those maintaining that the National Debt is a burden,[10] but his argument is quite different from the classical one, and bears instead all the marks of post-Keynesian analysis. He is not concerned with the differential effect of deficit versus tax financing, but asserts none the less that government debt in excess of government-owned physical capital—the so-called deadweight debt—is a burden on the economy. Unfortunately his contribution, which is so stimulating in analyzing the effects of a major capital levy, is less than convincing in its attempt to establish that the deadweight debt is a burden. For his demonstration seems to rely entirely on the proposition that elimination of the debt would be a blessing for the economy in that it would encourage saving through a "Pigou type" effect, besides reducing the frictional costs of transfers. Now the tax-friction proposition, though valid, is not new,[11] and had already been generally accepted as a second-order amendment to the no-burden argument. On the other hand, the first and central argument is rather unconvincing. For, as Meade himself recognizes, a reduction in National Debt, be it through a capital levy, budget surplus or inflation, would spur saving whether or not the debt reduced thereby was "deadweight" debt. In fact, at least the first two means would tend to increase saving, even if they were applied in a situation where the National Debt was zero to begin with, and the outcome would be that of driving the economy into a position of net indebtedness vis-à-vis the Government. Finally, Meade's analysis throws no light on whether the increase in saving following the capital levy is a permanent or a purely transitory phenomenon, nor on who, if anyone, bears the burden of a debt reduction. In spite of these apparent shortcomings, I am encouraged to think that Professor Meade's views are fundamentally quite close to those advanced here. I hope this will become gradually apparent, even without much further explicit reference to his argument.

IV. Fallacies in the No-transfer No-burden Argument

The classical argument summarized in the last section appears so far rather convincing, and if so we should be able to pinpoint the fallacies in one or more of the three propositions of Section II.

10. Meade, "Is the National Debt a Burden?"
11. See, e.g., the references in footnote 8, p. 111, above, and in Buchanan, *Public Principles of Public Debt*, p. 14, footnote 8.

The fallacy in proposition (1) is not difficult to uncover. It is quite true that a closed community cannot increase its current resources by relying on tomorrow's unproduced output. None the less, the way in which we use today's resources can affect in three major ways the output that will result tomorrow from tomorrow's labor input: (i) by affecting the natural resources available to the future; (ii) by improving technological knowledge; and (iii) by affecting the stock of man-made means of production, or capital, available to future generations. Hence government expenditure, and the way it is financed, *can* affect the economy in the future if it affects any of the above three items.

The argument in (3) is also seriously inadequate, and the post-war experience has brought this home sharply. For the demand of the private sector consists of consumption C and capital formation I, and at least the latter component depends not only on income and taxes but also on monetary policy. Once we acknowledge this point, the principle of Functional Finance no longer implies a unique level of taxes. To demonstrate this point and its implications, it will be convenient—though it is not essential—to suppose that monetary policy affects P exclusively through the intermediary of the rate of interest r, i.e., that $P = P(X, T, r)$ with $\dfrac{\delta P}{\delta r} < 0$; and that r in turn depends on X and the quantity of money M. But once we admit that r enters not vacuously in P we must also recognize that the equation

$$(1) \qquad P(\overline{X}, T, r) = P$$

will be satisfied not by one but by many possible values of T, each value being accompanied by the appropriate value of r, say $r(T)$. Now in most circumstances—that is, except possibly in very deep depression—there will be a range of values of T such that the corresponding $r(T)$ is achievable by an appropriate monetary policy. There is therefore not one but a whole schedule of values of T which are consistent with the maintenance of full employment and price stability, each value of T being accompanied by an appropriate monetary policy. Furthermore, within this range there will tend to be a direct connection between T and the capital formation component of $\overline{P}$. If, starting from a correct combination of T, r, and M, we lower taxes we will increase consumption, and to offset this we must reduce capital formation by appropriately tightening monetary policy. Conversely, by increasing taxes we can afford to have a larger capital formation. Thus, given the level of government expenditure, the level of taxes, and hence of budget deficit, does affect "future generations" through the stock of capital inherited by them.

Having thus brought to light the weaknesses in arguments (1) and (3), it is an easy matter to establish that, at least under certain conditions, the Keynesian framework is perfectly consistent with the classical conclusion stated in Section III. Suppose we take as a starting-point a given G, and some given combination of T and r consistent with full employment. Suppose further, as is generally assumed in Keynesian analysis, that to a first approximation consumption responds to taxes but not to interest rates. Now let the Government increase its expenditure by dG while keeping taxes constant. Then the deficit will increase precisely by $dD = dG$. What will happen to capital formation? If we are to maintain full employment without inflation we must have

$$dG + dC + dI = 0$$

and since, by assumption, taxes are constant and hence $dC = 0$, we must have

$$dG = dD = -dI$$

i.e., the debt-financed expenditure must be accompanied by an equal reduction in capital formation (with the help of the appropriate monetary policy).

This outcome is illustrated by a numerical example in Table I. Row (*a*) shows the behavior of the relevant flows in the initial situation, taken as a standard of comparison: here the budget is assumed to be balanced, although this is of no particular relevance. In row (*b*) we examine the consequence of an increase of expenditure by 100, with unchanged taxes, and hence consumption. The amount of resources available for, and hence the level of private capital formation, is cut down precisely by the amount of the deficit-financed expenditure. It is also apparent that this expenditure puts no burden on the "current" members of the community. Their (real) disposable income is unchanged by the expenditure, and consequently so is their consumption, as well as the net current addition to their personal wealth or private net worth. But because capital formation has been cut by the amount of the deficit, the community will thereafter dispose of a stock of private capital curtailed to a corresponding extent.

Thus the deficit-financed expenditure will leave in its wake an

TABLE I

A. Effects of Government Expenditure and Financing on Private Saving and Capital Formation

(Full Employment—All variables measured in real terms)

Method of Financing	Income, X. (1)	Government Expenditure, G. (2)	Taxes, T. (3)	Disposable Income, Y. $(X - T)$ (4)	Consumption, C. $(c_0 + cY)$ $(c = 0.6)$ (5)	Saving $S = \Delta W$ $(Y - C)$ (6)	Deficit, D. $(G - T)$ (7)	Private capital formation $I = \Delta K$ $(S - D)$ (8)
(a) Initial situation	2,000	300 (G_0)	300	1,700	1,500 (C_0)	200 (S_0)	0	200 (S_0)
(b) Increased expenditure— deficit financed	2,000	400 $(G_0 + dG)$	300	1,700	1,500 (C_0)	200 (S_0)	100 (dG)	100
(c) Increased expenditure— tax financed	2,000	400 $(G_0 + dG)$	400	1,600	1,440 $(C_0 - cdG)$	160 $(S_0 - sdG)$	0	160 $(S_0 - sdG)$

B. Comparative "Burden" Effects of Alternative Budgetary Policies

Budgetary policy.	Effect on	
	Private capital formation.	"Burden."
1. Joint effect of increased expenditure *and* deficit financing	$I(b) - I(a)^1 = (S_0 - dG) - S_0 = -dG$	$r^*(dG)$
2. Joint effect of increased expenditure and taxes	$I(c) - I(a) = (S_0 - sdG) - S_0 = -sdG$	$r^*s(dG)$
3. Differential effect of deficit financing	$I(b) - I(c) = (S_0 - sdG) - $	$r^*c(dG)$
	$(S_0 - sdG) = -(1 - s)dG = -cdG$	

1. $I(a)$ means investment in situation (a), and similarly for $I(b)$ and $I(c)$.

over-all burden on the economy in the form of a reduced flow of income from the reduced stock of private capital.

V. Interest Charges and the "True" Burden of Debt Financing

The analysis of the last section is seen to agree with the classical conclusion that debt financing transfers the burden of the government expenditure to those living beyond the time of the expenditure. At the same time it indicates that this burden consists in *the loss of income from capital* and not in *the taxes levied on later members to pay the interest charges,* as the classical argument contends.

In some respects this amendment to the classical burden position may be regarded as rather minor, for it can be argued that, under reasonable assumptions, the interest charges will provide a good *measure* of the true burden. Indeed, as long as the amount dD is not large in relation to the stock of capital (and the flow of saving), the loss in the future stream of output will be adequately approximated by $r^*(dD)$, where r^* denotes the marginal productivity of capital. Now if the Government borrows in a competitive market, bidding against other seekers of capital, then the (long-term) interest rate r at which it borrows will also be a reasonable approximation to r^*. Hence the annual interest charges $r(dD)$ will also be a good approximation to the true social yearly loss, or opportunity cost, $r(dD)$[12]—provided we can also establish that the initial reduction in the stock of capital will not be recouped as long as the debt is not repaid.

One can, however, think of many reasons why the interest bill might not even provide a good *measure* of the true loss. To begin with, if the government operation is of sizeable proportions it may significantly drive up interest rates, say from r_0 to r_1, since the reduction in private capital will tend to increase its marginal product. In this case the interest on the debt will overstate the true burden, which will lie somewhere between $r_0(dD)$ and $r_1(dD)$. More serious are the problems arising from various kinds of imperfections in the commodities as well as in the capital markets. In particular, the Government may succeed in borrowing at rates well below r^* by forcing banks and other intermediaries to acquire and hold bonds with yields below the market, or, as in wartime, by effectively eliminating the competition of private borrowers. In the first-mentioned

12. This is precisely the position taken by Musgrave, *The Theory of Public Finance,* p. 577.

case, *e.g.*, we should add to the interest bill the lost income accruing to the bank depositors (or at least to the bank's stockholders). There is also the rather nasty problem that, because of uncertainty, the rate of interest may not be a good measure of the productivity of physical capital. To put it very roughly, r is at best a measure of return net of a risk premium, and the actual return on capital is better thought of as a random variable whose average value is, in general, rather higher than r.[13]

Besides the relation of r to r^* there is another problem that needs to be recognized. In our discussion so far, and in our table, we have assumed that consumption, and hence private saving, were unaffected because taxes were unchanged. But once we recognize that the borrowing may increase the interest rate, we must also recognize that it may, through this route, affect consumption even with unchanged taxes. This problem might well be quickly dismissed under the principle of *"de minimis."* For, though economists may still argue as to whether an increase in interest rates will increase or decrease saving, they generally agree that the effect, if any, will be negligible.[14] But even if the rate of saving were to rise from, say, S_0 to $S_0 + e$ and the level of capital formation were accordingly reduced only by $dD - e$, one could still argue that r^*dD and not $r^*(dD - e)$ is the relevant measure of the true loss to society. This is because, as suggested by Bowen *et al.*,[15] the income generated by the extra capital formation e may be quite appropriately regarded as just necessary to offset the extra sacrifice of current consumption undertaken by those who responded to the change in r.

Thus it would appear that the classical-burden position needs to be modified to the extent of recognizing that the burden of deficit financing consists not in the increased taxes as such, but rather in the fall in income generated by the reduction in the stock of capital. But this modification would seem rather innocuous, since, admittedly, rdD will generally provide a reasonable approximate *measure* of the true burden. In fact, however, the amendment we have sug-

13. Cf. F. Modigliani and M. H. Miller, "The Cost of Capital, Corporation Finance, and the Theory of Investment," *The American Economic Review,* LVIII (June, 1958), 261-97. However, Miller has suggested to me that r may be the more relevant measure of return on capital as it deducts an appropriate allowance for the "cost" of risk bearing.

14. This is especially true if current consumption is appropriately defined to include the rental value and not the gross purchase of consumers' durables.

15. Bowen, Davis and Kopf, "The Public Debt: A Burden on Future Generations?" p. 704.

gested turns out to have rather far-reaching implications as we will
show presently.

VI. Shortcomings of the Classical Transfer and Burden Argument: The Differential Effect of Deficit Versus Tax Financing

The classical conclusion that deficit financing of an expenditure
places the burden on the future seems to imply that, if the expenditure were financed by taxes, there would be no burden in the future.
Interestingly enough, Buchanan's book provides nowhere a systematic treatment of the temporal distribution of the burden from a
tax-financed expenditure. Nor is this really surprising, for if the
burden were in fact the interest of the debt, then tax financing could
generate no burden on the future.[16] But if the relevant criterion is
instead the loss of capital formation, then in order to find the true
differential effect of debt financing versus tax financing, we must
inquire about the effects of tax financing on private saving and capital formation. Only if this effect were nil or negligible would the
classical conclusion be strictly valid.

Now, to an economist steeped in the Keynesian tradition, it is at
once obvious that raising taxes to finance the government expenditure cannot fail to affect significantly private saving and capital formation. While tax financing will reduce disposable income by the
amount of the expenditure, it will reduce consumption only by an
amount $cdT = cdG$, where c is the marginal propensity to consume.
The rest of the tax will be borne by a reduction in saving by sdT,
where $s = 1 - c$ is the marginal propensity to save. Accordingly,
if the initial position was one of full employment, as we are assuming, and inflation is to be avoided, private capital formation must
itself be reduced by the amount sdD (through the appropriate
monetary policy).[17] This outcome is illustrated numerically in row
(c) of Table I. By comparing the outcome (a), (b), and (c) as is

---

16. See, however, footnote 26, p. 127, for a different explanation of Buchanan's
omission.

17. The need to curtail investment when government expenditure is increased
at full employment, even though it is fully tax covered, is the counterpart of
the so-called multiplier effect of a balanced budget when starting from less than
full utilization of resources. The tax-financed expenditure per se increases the
aggregate real demand for goods and services by a dollar per dollar of expenditure. But if we start from full employment, this extra demand could only result
in inflation. Hence it must be offset by a fall in investment of s dollars per
dollar of expenditure, which, taking into account the multiplier effect, will
reduce total demand by $s/s = 1$ dollar per dollar, as required.

done in part B of the table, we find that the differential effect of the deficit versus tax financing is to decrease capital formation by $dG - sdG = cdG$. The balance of the reduction, namely sdG, must be attributed to the expenditure as such, independently of how financed.[18] Hence, even if we are willing to regard the interest rate paid by the Government as a good approximation to r^*, the differential burden of debt financing on the future generations is not rdG but only $rcdG$.

It can readily be seen that the above result is not limited to the case we have explicitly discussed so far, in which the deficit arises from an increase in expenditure. If, for whatever reason, a portion dD of the government expenditure is not financed by taxes but by deficit, capital formation tends to be reduced by approximately $c(dD)$. This conclusion is, however, subject to one important qualification, namely that for $T = \overline{G}$, i.e., with a level of taxation balancing the budget, there exists a monetary policy capable of achieving full employment—or, in terms of our previous notation, of enforcing the required rate of interest $r(\overline{T})$. When this condition is satisfied we shall say that there is a "potentially adequate private demand," or more briefly, an "adequate demand." We shall for the moment concentrate attention on this case, reserving the task of examining the implications of a lack of adequate demand to a later point.

Our result so far, then, is that even with an adequate demand, the net or differential burden placed on the future by debt financing is not nearly as large as suggested by the classical conclusion. But note that the implied error is poor consolation for the no-transfer proponents, for they maintained that the burden is always "paid as you go." The error we have uncovered would seem to lie instead in not recognizing that a part of the burden of the expenditure is always shifted to the future. This last conclusion, however, is somewhat puzzling and disquieting. And this uneasiness can be easily increased by asking ourselves the following embarrassing question: roughly how large is the coefficient s which determines the unavoidable burden on the future? This question is embarrassing because recent empirical as well as theoretical research on the consumption function suggests that the answer depends very much on the length of time which is allowed for the adjustment. In the long run, the average propensity to save has remained pretty constant in the general order

18. This conclusion has also been reached by W. Vickrey, "The Burden of the Public Debt: Comment."

of o.1, meaning that the marginal propensity is of the same order. But the quarterly increase in saving associated with a quarterly increase in income seems to be of a much larger order of magnitude, with estimates ranging as high as o.5 and even higher.[19] Which is the relevant figure and why? Or does the answer depend on whether we look only at the impact effect of taxation or also at its delayed and ultimate effects? We will argue that this is indeed the case, and that insofar as we are interested in the distribution of the burden over time and between generations, the total effects are paramount.

VII. Impact Versus Total Effects of Deficit and Tax Financing

Let us come back to a comparison of rows (b) and (c) in Table I, but this time let us concentrate on the effect of taxation on the terminal net worth position of the households. We can see that if the expenditure is debt-financed this terminal position is (at least to a first approximation) the same as if the expenditure had not been undertaken. On the other hand, in the case of tax financing, in addition to the concomitant fall in consumption, we find that saving, and hence the increase in net worth, was also cut down from 200 to 160. What effect will this have on later consumption and saving behavior?

In order to answer this question we need to go beyond the standard Keynesian emphasis on current flows and try to understand why consumers wanted to add 200 to their net worth in the first place and how they will react when this goal has to be scaled down in response to higher taxes. I have elsewhere proposed some answer to these questions by advancing the hypothesis that saving (and dissaving) is not a passive reaction to income but represents instead a purposive endeavor by the households to achieve a desirable allocation of resources to consumption over their lifetime.[20] However, in what follows we do not need to rely, to any significant extent, on that model or any other specific theory of saving behavior. All that we need to keep before our eyes is the logical proposition that there are, in the final analysis, only two ways in which households can dispose of any addition to their net worth achieved through current

---

19. See, e.g., the following two recent and as yet unpublished studies prepared for the Commission on Money and Credit: D. B. Suits, "The Determinants of Consumer Expenditure: a Review of Present Knowledge"; and E. C. Brown, R. M. Solow, A. K. Ando, and J. Kareken, "Lags in Fiscal and Monetary Policy," Part II.

20. F. Modigliani and R. Brumberg, "Utility analysis and the Consumption Function: An Interpretation of Cross-section Data," in Post-Keynesian Economics, K. Kurihara, ed. (Rutgers University Press, 1954).

saving: namely, either through later consumption or through a bequest to their heirs.

Now let us suppose at first that the bequest motive is small enough to be neglected and that, as a rule and on the average, each household tends to consume all of its income over its lifetime. This assumption can be conveniently restated in terms of the notion of the "over-life average propensity to consume" (*oac*), defined as the ratio of (the present value of) life consumption to (the present value of) life resources, and of the "over-life marginal propensity to consume" (*omc*), defined as the ratio of marginal increments in the same two variables. With this terminology, our current assumption is that both *omc* and *oac* are unity. It should be noted that, under reasonable hypotheses about the typical individual life cycle of earnings and consumption, an *oac* of unity for each household is consistent with a sizeable stock of aggregate assets, in the order of several times national income. With a stationary population and unchanged technology—stationary economy—this aggregate stock would tend to be constant in size, implying zero net saving in the aggregate, but it would be undergoing a continuous reshuffling of ownership from dissavers, such as retired persons, to those in the process of accumulating assets for retirement and short-run contingencies. On the other hand, with a rising population and/or technological progress, there would tend to be positive saving and a rising stock; in fact, the ratio of saving to income and of assets to income would tend to be constant in the long run if the above two forces resulted in an approximately exponential growth trend for aggregate income.[21]

Let us now consider the consequences of a non-repetitive increment in government expenditure dG, financed by a deficit, limiting ourselves at first to a stationary economy. Fig. 1 (*a*) illustrates graphically the effects of this operation on aggregate private net worth, W, and on the net stock of privately owned capital K. The horizontal dashed line AA represents the behavior of net worth in the absence of dG. It is constant by our assumption of a stationary economy, implying zero net saving, or gross saving and gross investment just sufficient to offset the wear and tear of the capital stock. If we make the further convenient assumption that there is initially no government debt (and ignore non-reproducible tangible wealth), then W coincides also with K. The incremental expenditure dG is supposed to occur in the interval t_0 to t_1 at the constant rate

21. Cf. A. K. Ando and F. Modigliani, "Growth, Fluctuations, and Stability," *The American Economic Review*, XLIX (May, 1959), 501-24.

$dG/(t_1 - t_0)$, and is financed by tapping a portion of the gross saving otherwise devoted to capital maintenance. As a result, between t_0 and t_1 K falls, as shown by the solid curve. But the net worth W remains at the same initial level as the fall in K is offset in the consumers' balance sheet by the government debt of dG. By t_1 the gap between W and K amounts to precisely dG, and thereafter the curves remain unchanged until and unless some further disturbance occurs. The final outcome is that the debt-financed expenditure, by generating a permanent wedge $dG = dD$ between W and K,[22] causes the entire cost of the expenditure to be borne by those living beyond t_1 in the form of a reduction in the stock of private capital by dG and in disposable income by $r^*(dG)$.[23] If, in addition, $r^* = r$, then before-tax income will be unaffected and the fall in disposable income will equal the tax collected to pay the interest, as claimed by the classical-burden doctrine.[24]

Consider now the effect of full tax financing of dG, illustrated in Fig. 1 (b). The line AA has the same meaning as before. The impact effect of the tax-financed expenditure—i.e., the effect within the interval t_0t_1—is to reduce consumption by cdG and saving and private capital formation by sdG. Hence, as shown by the solid line, by t_1 both W and K have fallen by sdG. As we had already concluded, this fall in K partly shifts the effect of the expenditure to those living beyond t_1. However, by following up the delayed effect of the tax, we can now show that in this case: (a) the shift of the burden is only temporary, as W, and hence K, will tend to return gradually to the original pre-expenditure level, and (b) the burden transferred to the period following t_1 is borne, at least to a first approximation, entirely by those who were taxed between t_0 and t_1.

22. Permanent in the sense that it persists as long as the debt remains outstanding.

23. Actually the fall in disposable income consequent upon the fall in K is likely to give rise to a further fall in W and hence in K, but this indirect effect will tend to be of secondary magnitude. See on this point footnote 34, p. 131.

24. If the reduction in K results in a significant rise in r^* and hence r, then, as pointed out by Vickrey, "The Burden of the Public Debt: Comment," p. 135, there will tend to occur a shift in the distribution of *pre-tax* income. Labor income will tend to shrink and property income to increase—and, incidentally, this increase will tend to more than offset the fall in labor's earnings. It does not follow, however, as Vickrey has concluded, that the "primary burden of diminished future income will be felt by future wage earners." For the burden consists in the reduction of *disposable* income, and this reduction will depend on the distribution of the taxes levied to pay the interest as between property and non-property income.

FIG. 1

Effect of Deficit and Taxes on Net Worth, W, and Capital, K,
(unity over-life propensity to consume)

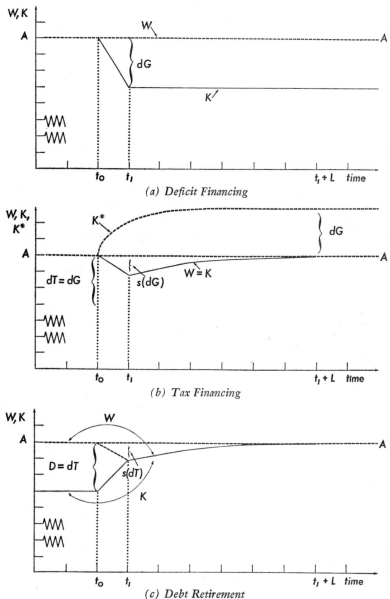

(a) Deficit Financing

(b) Tax Financing

(c) Debt Retirement

To establish this result we need only observe that since those taxed have suffered a loss of over-life (disposable) income amounting to dG as a result of the tax, they must make a commensurate reduction in over-life consumption. If the consumption is cut initially only by $c(dG)$ the balance of the tax, or $s(dG)$, is financed out of a reduction in accumulation—including possibly borrowing from other households—which at first reduces the net worth at time t_1 by $s(dG)$, but eventually must be matched by a corresponding reduction of consumption over the balance of the life span. Let L denote the length of time until the taxed generations die out. In the interval t_1 to $t_1 + L$, then, the consumption of this group will be smaller relative to its income, and hence its rate of saving will be larger, or its rate of dissaving smaller, than it would have been in the absence of the tax. On the other hand, over the same interval, the income consumption and saving of households who have entered the scene after t_1 will be basically unaffected by the operation. Hence, in the L years following t_1 there will arise some positive saving which will gradually die down as the taxed generation disappears. The precise path of aggregate saving will depend on the way the taxed generation chooses to distribute the reduction of consumption over its life. But, in any event, the cumulated net saving over the entire interval t_1 to $t_1 + L$ must come to precisely $s(dG)$, representing the required reduction of consumption relative to income of the taxed generation.[25] This cumulated saving is just sufficient to make up for the initial fall in the stock of $s(dG)$, so that by $t_1 + L$ the stock of capital (as well as W) has returned to the original level, as shown in Fig. 2 (b), and we are back in the original stationary state.

The above framework can be readily applied to analyze the effects of deficit or surplus generated under different conditions, e.g., by varying taxes, expenditure constant. Fig. 1 (c), for instance, depicts the outcome of an increase in taxes in the interval t_0 to t_1, utilized to retire the debt D outstanding at t_0. Here again the entire burden of the retirement falls on the taxed generation—although it is spread between t_0 and $t_1 + L$—and the gain accrues to those living after t_1 in the form of an increase in the stock of capital by an amount which

25. It may be noted that the cumulated reduction in consumption will tend to be somewhat larger than $s(dG)$ because the taxed generation will also lose some income as a result of the reduction in their wealth, amounting initially to $s(dG)$. However, the cumulated increase in saving over the interval is still $s(dG)$ because the additional loss in consumption just matches the reduction in income from this source. Actually $s(dG)$ measures essentially the *present value* as of t_1 of the required reduction in consumption.

eventually approaches the amount of debt retired and reflects the elimination of the wedge between W and K.

It is also easy to verify that our results remain valid for a growing economy, the only difference being that the dashed line AA would turn into an upward-sloping curve. With debt financing the graph of K would, from t_1 on, run at a distance dG below this line, while with tax financing the graph of $K = W$ would initially fall below it by $s(dG)$, but would tend to return to it at $t_1 + L$.

In summary, then, under unit oac the cost of an expenditure financed by debt, whether internal or external, tends to fall entirely on those living beyond the time of expenditure, as asserted by the classical-burden position, though it is best measured by r^*dD rather than by the incremental tax bill rdD. This burden may be eliminated at a later date by retiring the debt through a budget surplus, but thereby the full cost of the original expenditure is shifted to the later tax-payer, who financed the surplus. On the other hand, the cost of a tax-financed expenditure will tend to be borne by society as a whole, partly at the time and partly for some finite period thereafter. But the burden beyond t_1 still falls primarily on those who initially paid the tax and reflects the spreading of the burden over their lifetime.[26]

In the analysis so far we have concentrated on examining who bears the cost of the expenditure. To complete the picture we must, of course, also reckon the yield, if any, produced by dG beyond t_1. In particular, if dG results in a (permanent) addition to the stock of capital we must distinguish between W, K, and K^*, the latter denoting the total stock of private plus government-owned capital. K^* will exceed K by dG. Thus in the case of a debt-financed capital expenditure, K^* will everywhere tend to coincide with W, the

26. In a stimulating comment to a preliminary draft of this paper, Mr. Buchanan has provided an explanation for his failure to analyze the temporal distribution of the burden of a tax-financed expenditure. He points out that in line with the classic tradition, he defines the burden as the subjective loss of utility suffered by the tax-payer because of the initial loss of resources. The burden in this sense occurs entirely when the tax is levied and the later reduction of consumption cannot be separately counted as burden, as it is merely the embodiment of the original burden. I have serious reservations about the usefulness of this definition. It has, for instance, the peculiar implication that, when as a result of tax financing an heir receives a smaller inheritance or as a result of debt financing he is saddled with a larger tax bill, this cannot be counted as burden on him, as the entire burden is already accounted for in the guise of his father's grief that his heirs will enjoy a smaller net income. It is this peculiar reasoning that underlies Ricardo's famous conclusion that the cost of government expenditure is always fully borne by those present at the time.

government capital formation simply replacing the private one. For the case of tax financing, the behavior of K^* is shown by the broken line in Fig. 1 (b). Here the burden on the taxed generation results in a permanent gain for those living beyond t_1, which will gradually approach the yield on dG. In this sense one might well say that the cost of current government services can be paid for not only by the current and future generations but even by past generations.

There remains to consider how far our conclusions need to be modified if the *omc* is less than unity. Since a debt-financed expenditure does not affect the behavior of net worth, our analysis of this case basically stands, although one can conceive of some rather fancy circumstances in which modifications would be necessary.[27] In the case of tax financing, however, an *omc* of less than one implies that part of the burden of the expenditure will fall on later generations, who will receive a smaller bequest. It can be readily seen that the reduction in $K = W$ available to them will be of the order of $(oms)(dG)$, where *oms* denotes now the over-life marginal propensity to save. The differential burden of debt versus tax financing on society will correspondingly be of the order of $r(omc)(dG)$ instead of rdG.[28] In other words, the propensities to consume and save relevant to the long-run effect are precisely the over-life ones.[29] Unfortunately, these are propensities about which information is currently close to zero, both in terms of order of magnitude and stability, although some attention has begun to be devoted to this question.[30]

27. It is conceivable that, *e.g.*, the tax newly imposed to defray the interest cost might reduce the bequests. To this extent an even greater burden is placed on later generations, which will inherit a smaller K for two reasons: because of the smaller W and because of the wedge dG between W and K. An even fancier possibility is that the new tax might spur the initial generation to increase its bequests to help their heirs pay for the new tax. This would, of course, increase the burden on the current generation and decrease that on posterity.

28. Note that, regardless of the value of *omc*, the current generation must always fare at least as well, and generally better, under debt than under tax financing, even if it capitalized fully the new taxes that must be raised to pay the interest bill on the new debt. For, even in the highly unlikely event that the amount $r(dD)$ per year necessary to pay the interest bill were levied entirely on the initial generations, as long as they lived, this liability is limited by life, and hence represents a finite stream whose present value must be less than the amount dD which would have been taken away in the case of tax financing. See on this point also footnote 26 above.

29. Even with an *omc* of less than unity it is likely that the impact of the tax on bequests handed down from one generation to the next would gradually disappear so that W and K would eventually be unaffected by the tax-financed expenditure. But this is in the *very* long run indeed.

30. See, *e.g.*, J. Tobin and H. W. Guthrie, "Intergeneration Transfers of

Our analysis of the differential burden of tax versus debt financing could stand a great deal of refinement and qualifications to take proper account of the specific nature of the taxes levied to pay for dD or for the interest on the debt. But it is clear that these refinements can in principle be handled by proper application of the framework set out in this section. We shall therefore make no attempt at working out a long list of specific cases,[31] and will proceed instead to point out the implications of our framework for a somewhat different class of problems, namely where the change in debt occurs without any accompanying change either in government purchases or taxation.

VIII. *"Gratuitous" Increases in Debt, Repudiation and Inflation*

For analytical convenience we may start out by considering a case which has admittedly rather limited empirical relevance: namely, where the government debt is increased at some date t_0 by an amount dD by a "gratuitous" distribution of a corresponding amount of bonds.[32] Presumably, at least in this case, the proponents of the classical burden argument, if they apply their reasoning consistently, would have to agree with the proponents of the classical non-burden argument that the increment in the National Debt puts *no burden on the economy as a whole*, either at the time of issuance or thereafter, except for frictional transfer costs. For while it is true that from t_0 on, tax-payers are saddled with extra taxes to defray the interest bill, it is also true that the receipt of interest would not have arisen without the creation of extra debt. Note that this conclusion does not rule out the possibility that the operation may result in some transfer between generations, if by a generation we mean the set of members of the economy born at a particular date: thus the interest accruing to those receiving the gift will very likely be paid, at least partly, by a younger generation. But these are still mere income transfers involving no over-all burden.

But once we recognize that the over-all burden of the National

Wealth and The Theory of Saving," Cowles Foundation Discussion Paper No. 98 (November, 1960).

31. By so doing we are also deliberately bypassing the other major issue of fiscal policy, that of the distribution of the burden between income classes.

32. In order to avoid side issues, we will assume that the coupon rate on these bonds is such as to make their market value also equal to dD, and that no change occurs in the government purchase of goods and services, G.

Debt derives from its effects on the private stock of capital, then it becomes clear that, by and large, both classical doctrines agree with the wrong conclusion. This is indeed quite obvious in the case of a unity *oac*, a case illustrated graphically in Fig. 2 (*a*). The solid line *AA* shows as usual the behavior of $W = K$ in the absence of the gift. For the sake of variety, we deal here with a growing

FIG. 2

Effect of "Gratuitous" Changes in Debt on Net Worth, W, and Capital, K,
(unity over-life propensity to consume)

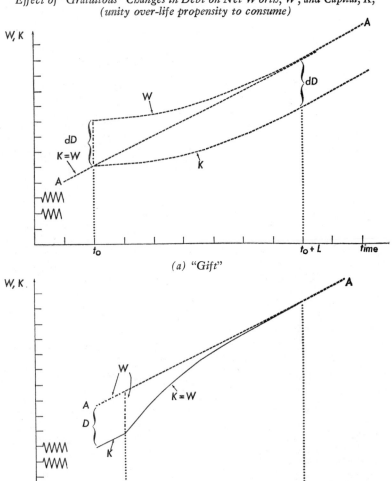

(*a*) "Gift"

(*b*) "Repudiation" or "Inflation"

economy with positive saving and rising wealth.[33] If the gift is distributed all in one shot at point t_0, then at that point W will rise by dD, with no change in K. But now between t_0 and $t_0 + L$ the members of the generation that received the gift will gradually dispose of the bonds (or of other assets that they may have exchanged against the bonds) by selling them to current savers and using the proceeds to increase consumption over what it would have been otherwise. As this takes place, the aggregate rate of saving, and hence the accumulation of net worth and capital, is reduced. The result is that W gradually approaches the base path AA, while K, which is always lower by the wedge dD, falls below it. By $t_0 + L$ the cumulated rate of saving and physical capital formation will have been reduced by (approximately) dD, so that W will tend to coincide with AA and K to be dD lower, a position that will tend to be maintained thereafter. Thus an increase dD in the National Debt, even if it arises from a free gift, will put a burden on the economy as a whole. Under unity *oac*—after a transient period in which W is increased as a result of the gift—this burden will approach the level $r^*(dD)$, and hence approximately equal the interest on the debt.[34]

33. Just for reference, we may note that according to the Modigliani-Brumberg model, if income were growing at approximately exponential rate, W would be growing at the same rate.

34. This conclusion is strictly valid only insofar as the fall in disposable income brought about by the fall in K is matched by an equal fall in consumption. To the extent, however, that consumption falls somewhat less, cumulated saving may fall somewhat more, pushing W and K to a lower position than in our figure: but this extra adjustment will in any event tend to be of a second order of magnitude. The nature and size of this adjustment can be exhibited explicitly with reference to the Modigliani-Brumberg model of consumption behavior. As indicated earlier, this model implies that, in the long run, the aggregate net worth of consumers tends to be proportional to their (disposable) income, or (1) $W = gY$, where the proportionality constant is a decreasing function of the rate of growth of income. Suppose initially income is stationary as population and technology are both stationary. We also have the identity (2) $W = K + D$, where D denotes the National Debt. With population and technology given, the effect of capital on income can be stated by a "production function" (3) $Y = f(K)$. We have stated in the text that a gratuitous increase in D, or more generally an increase in D which does not result in government capital formation or otherwise change the production function, will tend to reduce K by dD and Y by r^*dD: *i.e.*, we have asserted $\dfrac{dK}{dD} \simeq -1$ and $\dfrac{dY}{dD} \approx -r^*$, where $r^* = \dfrac{df}{dK} = f' \simeq r$. By means of equations (1)-(3) we can now evaluate these derivatives exactly. Solving (2) for K and using (1) and (3) we have

If the omc is less than unity, then the burden will be smaller, tending to $(omc)(r^*dD)$, because the gift will tend to increase W "permanently" by $(oms)(dD)$ and hence K will tend to fall only by $(omc)(dD)$. As usual, this burden can be removed at any later point by taxation and retirement of the debt, but only at the cost of putting the burden on the taxed generation, which in effect will be paying for the benefits enjoyed by the beneficiaries of the gift.

Our conclusion applies directly, but for an appropriate change of "sign," to the case of a "gratuitous" one-shot reduction in the National Debt, as indicated in Fig. 2 (b). Such a reduction might be accomplished by repudiation, total or partial, or by a capital levy, or, much more importantly and frequently, by the simple device of (unanticipated) inflation. Thus a (once and for all) doubling of the price level is entirely equivalent to a repudiation of one-half of the National Debt at the original price level—although it has, of course, all kinds of other widespread economic effects. As far as the National Debt is concerned, this operation puts a burden on the owners of the bonds by reducing the real value of their interest income as

---

$K = gf(K) - D$. Hence $\dfrac{dK}{dD} = gf'\dfrac{dK}{dD} - 1$ or $\dfrac{dK}{dD} = \dfrac{-1}{1-gf'} = \dfrac{-1}{1-gr^*}$. Simi-

larly, $\dfrac{dY}{dD} = \dfrac{-r^*}{1-gr^*}$ and $\dfrac{dW}{dD} = \dfrac{-gr^*}{1-gr^*}$. Thus, if $r^* \simeq r = 0.05$ and g is in the

order of 4, then $\dfrac{dK}{dD}$ is $-1\cdot25$ instead of -1 and $\dfrac{dY}{dD}$ is $-0\cdot625$ instead of $-0\cdot05$.

I am indebted to Ralph Beals, presently a graduate student at Massachusetts Institute of Technology, for pointing out that these formulæ are not entirely general, for, within the Modigliani-Brumberg model, the second-order effect is not independent of the nature of taxes employed to defray the interest bill. In fact, the formulæ derived above are strictly valid only if the revenue is raised entirely through an income tax on non-property income. With other kinds of taxes, one obtains somewhat more complicated formulæ. For instance, if the taxes are levied on property income this will depress the net yield of wealth below r, which in turn will, in principle, affect the proportionality constant g of equation (1). However, exploration of several alternative assumptions suggests to me that the outcome is unlikely to be appreciably different from that derived above, at least in the case of direct taxes.

It can also be shown that the above formulæ will tend to hold, at least asymptotically, for an expanding economy in which population grows at an approximately constant rate and/or so does productivity as a result of technological change which is neutral in Harrod's sense, cf. *Toward a Dynamic Economics* (Macmillan, 1949), p. 23. The main features of such a growth model are discussed in Ando and Modigliani, "Growth, Fluctuations, and Stability."

well as the real value of the principal. Insofar as the first effect is concerned, we have a mere transfer from the bond-holders to the tax-payers, with no over-all effect. But the reduction in the principal generates an unmatched reduction in consumption, and hence a *transient* higher rate of saving. The resulting increase in the capital stock will benefit all those living after the inflation—provided, of course, private capital has a positive marginal product and the potentially higher rate of saving is utilized for capital formation rather than being wasted in depressed income and unemployment.

From the content of this section and the previous one it should also be apparent that our analysis basically supports Meade's conclusion concerning the burden of the deadweight debt, although this conclusion is derived by a very different line of reasoning. The deadweight debt is a burden because: (*a*) it generates a corresponding gap between aggregate net worth W and the aggregate stock of capital K^*, and (*b*) we can expect that this gap will result primarily in a fall in K^* rather than in an offsetting rise in W. Thus, if we conceive two communities A and B identical with respect to natural endowments, technical know-how and habits of private thrift, and which differ only in that A has a deadweight debt D' and B has none, community A will be poorer, roughly, by D' times the marginal productivity of capital plus frictional transfer costs.

IX. Deficit Financing in War and in Depression

In this concluding section we propose to apply our tools to see what light they shed on the two classical and empirically relevant issues: the pre-Keynesian problem of war financing and the post-Keynesian problem of deficit created as part of a counter-cyclical stabilization policy.

In order to face squarely the core issue of war financing, let us be concerned with the case of a major war effort of the type outlined earlier in Section III, in which the stock of capital in existence at the termination of the war is independent of the methods used to finance it. It follows immediately that, independently of financing, the war will impose a burden on postwar society as a whole to the extent that the stock of capital in existence at its termination— counting only whatever portion is useful to satisfy the postwar requirements—is less than what would have been there in the absence of war. In order to examine the residual effects, if any, of methods of financing, we must suppose that, in spite of the war's severity, we have some choice as to the extent of taxation. Also, to keep separate for the moment the possible role of inflation, we must suppose that untaxed income in excess of the predetermined consumption level is prevented from bidding up the price of goods—whether through voluntary abstention or through a fully successful system of rationing. In these conditions the unspent income must result in an increase in government debt held by the private sector, either directly or through financial intermediaries. Thus the level of taxation versus deficit financing determines essentially the size of the increment in government debt, dD. Now suppose, for the sake of the argument, that the war had been entirely financed by taxes, dD being accordingly zero. It then follows from our earlier analysis that the burden of the war will be borne almost entirely by members of the war generation. For, in addition to the sacrifice of consumption and other amenities *during* the war, they will also bear the brunt of the reduced capital stock, their accumulation of net worth being unlimited to the permitted privately financed capital formation. Thus the burden falling on society as a whole after the war will fall primarily directly on the members of the war generation (affecting others only to the extent that the reduction in the stock of capital reduces total income by more than the return on capital). They will be forced after the war to maintain a reduced level of consumption over the rest of their life, tending to save heavily in their remaining earning span and to dissave at a greatly reduced rate thereafter. This behavior in turn will produce, after the war, an abnormally large rate of aggregate saving, gradually declining with the disappearance of the war generation. As a result, by the time the war generation has disappeared, the wartime reduction in capital formation may have been substantially made up—this being more nearly true the closer the *oac* is to unity and the smaller the initial loss of capital.

If, on the other hand, through lower taxes the war generation is permitted to increase its terminal net worth by an additional amount dD, the effect, with respect to the present issue, is essentially the same as though at war's end it had been handed down gratuitously a corresponding amount of government bonds.[35] As usual, this will enable them to maintain a higher post-war consumption, reducing

35. If the bonds issued during the war carried an exceptionally low rate of interest because of the monopoly position of the Government in the market, the gift in question should be regarded, for present purposes, as represented by the market value of the bonds.

capital formation, by an extent that can range as high as dD, if the oac is unity. Thus the debt financing will generate both: (i) a transfer from the postwar to the war generation to the extent of taxes levied on the former to pay interest to the latter, and (ii) a permanent burden on society as a whole to the extent that the stock of capital is permanently reduced by dD—less any increase in W resulting directly from dD.[36] Insofar as in the immediate postwar period the Government, to speed up the reconstruction, pushes capital formation by raising taxes and creating a surplus, the long-run effect is eliminated. But the burden of debt financing is placed to that extent on those living in the relevant postwar period, which may again consist in part of the very same war generation.

If inflation is permitted to develop in the course of the war or immediately following it our analysis remains valid, provided the increment in the debt is measured in real, rather than money, terms. This net real increment can be expressed as $\dfrac{D_0 + dD}{1 + dP} - D_0$ where D_0 is the prewar debt and dP is the relative increase in the price level in the course of the war inflation. The above quantity, it will be noted, may even be negative if $dP > \dfrac{dD}{D_0}$, i.e., if the increase in prices exceeds the relative increase in the debt. In this case the war generation will be made to carry even more than the cost of the war (unless its plight is improved by postwar transfers of income); and later generations may conceivably end up by benefiting from the war, at least following the transient period of high saving rates and rapid capital accumultaion. Perhaps the picture we have been drawing has some relevance for an understanding of the postwar experience of such countries as Germany, Italy, and Japan.

It seems hardly necessary to point out that our analysis in no way implies that in financing a war the use of debt should necessarily be minimized. Quite aside from obvious incentive considerations,

36. Note that the incremental debt dD could be regarded as a burden on society even if the economy tended to suffer from long-run stagnation, i.e., a chronic tendency for a very low or zero marginal productivity of capital. For while it is true that the larger consumption bestowed on the war generation would help to sustain consumption, and thus full employment, the same result could be achieved by reducing the taxes and expanding the consumption and saving of whoever was present at the appropriate later time.

there may be perfectly good equity reasons for lightening the burden of the generation that suffered through the war by granting them a more comfortable life after the war, at the expense of later generations.

We come finally to the effects of debt generated as a counter-cyclical measure. In view of the complexity of the problem, we shall have to limit ourselves to a sketchy treatment of a limited class of situations. Our main concern is to show that, even in this case, debt financing, though quite advantageous to the current generation, will generally not be costless to future generations, at least in terms of gross burden.

Consider a situation where, in spite of the easiest possible monetary policy and with the whole structure of interest rates reduced to its lowest feasible level, the demand for private capital formation is inadequate to absorb full-employment saving with a balanced budget. But let us suppose that the situation can be counted upon to be temporary and not to recur for a long time to come. If the Government does not step in there will be a temporary contraction of employment accompanied by a contraction of consumption and of addition to net worth, which is limited to the amount of private capital formation. Suppose, on the other hand, the Government expands its expenditure to the extent needed to fill the deflationary gap, and thereby runs into a deficit dD. Let us also imagine that it succeeds in choosing its action perfectly so as to maintain full employment without inflation. Hence consumption will be kept at the full-employment level and so will the accumulation of net worth; except that this accumulation will now take the form of an addition to the National Debt to the extent dD. Thus the government action involves a current gain to society which can be measured by the income which would have been lost otherwise. What we wish to know is whether this gain places any cost on later generations (and if so, how it can be valued).

Under the assumed conditions the answer would have to be affirmative at least under unity oac. In this case, in fact, we can see that the cost which was spared to society would have fallen entirely on the members of the depression generation. They would have been forced over their lifetime to cut their consumption by an amount (whose present value is) equal to the lost income. This reduction would be distributed partly within the depression but partly *after* the recovery, to an extent equal to the loss in accumulation of net worth in the depression. This reduction of consumption would in turn give rise to a somewhat higher rate of capital formation after the recovery, so that by the time the depression generation disappears the stock of capital would tend to be back to where it would have been without depression. In other words, under the assumed conditions failure of the Government to act, though costly to the depression generation, tends to be costless to later generations. On the other hand, if the Government acts, the depression generation does not have to maintain a lower consumption after the recovery, and accordingly, the lost private capital formation during the depression is never made up. The creation of dD introduces again a corresponding wedge between W and K which will tend permanently to reduce the amount of physical capital available to future generations. Hence there is a loss to them to the extent that at later points of time an increment to the stock of capital would make any net positive addition to output. If the debt is never meant to be retired, then at least with well-functioning capital markets, the consol rate, being an average of anticipated future short rates, may provide at least a rough measure of the (appropriate time average) annual loss. And in this sense if the Government borrows long, the interest bill on the incremental debt may provide a rough measure of the average future (gross) burden placed on society as a whole.[37]

Once more, recognizing that the government action may involve a gross cost to future society does not imply that the action should not be taken. In the first place, because of multiplier effects the gain in income to those present is likely to be appreciably larger than the lost stock of capital which approximates the present value of the sacrificed income stream. In the second place, if the Government spends on projects which produce a yield in the future, then the gross burden will be offset by the gross yield and the net outcome may even be positive. In the third place, the gross burden can be eliminated if at some future point of time the Government runs a surplus and retires the debt. It is true that this will tend to place

---

37. Of course, under our present assumptions the burden as measured by the opportunity cost will be essentially zero during the period in which the debt is created, regardless of whether it takes the form of long-term debt, short-term debt, or currency creation. But in the last two cases the current interest cost will not appropriately reflect the average future burden, unless we also take into account the rate the Government will have to pay on bonds sold at later points of time to refinance the short-term debt or to reduce the money supply in order to prevent inflation.

the burden of the original deficit on those who pay the taxes financing the surplus. But if the surplus follows the deficit in short order these people will be, to a large extent, the very same ones that benefited from the original deficit; thereby the questions of inter-generation equity are minimized. The case for eradicating the deficit with a nearby surplus is, of course, strongest if the government expenditure provides nothing useful for the future, or if the deficit reflects a reduction in the tax bill, expenditure constant, resulting either from built-in flexibility arrangements or from *ad hoc* tax rebates. Thus, our analysis turns out to provide a strong case in favor of what used to be called the cyclically balanced budget.

Although we cannot pursue further here the complex issues raised by the burden aspects of counter-cyclical fiscal operations, we hope to have succeeded in showing how the tools we have developed may provide some insight into the problem. One point should be apparent even from our sketchy treatment: namely, that insofar as counter-cyclical fiscal policy is concerned, our analysis does not require any significant re-evaluation of currently accepted views. Yet, by reminding us that fiscal operations involve considerations of inter-generation equity even when used for stabilization purposes, it may help to clarify some issues. It does, for example, establish a *prima facie* case, at least with respect to *ad hoc* measures as distinguished from built-in stabilizers, for a course of action that will minimize the "deadweight" deficit and stimulate investment rather than consumption.[38] More generally, considerations of inter-generation equity suggest the desirability of a compromise between the orthodox balanced-budget principle and the principle of functional finance, which might be couched roughly as follows: as a rule, the Government should run a "deadweight" deficit only when full-employment saving exceeds the amount of capital formation consistent with the most favorable feasible monetary policy; and it should run a surplus, insofar as this is consistent with full employment, until it has wiped out previous deficits accumulated in the pursuance of this policy.

38. These considerations, *e.g.*, cast some doubt on the desirability of relying on personal tax cuts explicitly announced to be but temporary. For there is at least some ground for supposing that the temporary nature of the cut will tend to reduce the desirable impact effect on consumption and increase instead short-run saving and the (possibly) undesirable delayed consumption.

B/ INTERNAL DEBT IN THE CLASSICAL SYSTEM*

BY *Richard A. Musgrave*

In the classical system all private income is spent on either consumption or investment. Full employment is secured automatically. Price-level stability is maintained if the money supply is held stable or is increased at the same rate at which real income grows. In this setting there is no need for compensatory finance. Loan finance is as effective as tax finance in reducing aggregate demand, and debt retirement is as effective as goods and service expenditures of government in expanding demand. What role, then, can be assigned to public debt policy in such a system?[1]

The choice between tax and loan finance remains important because it determines the way in which the resource withdrawal from the private sector will be divided between consumption and capital formation. Let us define the classical system as one in which saving is a function of disposable income as well as of interest. If the savings schedule is wholly inelastic to interest while the investment schedule is elastic, the entire resource withdrawal under loan finance will be from private capital formation. Private savings will be absorbed in part by public borrowing. Private investment will fall and the interest rate will rise, but saving and hence consumption will remain unchanged. Tax finance will result in a withdrawal from both private capital formation and consumption, depending on the taxpayers' marginal propensity to consume.[2]

If the savings schedule is interest elastic while the investment schedule is wholly inelastic, the entire resource withdrawal for loan finance will be from private consumption. The rate of interest

---

* Reprinted by permission from Richard A. Musgrave, *The Theory of Public Finance*. Copyright 1959 by McGraw-Hill Book Company, Inc., New York.

1. For a somewhat similar discussion see James M. Buchanan, *Public Principles of Public Debt* (Homewood, Illinois: Richard D. Irwin, Inc., 1958). Buchanan's volume became available after compilation of this manuscript and is not dealt with here.

2. For convenience we shall assume a lump-sum tax so that substitution effects need not be considered.

will rise until saving increases by the amount of public borrowing. Tax finance must give the same result since investment remains unchanged. If both the saving and investment schedules are interest elastic, the resource withdrawal will be spread between consumption and capital formation for both types of finance. The more interest elastic saving is, and the less elastic investment is, the larger the share contributed by capital formation will be. However, the share contributed by consumption will be larger in the case of tax finance than in the case of loan finance.

The result depends, moreover, on the type of expenditures the government makes. If the government spends for investment, resource withdrawal will be more from private capital formation, provided that government investment enters into the same total investment schedule as does private investment. Government investment will then drive down the rate of interest and lower saving. However, government investment may raise the share contributed by private investment, if the public investment does not draw on the same investment outlets but raises the efficiency of private investment.[3]

The choice between loan finance and tax finance thus involves a choice between a resource withdrawal largely from private capital formation and one largely from private consumption. A fiscal policy designed to accentuate growth relies on tax finance, while a policy designed to support present consumption relies on loan finance. If regulation of the rate of growth is considered a function of budget policy, such regulation is the crucial consideration in the choice between loan and tax finance. However, this is not the case in the classical system. Here the rate of growth may be determined by consumer preference between present and future consumption, and by the return on capital that is obtained in the market.[4] The government's choice between loan and tax finance is to be made as a part of this process; the purpose is not to interfere with the

3. The same general principles apply, but the details differ for a primitive classical system in which saving is a function of the rate of interest only. If government expenditures are for consumption, resource withdrawal through taxation must always come out of private consumption. Since the rate of interest is not changed by the imposition of the tax, private saving remains unchanged, as does private investment. The results for borrowing depend again on the elasticities of the investment and saving schedules; and as before, the results may differ if government expenditures are for investment.

4. See Musgrave, *Public Finance*, p. 553.

market-determined rate of growth, but to align the choice between present and future satisfaction of social wants, with the choice between present and future satisfaction of private wants.

Our argument has been that the budget of the Allocation Branch should be balanced, since the opportunity cost of resource withdrawal must be allocated to the individuals whose wants are satisfied; but we have also noted that annual balance was not necessary, since the cost of durable goods or of lasting services should be allocated over their useful life.[5] We must now consider more carefully just when loan finance is called for in the budget of the allocation Branch.

Pay-as-you-use Finance

Let us suppose that people want to provide for the satisfaction of certain social wants involving initial capital expenditures. The facilities may be durable consumer goods such as playgrounds, capital goods such as highways, or productivity-increasing services such as investment in education. In these cases, present expenditures will provide for future benefits. Where the initial outlay is large, taxpayers may not wish to assume the entire cost at once and may prefer to pay over the years as the services of the new facility are enjoyed. This reflects the same motivation underlying the purchase of a house on a mortgage or of an automobile on an installment basis. The option of pay-as-you-use finance increases the flexibility of consumer budgeting and adds to the efficiency of private finance. Precisely the same results occur in public finance. The question is only how the principle can be implemented at the public level.

Matters are simple enough if we assume that there is a continuous stream of capital outlays. In such a case, tax finance of new projects becomes equivalent to pay-as-you-use finance of old projects. This solution is not open if we consider the financing of a single and discontinuous project. Here we are confronted with the inevitable fact that provision of a durable facility requires the full resource input in the *initial* period. Resources must be withdrawn from other uses, thus giving rise to a current opportunity cost that the community must assume at once. There is no escape from this, whatever the sources of internal finance. The government's internal borrowing, unlike external borrowing, does not increase the supply of re-

5. *Ibid.*, p. 16.

sources available to the group as a whole. It cannot obviate the need for releasing resources from other uses.

However, it makes a difference whether this release is from present consumption or from capital formation. The immediate burden of a heavy public outlay in terms of current consumption is cushioned if the resources are withdrawn from private capital formation. This is accomplished by the use of loan finance. In a perfect system, with rational taxpayer behavior and a pure credit market, it will be equally advantageous for the government to use tax or loan finance. If the taxpayer wishes to spread his burden, he may secure a tax or consumer loan and thus obtain command over resources that otherwise would have gone into capital formation. The outcome will be similar to that of public loan finance, the only difference being that private rather than public debt is issued. In the real world, where credit facilities are not available on equal terms to all taxpayers, this equality does not apply. Public loan finance may then be thought of as a means of enabling individual taxpayers to secure tax credit at equal terms. By placing payment on a pay-as-you-use basis, loan finance remains a significant instrument of policy, even though it does not increase the total availability of resources.[6] By the nature of the pay-as-you-use principle public debt issued for such purposes should be repaid as the benefits from the initial expenditure are being exhausted. The principle is the same as for consumer credit on the private level.

. . . .

Intergeneration Equity

The general principle of pay-as-you-use finance gains in importance if we allow for the fact that facilities provided for by government will be used frequently by several generations of taxpayers. This is particularly true in municipal finance, where the composition of the resident group is subject to more or less frequent change. Here the principle of pay-as-you-use finance fol-

---

6. This fact seems to be overlooked by A. C. Pigou, *A Study in Public Finance* (3rd ed.; London: Macmillan & Co., Ltd., 1951), p. 38, who argues that there can be no transfer of costs by internal borrowing because the resource use must occur at once. However, in his *Political Economy of War* (2nd ed., London: Macmillan & Co., Ltd., 1940), chap. 7, Pigou notes that in the case of war finance the future is burdened if the "real war fund" is drawn from capital formation. This, precisely, is the central point of our argument.

lows directly from that of benefit taxation, and loan finance is required to distribute costs among the various generations.

To illustrate the point, consider a project whose services become available in equal installments over three periods. Also, suppose that the life (or residency) span of each generation covers three periods, and that the population is stable. Finally, assume that loans advanced by any one generation must be repaid within its life span. In each period the benefits accrue to three generations, including generations 1, 2, 3 in the first period; 2, 3, 4 in the second; and 3, 4, 5 in the third period. To contribute their proper share, generations 1 and 5 should each pay 1/9 of the cost; generations 2 and 4 should each pay 2/9; and generation 3 should pay 3/9. Let us now suppose that the total cost is $100, and that is to be allocated accordingly. To simplify matters, we will disregard the allocation of interest cost.[7]

The entire outlay of $100 must be raised and spent in the first period. Of this, $33.3 is obtained by taxation, divided equally between generations 1, 2, and 3. The remainder is obtained by loans from generations 2 and 3. There can be no loans from generation 1 owing to our rule that each generation must be repaid during its life span. In the second period, tax revenue is again $33.3, contributed now by generations 2, 3, and 4; the debt held by generation 2 is retired in full, and loans of $16.6 are advanced by generation 4 to retire part of the debt held by generation 3. In the third period the tax revenue of $33.3 is contributed by generations 3, 4, and 5. It is used to retire the remainder of the debt held by generations 3 and 4. In retrospect, the total cost has been divided between the five generations in accordance with benefits received. Loan finance in this case not only provided credit to taxpayers but resulted in a bona fide division of the cost between generations—a result impossible to secure through tax finance.[8]

Concerning the change in resource allocation in the private sector, let us assume that 75 per cent of tax receipts comes from con-

7. The interest will be divided between the generations in proportion to their share in the postponement of payment, so that ¼ is contributed by generations 2 and 4 each, while 3 pays ½.

8. Note that this financing pattern does not involve tax discrimination between generations. The tax in any one period applies alike to the members of all generations living. While the schedule of debt transactions in each period involves a distinction between generations, our scheme does not necessitate the use of bonds that are nontransferable among generations. Rather, the government can borrow and retire debt independent of the particular holder.

sumption, and 25 per cent from saving. Since we are dealing with a system in which planned saving is matched by investment, the latter fraction is reflected in reduced capital formation in the private sector. Moreover, we assume that saving is inelastic to interest, so that the full amount of government borrowing is withdrawn from private capital formation. Repayment of government debt is reflected similarly in increased capital formation in the private sector. As shown in the last column of Table 1, we find private consumption reduced by $25 for each period, thus reflecting the principle of pay-as-you-use finance. Private capital formation is reduced by $75 in the first period and increased by $25 for each of the following periods. The net reduction in private capital formation for all periods as a whole equals $25. Thus the total cost is divided between consumption and

TABLE 1. *Intergeneration Equity through Loan Finance*
(In dollars; figures rounded)

Period	Source of funds*	Payments for each generation					Total payments in period
		1	2	3	4	5	
1	Taxes	11.1	11.1	11.1	†	†	33.3
	Loans	.....	33.3	33.3	†	†	66.7
	Repayments	......	......	......	†	†	
	ΔC	−8.3	−8.3	−8.3	†	†	−25.0
	ΔI	−2.8	−36.1	−36.1	†	†	−75.0
2	Taxes	†	11.1	11.1	11.1	†	33.3
	Loans	†	......	......	16.6	†	16.6
	Repayments	†	33.3	16.6	......	†	49.9
	ΔC	†	−8.3	−8.3	−8.3	†	−25.0
	ΔI	†	30.5	13.8	−19.4	†	25.0
3	Taxes	†	†	11.1	11.1	11.1	33.3
	Loans	†	†	......	......	.....	
	Repayments	†	†	16.6	16.6	.....	33.3
	ΔC	†	†	−8.3	−8.3	−8.3	−25.0
	ΔI	†	†	13.8	13.8	−2.8	25.0
1–3	Taxes	11.1	22.2	33.3	22.2	11.1	100.0
	Loans	.....	33.3	33.3	16.6	.....	83.2
	Repayments	.....	33.3	33.3	16.6	.....	83.2
	ΔC	−8.3	−16.7	−25.0	−16.7	−8.3	−75.0
	ΔI	−2.8	−5.5	−8.4	−5.5	−2.8	−25.0

* ΔC indicates change in consumption.
  ΔI indicates change in investment.
† Unborn or deceased.

capital formation in accordance with the marginal propensity to consume. This is true since we assume that saving is not elastic to interest. If interest elasticity is allowed for, the insertion of government demand in the loan market, by driving up the rate of interest, may lead to an increase in the rate of saving, with a corresponding transfer of part of the cost to private consumption.

. . . .

Interest as Social Cost

Let us return to a classical model where loan finance curtails the scarce supply of savings available for private capital formation. Here interest on public debt may be considered the opportunity cost of previous earnings from private investment. Debt retirement in turn increases the supply of funds available to private capital formation, provided that the funds are obtained from taxes that reduce consumption.

In this setting, the existence of public debt implies a burden in that current national income would have been higher if past outlays of government had been tax rather than loan-financed. The principle is similar to that observed previously in the use of domestic borrowing to implement pay-as-you-use finance. At the same time, it does not follow that current income would be higher had past loan-financed expenditures not been made. Current income would be higher only if public borrowing served to finance past consumption, or if public investment was less productive than private investment would have been.

C/ IS THE PUBLIC DEBT A BURDEN ON FUTURE GENERATIONS?*

BY *Hans Neisser*

As pointed out in a note by W. G. Bowen, R. G. Davis, and D. H. Kopf in *The American Economic Review* of September, 1960, with comments and reply in the March, 1961, issue of the same

* Reprinted by permission from *Social Research*, (Summer, 1961).

journal, the majority of American textbook writers agree that the real burden of a public project financed by a privately held internal debt cannot be shifted from one generation to another. Their reasoning seems to be that it is always current income, or better, currently available resources, that must bear the burden of the project. This is, indeed, an astonishing argument in times in which the level of welfare, whether for individuals or for the community, is usually defined in terms of consumption and not of "income," and in a period when a major concern of scholars is the conditions of economic growth. The three authors rightly take issue with the conventional position, but it seems to me that the following considerations offer a somewhat simpler refutation than the arguments they bring forward, and at the same time may clarify certain points not touched on by them.

At the outset it should be noted that the "burden" economists usually refer to is a *net* burden. Obviously, if a public debt is undertaken to finance investment in enterprises whose products will be sold to the public at a price sufficient to cover also the interest on the debt incurred, nobody would even discuss the question whether this transaction implies a burden on future generations. The real difficulty arises from "public projects" that, although they are "useful" also for future generations or even indirectly contribute to the productivity of the private sector (for example, by leading to the application of new production techniques), do not by themselves furnish the means for defraying the interest on the newly assumed public debt. Though the existence of these nonmarketable services to future generations may justify shifting the burden to them, if such a shift is possible, this is not the point at issue. The question is whether the government borrowing required for the investment indeed affects only the present economy.

An increase in taxation reduces not only saving (as generally conceded in the theory of the balanced-budget multiplier) but also consumption. In a fully utilized economy, an equivalent increase in government borrowing would affect only the amount of investable funds available to the private sector, except for the negligible amount by which a higher interest rate stimulated private saving. Hence the stock of real capital available to the "future generations"—those who live after the period of extra government expenditures—would be smaller under borrowing than under taxation. In addition, future capital stock may be affected by a diversion of current depreciation allowances: the operational lifetime of a piece of equipment or a building is usually longer than the depreciation lifetime used by accountants, and therefore replacement can be postponed without reducing the capital stock in operation. Since effective means are not known for increasing the propensity to save (voluntarily), the maximum burden shifted to future generations is thus the sum of the current saving potential and the current depreciation allowance. Any extra government expenditure beyond this limit must be borne by the present generation, through curtailment of consumption via either taxes or inflation.

This principle, however, holds only when the condition of full utilization is satisfied. When it is not, there are two situations in which government borrowing does *not* imply a burden on the future. First, if the inducement to invest is inelastic, private investment may fall short of the saving potential, even at the lowest possible interest rate, and thus government borrowing would not reduce private investment in the way described above. And second, if current private investment, though equal to the saving potential, is so high that a further appropriate increase (by something like the Harrod-Domar growth rate) cannot be expected, and that therefore underutilization is likely in subsequent periods, current government borrowing will not reduce future income and consumption.

If the present generation shouldered the full burden of the extra expenditure, future generations would of course be likely to enjoy a higher level of income, consumption, or satisfaction than the present one. But to say that the burden of current outlay will be shifted to future generations does not imply a future level of these variables that is *lower* than the present. To see clearly how the burden is equalized, assumptions from the realm of welfare economics may be introduced, as for example Ramsay's famous mathematical theory of saving. If we disregard the ways that changes in income distribution affect satisfaction, and make the usual Harrod-Domar assumptions concerning constancy of the saving ratio and the productivity of capital, then it is not difficult to work out an equalization formula—assuming that the government expenditure keeps within the limits indicated above (current saving potential plus current depreciation allowance).

Let us, in a first approximation, neglect population growth, technological progress, and the interest payable on the government borrowing. Then during the period of extra government expenditure, the loss of investment in the private sector (dI_0), as caused by the increase in government expenditure (dG_0), is expressed as follows: $dI_0 = - sdT_0 - d(G_0 - T_0)$, where dT_0 is the revenue from additional taxation and s is the saving ratio. The consumption sacrifice is $dC_0 = -(1-s)dT_0$. Because of the reduction of investment in the period of extra government expenditure, income (Y) will be lowered in period 1 in accordance with the formula $dY_1 = (sdT_0 + dG_0 - dT_0)/v$, with v representing the capital coefficient, and consumption will decline in accordance with $dC_1 = -(1-s)(sdT_0 + dG_0 - dT_0)/v$. The consumption losses will be equalized if $dT_0/dG_0 = 1/(v - s + 1)$. The longer the period of extra expenditure, the smaller v and the larger dT_0/dG_0, in conformity with common sense. (For a period of a year, in which $v = 3$ and $s = .1$, we have $dT_0/dG_0 = 10/39$.)

To take account of the neglected factors could not greatly affect dT_0/dG_0 and would never increase it. For expenditures within the limits indicated, the interest-rate effect can only be small. Population growth would, to be sure, require a higher capital stock in subsequent periods than is implied in the final equation, and hence more investment and less government borrowing in the actual expenditure period. But the effect of increasing productivity, whether from technological progress or from capital intensification, would work in the opposite direction, and has typically been much stronger than that of population growth.

It may be worth while to close with a few remarks on the main strands of thinking in the literature on the problems discussed here. According to John Stuart Mill (*Principles of Political Economy*, Book 1, Chapter 4, paragraph 8), it was Dr. G. Chalmers who first set forth what is now the textbook argument, that "whatever is spent cannot but be drawn from yearly income" (from Chalmers' writings in the New York Public Library I have not been able to trace the source of this statement). Mill had some reservations, but on the whole his argument makes too much use of his wage-fund theory to be relevant here.

The effect that such government expenditures exert on growth had already been discussed by Ricardo (in his article "Funding System," reprinted in *Works*, 1951, vol. 4). He was primarily interested in the desirability of financing such expenditures by taxes and not by loans, on the grounds that taxation induces an equivalent, or at least a partial, reduction in current consumption (pp. 184, 187). It would follow that borrowing, assumed not to restrict consumption, would affect the stock of capital and thus the level of future production (p. 184), and hence would be a burden on future generations. Unfortunately Ricardo confused the issue by asking (p. 187): "Where is the difference, whether somebody leaves to his son 20,000 pounds with the tax [necessary to pay the interest on the loan] still in force, or 19,000 pounds without it [in case the extra expense was defrayed by extra taxation]?" In other words, he here assumes that in case of taxation and no borrowing, the tax would fall exclusively on saving, with the result that posterity would suffer, regardless of the financing chosen.

During the nineteenth century, economists never lost sight of the growth aspect. Two German authors may be singled out for mention: F. Nebenius (1829) and C. Bernoulli (1839), excerpts of whose writings are conveniently accessible in K. Diehl and Mombert, *Ausgewählte Lesestücke* (vol. 16, 1923, p. 253). No clear analysis was possible, however, before the introduction of the consumption function and the capital coefficient. C. Dietzel (1855) represents one extreme by holding that any burden on a future generation is offset by the advantages accruing to it from the use of the borrowed funds by the present generation. The discussion in A. C. Pigou, *A Study in Public Finance* (1928, Part III, Chapter 1, especially pp. 5-13), misses the decisive point by not distinguishing clearly between gross and net burden.

The necessity of distinguishing between a fully utilized and an underutilized economy seems to have been stated first, though in imperfect formulation, by Adolph Wagner in his contribution to Schoenberg's *Handbuch der politischen Ökonomie* (vol. 3, fourth ed. 1897, reprinted in Diehl-Mombert, p. 257). Wagner contended that loans from disposable domestic capital—that is, funds that at the time of borrowing are not productively used and hence lie idle —"do not withdraw capital from production and employment, and therefore do not reduce either directly."

Chapter Six

TAXPAYERS' ANTICIPATIONS
AND FISCAL ILLUSION

A/ PUBLIC DEBT, COST THEORY, AND THE FISCAL ILLUSION*

BY *James M. Buchanan*

I. Introduction

To what extent does the presence or absence of a "public debt illusion" affect the temporal location of debt burden? This question is important in itself, but in exploring it I hope also to clarify some of the points that remain obscure in the recent literature.[1] Puviani in his unique and highly original work on the fiscal illusion [15] (references on page 162), specifically included public debt as one institution through which such illusions may be generated. In the more recent discussion, Vickrey and others have explicitly made reference to a "public debt illusion," and, at least to some extent, the phenomenon of postponing debt burden through time is held to depend on the presence of some illusion.

Clarification of the term "illusion" is needed at the outset. Fol-

---

*This paper was written in its original form during the academic year, 1961-62, and it was presented as lectures at both the London School of Economics and at the University of Frankfurt. It has been substantially modified from its original version. In undertaking this revision, in 1963-64, I have benefited from several discussions with my colleagues, James Ferguson and Emilio Giardina.

1. See the references on page 162.

lowing normal usage, illusion will be used here to refer to a phenomenon that appears to be what it is not, at least to some of the persons who encounter it. By implication, errors in behavior may arise because of the presence of illusion, errors that could be avoided by more complete knowledge. Economists are, of course, familiar with the "money illusion," a phenomenon that causes people to interpret money values as real values. Presumably, the introduction of a monetary calculus has the effect of "hiding" or "distorting" the underlying real values of the alternatives that are confronted for choice. Men could be predicted to behave differently from the way they do behave were this illusion not present.

A public debt illusion may be defined similarly. It is, or may be, a phenomenon, inherent in the institution of public credit, that causes some men in the political group to behave differently from the way that they would behave in the absence of any illusion. Two different, but related, forms of an illusion will be discussed; these are considered in Sections II and III. I shall demonstrate that the presence or the absence of an illusion does not modify in any essential respects the elementary proposition that the real cost of public expenditures that are financed through debt tends to be shifted forward in time.

II. Undervaluation of Future Tax Liabilities

Vickrey suggests the most familiar form of a public debt illusion when he says: "if we assume a 'public debt illusion' under which individuals pay no attention to their share in the liability represented by the public debt. . . ."[2] This prompts the question: What is an individual's share in the liability that an issue of interest-bearing public debt represents?

I should specify, first of all, that I am concerned here with the individual as he participates, directly or indirectly, in a collective decision-making process where the creation of public debt is one among several fiscal alternatives. In short, I concentrate on the role of the individual as "voter-taxpayer-beneficiary." I shall assume that public debt, if chosen, will be issued independently of tax payments in subsequent time periods. In such a model, debt is serviced from general governmental revenues that are not earmarked in advance. Under such circumstances, the voter-taxpayer, if he is wholly free of illusion, will recognize that the contractual terms

2. See Vickrey [24], p. 133.

upon which debt is created embody claims upon his income, or that of his heirs, in future accounting periods, claims that the government will implement through some ordinary taxing process. These claims may be discounted and some present value estimated.

If present values, so computed by each individual, are summed over all members of the political group, the aggregate liability so expressed need not be equal to the value of the public debt that is marketed. A divergence may appear between these two magnitudes because of the limited time horizons upon which individual plans are made. Individuals do not expect to live forever, and they may not treat their heirs as linear extensions of themselves for economic decisions. It does not seem appropriate to define as illusory behavior that stems from mere limitations on time horizons. However, I do not want to introduce here the many problems of "rational" behavior that the limitations of human life impose. I shall, therefore, examine the public debt illusion under the simplifying assumption that all persons act "as if" they expect to live forever. Even in this model, the single individual will find it difficult to determine his own particular share in the liability represented by public debt. The distribution of taxes required to service the debt will be independently chosen in each time period, in the absence of tied sources. This political fact requires that the individual consider a probability distribution of outcomes for his own share. Again, however, we assume that he does carry out the necessary calculations, and that each person arrives finally at a certainty equivalent for his own expected tax liability. In this highly rarified model, the sum of the present values separately estimated for all individuals should approximate the value of the debt that is to be issued.

No public debt illusion exists in this model. There is no net undervaluation of the future tax obligations that the debt represents. The question now is one of determining the difference in behavior between this model and one in which an illusion is explicitly assumed to be present. Is it correct, as Vickrey suggests, to say that "elimination of this factor eliminates the shifting to the future entirely. . ."?[3] Is the "burden of public debt" wholly concentrated on the "present generation," in the "here and now" of the initial period, in the absence of an undervaluation illusion?

The answer to each of these questions is, I think, negative. And the failure of economists to recognize this is based, in part, on an

3. Vickrey [24], p. 135.

elemental, but near-universal, confusion in the theory of costs.[4] The presence or absence of an illusion, defined in the sense of some failure to discount properly future tax liabilities, is irrelevant to the question of "shifting" a burden of debt to the future periods. The illusion is important, and relevant, only in its effects on *decisions* made at the moment of the original debt issue or creation. Its presence or absence at this moment determines the individual's estimate of the *subjective cost* that a decision to finance public expenditures with debt issue involves. The illusion has no bearing on the distribution of the *objective cost* of this decision *over time*.

Before elaborating this point, it is useful to clarify the distinction between subjective cost and objective cost in a more general setting unrelated to public debt. Many economists overlook this difference, despite repeated warnings.[5] Subjective cost is the obstacle to decision; it consists in the alternative that is foregone *at the moment of choice*, an alternative which can, because it is rejected, never be attained or realized. This cost is wholly within the "mind" of the individual chooser, and it can never be measured by an external observer. It exists temporally only in the moment preceding an act of choice, if it can be dated at all. It results from the sense of anticipating enjoyments that must be foregone. All subjective cost is anticipatory in this sense; hence, conceptually, there is no distinction between an alternative foregone immediately subsequent to decision and one foregone years afterward. Both are, once and for all, given up once a positive choice is made. For this reason, the subjective cost involved in debt issue, as conceived by the voter-taxpayer who is "choosing," must be concentrated in the moment of decision, despite the fact that this cost arises wholly from some current expectation of *future* tax liabilities. The debt illusion that Vickrey mentions has to do with the individual's estimation of this subjective cost. If illusion exists, there may be some undervaluation of the alternative with which debt issue is compared, and, because of this, errors may be made which would, in the absence of illusion, be avoided.

Subjective cost need not be equal to what is here called objective cost, if equality is meaningful at all between these two magnitudes.

4. In my own earlier writings on public debt, I shared this confusion; hence, my failure to be more explicit concerning the meaning of "burden" in my whole analysis [3, 4].

5. Notably by G. F. Thirlby [21, 22], but also by Hayek [8], Robbins [17], and Wiseman [25].

The fact that, in competitive equilibrium, the ability of the buyer-seller to adjust his behavior to a set of uniform market-determined prices converts subjective costs into an objectively-measurable quantity does not imply that, in nonequilibrium situations of choice, any equality need hold. Objective cost is defined as actual resource services that are "given up" or "paid out" to attain the alternative that is chosen. Conceptually, objective cost can be measured by some person external to the decision maker; a real flow of resource services can be observed. Objective cost is *never* realized until *after* decision. The nature of time itself prevents the simultaneity of choice and consequence that is assumed in so much of economic analysis. For many purposes, of course, this temporal gap between the incurring of subjective cost at the moment of definitive choice and the incurring of objective cost subsequent to choice may be ignored. But the distinction clearly cannot be neglected in any discussion of debt, public or private, since the essence of debt is the postponement of objective cost in time.[6]

It is, of course, the objective cost of the public project that is debt financed which is shifted to the future or postponed. Subjective cost or "burden," that which serves as an obstacle to decision, cannot be shifted, by the fact of decision itself, and it is this cost that is affected by illusion. The resource services that are actually committed upon a decision to borrow, to create debt, that actually must be "paid out" or "given up" in exchange for the benefits of the debt-financed collective services can be dated at the time that resource services are transferred from individuals to the fisc, to the extent that these are drawn from current consumption.[7] This transfer takes place in periods subsequent to debt issue as interest and amortization charges come due. This is as true for private debt as for public debt. There is no conceptual difference between the two other than the greater likelihood that

6. The failure to see that *two* costs are associated with any act of choice, a subjective cost and an objective cost, has plagued much of the recent discussion on public debt, including my own. Note, especially, how the recognition of this point clarifies the ambiguity raised in Footnote 1, page 746, in Modigliani's paper [13]. Among the recent contributors, only Scitovsky [18] seems to note a distinction, but he erroneously labels objective costs as "social" and, because of this, misinterprets its meaning.

7. If the taxes levied for the purpose of servicing the public debt should cause individual taxpayers to draw down capital rather than consumption funds, the objective costs of the collective services are postponed even farther into the future. See the discussion on this point below.

the illusion herein discussed will be present under public rather than under private debt due to the complex probability calculus that is necessary to determine individual liability. To the extent that the illusion arises in public debt, more mistakes are likely to be made, but no difference in the temporal location of objective cost is generated.

In the complete absence of illusion, the sacrifice of resources may have been fully anticipated when the initial decision to borrow was made. This does not modify the conclusion, however, that, had the project been tax financed and debt not issued, resource services in the amount of current interest-amortization charges could remain in the possession of the individual during those periods when debt service is necessary.

The concepts of national income accounting, when combined with the failure to distinguish properly between subjective and objective cost or "burden," have been largely responsible for the widespread acceptance of the fallacious idea that there is no postponement of cost involved in the creation of internal public debt. If we look at the fiscal operation from an aggregative or "social" point of view, resources are, of course, "given up" during the time period in which the public expenditure project is undertaken. The members of the group who bear this objective cost, who suffer this "burden" in terms of sacrificed potential consumption in the period of debt creation, *are not* the "purchasers" of the public project, the voters-taxpayers-borrowers-beneficiaries. Those who bear this initial-period objective cost are, instead, those members of the group who choose to buy the government securities that are offered for sale in a wholly private, voluntary, noncollective transaction. These persons will also suffer a subjective cost upon their decision to lend current resources to the collectivity. And the objective cost which they bear arises when they "pay out" current purchasing power, current command over resources, to the public treasury in exchange for the bonds. Their exchange is not, however, for the benefits of the project that is being financed through the fiscal process but is, instead, for the future income stream that inheres in the debt instruments, the government securities. The central feature of public credit lies in its facilitation of this dual exchange between the taxpayer-borrower and the bond purchaser-lender. Two decisions are involved, as there must be in any exchange, since two parties to the exchange are present, and each decision has associated with it both a subjective and an objective cost element. The theory of public debt that I have called elsewhere the "new orthodoxy" is based on an oversight of these embarrassingly simple facts.

III. Failure to Distinguish Owned and Non-Owned Assets

Puviani stressed a slightly different, although related, form of public debt illusion from that which has been discussed above. Let us begin with the familiar Ricardian equivalence between a debt obligation, which embodies the levy of an annual tax in perpetuity, and an extraordinary tax, which collects the full capital sum in the initial period. In such an equivalence, any illusion of the Vickrey type is absent, and, also, the model remains at the level of individual decision. To introduce the standard numerical example, the individual is confronted with the choice of paying a tax of $2,000 once and for all, or paying the sum required to service a debt of this amount through an annual levy of $100 in perpetuity, assuming a discount-interest rate of 5 per cent. Puviani suggested that, even here, the individual will not be indifferent between these two alternatives, but that he will tend to choose the annual tax in perpetuity. He will do so, not because he undervalues future tax obligations, but because he will not treat the acknowledged claims as diminution in the value of his owned assets in the same way that he would treat the once-and-for-all current tax alternative. In the first case, argued Puviani, the individual knows that he will continue to administer the same total assets, undiminished in productive power. The fact that the debt, as embodied in the annual tax in perpetuity, alienates a certain share of these assets will not be fully appreciated even though, in strict balance-sheet terms, the tax liability is fully capitalized. In this sense, therefore, a "public debt illusion" may exist.[8]

This argument applies to debt generally; there is no particular difference between public and private debt in this respect. When a decision to borrow is made, alternatives are, as of that moment, foregone. If we assume that loan contracts are enforced, the moment of decision to borrow and spend removes, once and for all, any opportunity that the individual or group may have for utilizing a certain share of income during subsequent time periods. This remains true independently of the rationality of the borrowing-spending decision. As suggested earlier, the subjective cost, which

8. See the citation from Puviani contained in Fasiani [7], p. 131.

exists solely in the anticipation of foregone opportunities, is present only at the moment of choice when, to any external observer, nothing actually "happens." Resources are only "paid out" by the borrower to the lender as interest and amortization charges come due over time. This pay out does have a temporal sequence that may be observed. And this pay out always reduces potential consumption opportunities below what they would be otherwise, but this need not impose any "burden" in the subjective or "felt" sense. Psychologically, however, the alienation that would be required to eliminate all subjective burden here becomes almost impossible to imagine. At the moment of a borrowing decision, it is conceivable that the individual could "chop off" or "earmark" a sufficient portion of his total capital value, produced by discounting his future earnings stream, so that the servicing of the debt could take place "outside" his internal calculus. He could, in this way, simply treat this portion of his "assets" *as if* it were owned by his creditors. Or, in the extreme, he might actually implement a transfer of title. Note, however, that human as well as nonhuman capital must be included in total assets here, and, both institutionally and behaviorally, it is difficult to think of a transfer of ownership of human capital assets.

If such a complete alienation is not made, however, there will appear to be a "burden" of debt, in some genuinely subjective sense. If the borrower retains what we may call psychological or behavioral ownership of assets, even when these are offset by liabilities, he will "receive" income and then "transfer" this to his creditors. He will, as Puviani implies, suffer some "burden" here, a feeling of deprivation, even though he has no alternative open to him. That is to say, he is confronted with no choice; hence, the subjective burden that he suffers here is not analogous to the subjective cost of decision, previously discussed, which arises precisely because he does have alternatives for choice. Indirect evidence of this Puviani-type of asset illusion is to be found in common or ordinary language where reference is universally made to the "burden" of carrying debt, public or private. By contrast, when an individual is observed to have purchased ordinary commodities, we do not find reference to his suffering a "burden of potatoes."

The temporal aspects of life itself make a Puviani-type illusion plausible. The individual who lives in the moment subsequent to choice is not the same person who has chosen, at least in all respects.

The individual who inherits the consequences of past commitments, even those made by himself, in some physical sense of continuity, will always consider "what might have been," and the alternatives as seen retrospectively must look different from those comtemplated at the time of choice.[9] The institution of debt, public or private, makes this attitude especially likely to arise since the indivdual debtor must, in an objectively observable sense, transfer resource services to creditors, resource services that he "might have" retained had not the borrowing commitment been made at some earlier point in time.

Thus, the Puviani hypothesis implies that the individual, when faced with a pure Ricardian choice, will prefer the debt-annual tax alternative, but also that in subsequent periods, despite the full discounting of future taxes that is inherent in the Ricardian equivalence, he will "feel a burden of debt." This should not be taken to suggest that there exists any shifting of the subjective cost of the debt-issue decision to future periods. It is possible that the subjective cost at the time of decision can be accurately estimated (as it is in the Ricardian equivalence), that no Vickrey-type illusion exists at all, and yet there may remain a subjective "burden" during periods of resource transfer. The fallacy to be avoided here is that of assuming that subjective or "felt" burden need add up to any particular sum. "The coward dies a thousand deaths."[10]

A contrast between debt issue and capital consumption illustrates the Puviani illusion. Analytically, an act of borrowing is not different from "using up" or "eating up" capital. In either case, the subjective cost, the negative side of the account that is relevant for decision, the rejected alternative, is represented in the mind of the chooser by some present value of an income stream over subsequent time periods, an income stream which will come into being if a debt creation or capital consumption decision is not made, but which can never come into being at all if a positive option for either debt creation or capital consumption is exercised. The objective cost appears to be different in the two cases, but this ap-

9. For an interesting treatment of the intertemporal inconsistency of decision, see the paper by Strotz [20].
10. The analysis developed in this section has much in common with that discussed by James Ferguson, included elsewhere in this volume. Although these treatments were developed independently in the initial stages, I think that there now exists substantial agreement between us on the relevant issues in the controversy.

parent difference is due strictly to the institutional realities that reflect the presence of the Puviani illusion. The effective transfer of resource services, in the case of capital consumption as well as debt, occurs in future periods. By definition, capital, as capital, embodies potential consumption in future periods. Converting capital into current consumption potential represents a transfer of resource services away from potential consumption in the future. But capital, once consumed, once "eaten up," appears to be consumed. The alienation of assets appears to be made immediately after decision despite the fact that current consumption is no different here than it would be under borrowing. The individual living in periods after capital is overtly consumed has no sensation of "owning" assets that have already been destroyed in some "eating up" process, or of transferring income (potential consumption) from these nonexistent assets to "creditors." Hence, the presence of a "felt" burden of past decisions is much less likely to exist under capital consumption than under debt. In any time period, a person's income is, of course, in part the consequence of past decisions on the accumulation and decumulation of capital, private and public, human and nonhuman. But one does not, normally, feel overburdened by these past decisions. What is done is considered to be done, and that is that.

This attitude is in evident contrast to that which arises when debt obligations are outstanding. As suggested, the objective cost stream is identical in the two cases. Borrowing does not, however, carry with it the same alienation of claims to assets that capital consumption does. Assets are not really "destroyed" for the individual in the same behavioral sense under these two institutional operations.

In their recent contributions to the debt theory discussion, Modigliani [13] and Vickrey [24] have stressed the point that taxation, insofar as it impinges on capital formation, involves a shifting to the future of the objective cost of the public project that is financed. Insofar as the taxpayer chooses to meet his current obligation by drawing down his rate of capital formation instead of restricting consumption, he is, of course, reducing his income over future periods. The objective cost of the project is, to this extent, effectively shifted forward or postponed. Where Modigliani, Vickrey, and, also, Musgrave [14] err is in their suggestion that public debt issue involves such a postponing of objective cost *only* if, *in the aggregate,* the rate of capital formation in the economy is less than it would be under the tax alternative. This extension of an argument that is basically correct represents a lapsing back into a sophisticated version of the national accounting fallacy that has distorted the more naïve discussions of public debts. Even if those persons who purchase the bonds should do so wholly out of funds otherwise destined to current consumption, the public debt, as such, still involves a shifting of objective cost to future periods, by the individual members of the political group, considered in their role as "purchasers" of the debt-financed public project, that is, as taxpayers-borrowers. The fact that, in the aggregate, the expanded public utilization of resources on behalf of these persons, or persons acting as taxpayers-borrowers-beneficiaries, is just offset by the reduction in resources devoted to consumption by the lenders-bond purchasers, or persons acting in this capacity, has no relevance for any fiscal decision. It is both meaningless and misleading to talk here in terms of "social" or "global" aggregates. For the individuals, as taxpayer-borrowers, as purchasers of the desired collective goods project, the issue of public debt is a *means of consuming* capital. That is to say, the operation is for them analytically equivalent to the imposition of a capital levy upon themselves to finance the same project, assuming away distributional differences and the Vickrey-type illusion. The capital levy is not normally considered for reason of the Puviani illusion.

As a taxpayer-borrower, the individual's income stream (his potential consumption) in future periods is reduced by the full amount of the debt service charges that are imposed upon him. He could prevent this only if, when the debt is initially created, he should set aside resources and *create capital* sufficient to generate an income equivalent to that necessary to meet future debt service charges. The individual, as taxpayer-borrower, could, in this manner, convert the future objective cost into a current-period objective cost. If, however, the model of political choice is assumed to be a voluntaristic one, the "representative" taxpayer-borrower could accomplish this purpose far more simply by accepting current tax financing rather than debt financing for the public project. Just as capital consumption is the analytical equivalent of debt creation, so capital creation is the analytical equivalent of debt retirement. Hence, capital creation designed to offset the temporal effects of debt creation can occur only if the debt creation is imposed on the individual externally, and not chosen by him.

The point to be emphasized is that whether or not the bond purchaser draws funds from his own consumption or from investment during the initial period is wholly irrelevant to the taxpayer-borrower, except in a remote and indirect way. The aggregate rate of capital formation in an economy is, of course, affected by the source of the funds used to purchase public debt instruments. This rate is a meaningful datum for some purposes. But such an aggregate rate of investment does not directly affect or influence the decisions of individuals as they participate in fiscal decisions made on behalf of the whole collectivity. In this capacity, individuals recognize only that public debt, regardless of the source of funds, will impose an objective cost upon them that is represented by a necessary transfer of resources away from them in future periods. If they do not want to incur this temporal pattern of resource pay-out they will not choose to create debt in the first place.

The fact that the totality of the saving-investing decisions in the whole economy acts to insure that the rate of capital formation shall be such-and-such cannot, directly, modify the essential elements in debt creation as a fiscal operation.

IV. Conclusion

Public debts probably generate fiscal illusions of both the Vickrey and the Puviani sort. Individuals, for many reasons, probably do undervalue the future tax liabilities that an issue of debt embodies, and, even if they do not, they should probably still prefer debt to the current tax alternative. The analysis of this paper has demonstrated, however, that the presence or absence of illusion does not affect the temporal pattern of resource payment which debt issue must involve. The presence of a Vickrey-type illusion may affect the subjective cost estimates involved in making a decision to borrow, and, because of this, it may produce errors in the behavior of individuals as they participate in collective choice processes. Once a decision is made, however, the objective cost of the debt-financed project can be located only in time periods following that in which the debt is created and the funds expended for the provision of collective services.

The Puviani illusion acts to create a behavioral distinction between capital consumption and borrowing, despite the analytical equivalence between these two institutions. This distinction allows us to explain the "felt" burden of debt, even when future tax liabilities have been fully and accurately capitalized in the estimate for subjective cost at the time of decision. A recognition of this analytical equivalence also leads to the conclusion that taxation, insofar as individuals draw down capital funds to meet current tax obligations, can also involve a postponement of objective cost in time. Here, as in the case of debt, the relevant conversion decisions are made by individuals, and serious confusion can result from an undue concentration on "social" aggregates, considered apart from individual choices. Individuals, as taxpayer-borrowers, who are observed to choose public debt as a fiscal alternative, will confront an objective cost in future income periods. This remains true independently of the sources from which the funds that are used to finance the public project are originally drawn.

References

1. Bowen, William G., Richard G. Davis, and David H. Kopf. "The Burden of the Public Debt: Reply," *The American Economic Review*, LI (March, 1961), 141-43.
2. ———. "The Public Debt: A Burden on Future Generations?" *The American Economic Review*, L (September, 1960), 701-6.
3. Buchanan, James M. *Fiscal Theory and Political Economy: Selected Essays*. Chapel Hill: The University of North Carolina Press, 1960, especially pp. 51-59.
4. ———. *Public Principles of Public Debt*, Homewood, Illinois: Richard D. Irwin, Inc., 1958.
5. De Marco De Viti, Antonio. "La pressione tributaria dell'imposta e del prestito," *Giornale degli economisti*, I (1893), 38-67, 216-31.
6. Elliott, James R. "The Burden of the Public Debt: Comment," *The American Economic Review*, LI (March, 1961), 139-41.
7. Fasiani, M. *Principii di scienza delle finanze*. Vol. I, 2nd ed. Torino, 1950, Chapter 3.
8. Hayek, F. A. "Economics and Knowledge," *Economica*, IV (February, 1937), 33-54.
9. Lerner, Abba P. "The Burden of Debt," *The Review of Economics and Statistics*, XLIII (May, 1961), 139-41.
10. Meade, James E. "Is the National Debt a Burden?" *Oxford Economic Papers*, X (June, 1958), 163-83.
11. ———. "Is the National Debt a Burden: A Correction," *Oxford Economic Papers*, XI (June, 1959), 109-11.
12. Miller, H. Lawrence, Jr. "Anticipated and Unanticipated Consequences of Public Debt Creation," *Economica*, XXIX (November, 1962), 410-19.
13. Modigliani, Franco. "Long-Run Implications of Alternative Fiscal Policies and the Burden of the National Debt," *The Economic Journal*, LXXI (December, 1961), 730-55.

14. Musgrave, Richard A. *The Theory of Public Finance.* New York: McGraw-Hill Book Company, Inc., 1959, Chapter 23.
15. Puviani, A. *Teoria dell'illusione finanziaria.* Palermo, 1903.
16. Ricardo, David. *Principles of Political Economy and Taxation, Works and Correspondence.* I, Royal Economic Society, 1951, 244-46.
17. Robbins, L. "Remarks Upon Certain Aspects of the Theory of Costs," *The Economic Journal,* XLIV (March, 1934), 1-18.
18. Scitovsky, Tibor. "The Burden of the Public Debt: Comment," *The American Economic Review,* LI (March, 1961), 137-39.
19. Shoup, Carl S. "Debt Financing and Future Generations," *The Economic Journal,* LXXII (December, 1962), 887-98.
20. Strotz, R. H. "Myopia and Inconsistency in Dynamic Utility Maximization," *The Review of Economic Studies,* XXIII (1956), 165-80.
21. Thirlby, G. F. "Economists' Cost Rules and Equilibrium Theory," *Economica,* XXVII (May, 1960), 148-57.
22. ———. "The Subjective Theory of Value and Accounting 'Cost'," *Economica,* XIII (February, 1946), 32-49.
23. Tullock, Gordon. "Public Debt—Who Bears the Burden?" *Rivista di diritto finanziario e scienza delle finanze,* XXII (June, 1963), 207-13.
24. Vickrey, William. "The Burden of the Public Debt: Comment," *The American Economic Review,* LI (March, 1961), 132-37.
25. Wiseman, J. "Uncertainty, Costs, and Collectivist Economic Planning," *Economica,* XX (May, 1953), 118-28.

B/ ANTICIPATED AND UNANTICIPATED CONSEQUENCES OF PUBLIC DEBT CREATION*

BY *H. Laurence Miller, Jr.*

Although there has been extensive consideration of the subject, the theory of public debt creation and of the burden of debt remains unsatisfactory in certain respects.[1] For one thing, discus-

* Reprinted by permission from *Economica,* XXIX (November, 1962). James M. Buchanan, Harold Demsetz, and Harold M. Somers provided helpful comments on earlier versions of this paper. Responsibility for any errors rests entirely on the author.

1. The latest edition of Samuelson's text (P. A. Samuelson, *Economics,* 5th ed., 1961) presents a good exposition of the theory at the textbook level.

Recent participants in a renewed discussion of debt creation include J. M. Buchanan, J. E. Meade, R. A. Musgrave, A. P. Lerner, E. R. Rolph, A. H. Hansen, W. G. Bowen, R. G. Davis, and D. H. Kopf, W. Vickrey, T. Scision continues to suffer from ambiguities and terminological difficulties. Partly as a consequence several matters have been obscured and/or overlooked.

The treatment of borrowing by a government during wartime constitutes one case in point. The layman's view that public borrowing postpones payment for a war to some future point in time in a manner analogous to individual borrowing is wholly erroneous. The standard discussion of the subject correctly states this fact. But in emphasizing that "present resources must be used to fight a war" it provides a basis for further misunderstanding of the subject. It obscures the fact that government resort to debt creation as a substitute for taxation can cause a part of the cost of a war to appear at a later date in the form of frustrated anticipations. The usual discussion also works against a clear understanding of the normative aspects of debt creation—in wartime and in peacetime.

This article re-examines certain aspects of debt creation with the aim of clarifying and extending the analysis in the respects just mentioned. Though primarily concerned with the rationale of public borrowing and the nature and consequences of wartime finance, it should help some readers to a better understanding of the contributions of earlier writers. As its title suggests, the major novelty lies in the way in which anticipations are introduced into the analysis.

We begin by examining an argument for public borrowing to finance public spending in an economy which automatically tends toward full employment. The full employment model is applicable in many local government contexts and offers a good starting point for analyzing central government activities. We assume initially that the community levies taxes on the basis of benefits received from government spending, and that all members of the community anticipate being taxed if they receive benefits. These assumptions underlie the argument for debt creation referred to above, and provide the basis for an unambiguous examination of what is involved in "shifting a burden from present to future" in one sense of that expression. We will identify several different senses in which debt creation can "shift a burden from

tovsky, J. R. Elliott, and F. Modigliani. For citations of their contributions see the first three footnotes in Modigliani's recent paper, "Long-Run Implications of Alternative Fiscal Policies and the Burden of the National Debt," *The Economic Journal*, LXXI (December, 1961), 730-55.

present to future." One widespread practice is to say that a burden is "shifted onto (or placed on) future generations" if, and only if, some action reduces private capital formation. We claim for our procedure only that it uses the word burden in a relevant way and that it facilitates examination of a number of different phenomena meriting attention.

We assume individual utility functions where utility is a function of the stream of real consumption opportunities open to the individual over time à la Irving Fisher. Fisher limits his attention to individuals with finite horizons who exhaust their consumption opportunities during their lifetimes, i.e., leave no estates for their heirs. It will be convenient on occasion to assume that the utilities of (present) individuals depend upon the opportunities that will be available to future generations, and that (unless otherwise specified) the present generation neither undervalues nor overvalues the interests of future generations.

I. Shifting The Burden of Capital Expenditures by Borrowing to Link Taxes with Benefits

Let us imagine an economy that automatically tends toward full employment, and where the residents have adopted the principle that all government spending for specific goods and services should be paid for by taxes levied on the basis of benefits, other taxes and grants having the job of achieving a desirable distribution of income in the economy. What argument could be advanced for borrowing rather than taxing to finance government expenditures? As many writers have pointed out, borrowing seems an appropriate way to finance public spending for capital goods, goods which yield benefits in the future as well as the present. But durability is only a necessary, not a necessary and sufficient, requirement in the most widely persuasive argument for borrowing. Attention needs to be given to the disposition of the goods purchased by the government.

Suppose, for example, that the government is buying tractors to give to certain members of the community. The tractors will provide benefits over a considerable period of time, but the benefits from the government spending can be assigned to present members of the community and taxes levied now on the basis of these benefits. The imposition of the full cost of durable goods on the taxpayers need not be a matter of concern. Taxpayers individually can resort to the capital market in order to allocate the burden of taxes over time if this appeals to them. Moreover, if individual resort to the capital market is objectionable on grounds of imperfection in that market, the government can add its credit to that of individuals as is done in the United States in the veterans housing program.

The situation is different when property rights to the capital equipment or to the services of the equipment are not, for technical or economic reasons, assigned to present members of the community. Suppose a road is being built in a particular community. Some members of the community will subsequently leave it. Others will enter it. Rates of use will vary over time. If it were feasible and economic to provide present members of the community with salable property rights to the use of the road, one could argue for financing the road by taxing present members of the community. But this will often not be the case, and everyone may agree that in the interest of equity the government should shift the burden of the undertaking to the future where the benefits will also appear, the burden to be shifted by borrowing now and taxing later.

In principle, this argument for borrowing is independent of the argument for spending, though the two will often be intertwined.

Let us look closely at what happens in this full employment economy when the government sells securities now to finance capital expenditures, and repays this debt by taxing in the future. Some or all of the members of the community voluntarily buy bonds, voluntarily exchange money or present goods for future goods. Lerner and many other economists refer to these individuals as bearing the burden of public spending, the burden consisting of foregoing present goods and services.[2] No one can quarrel with consistent use of this terminology. It should be noted, however, that these individuals suffer no burden in the sense of a reduction in utility. They exchange one thing for another in a move to preferred utility levels. At the same time, no one pays taxes now. A tax burden in the form of a compulsory reduction in consumption opportunities is shifted into the future.[3]

We have been assuming that all members of the community are supporting this action with full knowledge that a tax liability is

2. A. P. Lerner, "The Burden of Debt," *The Review of Economics and Statistics*, XLIII (May, 1961), 140. Some further remarks on this point appear in Section V below.

3. There is no suggestion here that the present generation gives less attention than it should to the interests of future generations. As noted in the introduc-

being shifted to the future, that they expect a tax in the future if they receive a benefit, and that they know that the only reason for not levying the full cost of the public investment in taxes is the one just discussed—inability to assign future benefits to present persons. In this situation, the probability of a future tax equals the probability of a future benefit for every member of the community, and "shifting the burden" refers to exchanging a certain reduction in consumption now (or later, if the individual can borrow to pay taxes) for some probability less than one of a reduction in consumption (offset by receipt of a benefit) later. The possibility of subsequent immigration into a community is simply one aspect of the inability to relate future benefits to present persons, but it gives present members of the community as a group an added incentive to shift a burden through time by borrowing.

In summary, we have said that public borrowing plus spending can shift a burden from the present to the future where everyone understands what the government is doing, and has no hope whatsoever of pushing taxes off on to others, in the sense that each individual exchanges a *certain* reduction in consumption for a *less certain* reduction in consumption. Borrowing necessarily has the effect of at least postponing a reduction in consumption. The fully anticipated exchange of a certain reduction in consumption for an uncertain one envisaged here obviously constitutes a possible rather than a necessary result of borrowing plus spending.

Will future residents of the community feel that they have inherited an unprofitable burden in the form of the public debt? Not unless it turns out that the public undertaking is unprofitable. Benefits will accompany the taxes into the future, and will be visible both before and after the public borrowing and spending. Moreover, since taxes will be on the basis of benefits, the need to levy taxes to pay interest on the debt and to retire principal will not appear burdensome to anyone except in the sense that taxpayers have to pay a non-zero price for benefits they are receiving.

The view that the debt will be retired is inherent in the argument for borrowing in the case of a non-renewed investment. Not to do so would violate the original rationale for borrowing and would lead to higher costs of servicing than those assumed in the

tion, we can assume that present members of the community fully and correctly provide in their planning for future generations.

calculation of the profitability of the public undertaking.[4] Of course, if it is profitable to renew the investment, the original argument for creation of debt becomes an argument for re-financing it.

One more point requires attention before discussion of this case can be considered complete. An increase in government spending entails a decrease in private consumption and/or investment spending in a full employment economy. Individuals who buy bonds voluntarily suffer no burden in the sense of a reduction in utility, and private consumption and investment spending fall voluntarily. But a decrease in private investment does mean less provision for the future just as an increase in public investment means more. Both of these effects must be taken into account in assessing the effect of government borrowing and spending on total provision of capital for the future. As noted earlier, many writers say that a burden is imposed on, or shifted onto, future generations if, and only if, an action reduces private capital formation. It should be clear that borrowing and spending can place a burden on future generations in this sense without reducing the total amount of capital available to future generations. In the circumstances envisaged here where public debt creation occurs in concert with public capital formation, total provision for the future necessarily increases unless the entire reduction in private expenditures takes the form of a decrease in private investment.

Our concentration in this section on the case where taxes are levied in accordance with benefits, and debt is created because individual property rights cannot be assigned to present members of the community, should not be construed as an argument for these principles over alternative ones. Public spending for medicine with taxes not levied on beneficiaries may be the politically feasible means to attaining a desired redistribution of income. Similar and other considerations can be advanced in favor of public borrowing. Some receive attention below. The analysis of this section serves several useful purposes, however. For one thing, it is desirable to see the unassignability of property rights to future benefits as the most widely persuasive argument for borrowing in a full employment economy. For another, it is useful to see exactly what is involved in shifting a burden in one sense of that elusive expression,

---

4. We are not concerned here with inefficiencies that result from uneconomic evaluation of public investment, e.g., from an unduly low interest rate on government debt.

one, moreover, of obvious interest to economists. Finally, a clear understanding of this case forms a helpful background for considering other matters relating to public borrowing and spending.

II. An Unprofitable Public Investment

What would happen if the public undertaking turns out to be unprofitable, if the benefits do not materialize or are not valued by the community as expected? In this case, the members of the society would be aware of an unprofitable burden in the form of an obligation to pay interest and principal on a debt that is not accompanied by the full amount of benefits anticipated. And the benefits after the fact of debt creation provide an inadequate base for taxes to pay interest and principal.

The existence of "deadweight debt" introduces a "transfer burden" as described in the textbooks now that taxes are not a price for receiving benefits. Unrelated to benefits, taxes lower the real rate of compensation for work. Of course, if this case differs from that in the preceding section only in that the investment turned out badly, the members of the community expected before the fact to retire the debt over time unless it was profitable to renew the investment. What will they do now? They could reap a small gain in not having to devote resources to servicing the debt if the debt were retired. Retiring the debt would do away with any misallocation effects resulting from the discrepancy between the real and money rates of substitution between goods and leisure. Retiring the debt would also prevent the emergence of a discrepancy between what people think they have and what in fact they have— a discrepancy equal to the unprofitable capital formation—of the sort that will occur if they regard debt held as an asset but ignore a liability to retire the debt. Private debt incurred to finance an unprofitable investment is not likely to produce this sort of discrepancy or to distort economic signaling devices. In a world of certainty and rationality acting on the principles described, the debt would be retired. In the actual world the debt is likely to continue into the indefinite future.[5]

To sum up, when a community intends to shift a burden from

5. This statement applies primarily to debt incurred by national governments. Debts incurred by lower-level governmental units typically include legal provisions for repayment not subject to reconsideration after the fact. It should also be noted that the argument for debt retirement in this paragraph assumes continuous full employment.

present to future (in the sense described in the preceding section) but the investment goes badly, it is impossible after the fact to implement what was envisaged before the fact. Less present and future income are available than before the investment, though this may not be apparent to the population if the debt is not retired. And a burden is imposed on present and future members of the community in the form of a transfer burden that will continue until the debt is retired.[6]

III. Wartime Finance

A clear understanding of the argument for debt creation described in the first section seems desirable in itself. It also provides a useful background for considering some aspects of wartime finance obscured or passed over in the usual discussion of debt creation.

As all economists are well aware, the government typically assumes in wartime that considerations of morale preclude levying the full cost of the war in taxes, that workers will not move from farms to factories nor work as hard if the cost of the war is evident to them in the form of taxes. Those who respond must be given a claim on future income if the desired response is to be elicited. The government thus turns to debt creation to finance expenditures.

Taxes to repay debt will seldom if ever be anticipated with certainty by individual taxpayers. But it is interesting to note that the policy just described would be pointless *if* the public always assumed a liability to pay taxes to repay the debt (plus interest) exactly equal to the taxes that would be required to finance the war on a pay-as-you-go basis, and there was no need to replace private opportunities to borrow with public borrowing. Borrowing in this situation with full intent to repay the debt would shift the deficit-financed part of the burden of a war from present to future in a manner virtually analogous to the borrowing examined in Section I. Taxpayers would pay less now in return for paying more later. But why borrow internally for this purpose? Unless consideration is to be given to benefits from the war accruing to future immigrants to the country, members of the community would simply exchange a *certain* reduction in consumption now for a *certain* reduction in consumption later if taxes were anticipated with cer-

6. An investment may be more or less profitable than anticipated. If it is more profitable, taxes higher than those needed to repay the debt would be attainable, and higher taxes or tolls might be called for to clear the market. We need not examine all such implications of a divergence between expected and actual consequences.

tainty. This could be achieved by private borrowing, perhaps with the aid of government guarantees. On the other hand, external borrowing by someone, private or public, is required if the resources flowing from external borrowing are to be made available. No amount of willingness to bear taxes lessens the need for external borrowing if the resources available domestically are to be supplemented by resources of other countries. It is impossible to obtain goods from abroad without giving up goods, receiving gifts, or incurring external indebtedness.[7]

As noted above, future taxes are uncertain. Taxpayers may hope for an improvement in their tax situation in the future as compared to the present. It would be wrong to conclude that internal borrowing in wartime is irrational. Nor can we say anything about the intentions of governments that engage in this practice. All we can say is that internal borrowing would have no appeal if specified circumstances prevailed.

Another aspect of wartime finance dealt with inadequately in the usual discussion is the fact that debt creation can play a part in shifting a burden from present to future in the sense of allowing expectations to be formed that are subsequently unrealized. It seems impossible to doubt, for example, that the financing of the second world war had such consequences for many countries in the form of inflation after the war. During the war, individuals bought bonds, acquired money balances, and refrained from participation in black markets with the expectation that their assets would command certain amounts of goods at some future date. It seems safe to think that they did not anticipate taxes to repay the debt created. When prices rose after the war, many individuals failed to achieve anticipated utility levels. Only a very intrepid investigator would attempt to measure the burden of a war that is shifted as a result of disappointed expectations. Some individuals gained from the policies followed. But can one doubt that there was an aggregate loss?[8]

7. One can imagine internal borrowing for the sole purpose of substituting public borrowing for private borrowing. Individual taxpayers would exchange a definite liability to pay, for example, $100 now for a definite liability to pay $100 plus interest at some future time.

8. An investigation (*ex post*) of the tax effect of inflation appears in R. Turvey, "Inflation as a Tax in World War II," *The Journal of Political Economy*, LXIX (February, 1961), 70-73. A. Alchian and R. Kessel have investigated the effects of anticipated as compared to unanticipated inflations in some recent work. See especially a paper by these authors which will appear in a forthcoming issue of *The Journal of Political Economy*.

This outcome was the result of borrowing from the public *plus* indirect money creation that added to interest-bearing debt and direct money creation *plus* other factors affecting aggregate demand in the economy.[9] The consequences (other than the transfer burden resulting from interest-bearing debt creation) were not inevitable.[10] But in many cases some such outcome is no doubt predictable (by some individuals, within or outside the government) when the decision is made.

Nothing in the foregoing supports the layman's view that borrowing in wartime necessarily shifts the burden of a war from present to future in a way analogous to individual borrowing. On the other hand, we are saying that debt creation in such circumstances can shift part of the burden of a war in the sense that expectations fail to be realized, and that the statement to the effect that "present resources must be used to fight a war" (and thus, subject to qualifications relating to effects on capital formation and the extent of external borrowing, that the burden must be borne at the time) obscures this phenomenon. Moreover, it follows that it is incorrect to argue that the only way in which debt creation can affect future generations adversely is by reducing private capital formation, by increasing external indebtedness, and by imposing the transfer burden on the future. When the public does not anticipate taxes to repay debt or other adverse consequences, a discrepancy between what people think exists and what in fact exists always involves a potential frustration of expectations of the sort discussed here.

9. As is well known, a large part of the public debts of many countries has come into existence as an intermediate step in money creation that imposes a transfer burden on the economy. In the United States, for example, if the government wants an increase in the money supply in and of itself, the Federal Reserve Banks buy certain assets with non-interest-bearing deposit credits and/or make it possible for the commercial banks to create money. But when money is wanted so that the government can spend it, the government (the Treasury) typically offers interest-bearing debt to other institutions (the Federal Reserve Banks or the commercial banks) for money the latter create. To the extent that the government sells securities to the central bank, one agency of the government simply obligates itself to another agency of the government. More than two-thirds of the money creation in the United States during the second world war involved sale of securities to commercial banks.

10. To the extent that the government spends for capital formation adaptable to civilian production, no discrepancy is introduced between what people think they have and what in fact exists. And even if the resources go entirely into wartime or other consumption, a debt can continue to exist forever with only the consequences discussed in the preceding section where the public failed to retire a debt incurred to finance a subsequently unprofitable investment.

IV. External versus Internal Indebtedness

Buchanan has presented a correct and virtually definitive treatment of external as compared to internal indebtedness.[11] In brief, external borrowing is required if the resources available domestically are to be supplemented by resources of other countries. And external debt is "like individual debt," whereas internal debt is not, if one takes an aggregative view of the community. Otherwise, external debt is no more "burdensome" than internal debt. The discussion of the preceding section obviously reinforces this conclusion.

Deadweight debt involves a discrepancy between what people think exists and what in fact exists. All deadweight debt imposes a claim on resources that cannot be fully honored without taxes or other consequences that fall unexpectedly on someone in a full employment economy. And an external debt is on the same footing as an internal debt as a claim on more goods and services than can be made available.

Suppose foreign and domestic holders of government debt present debt (payable in domestic funds) for redemption, and that payment of cash results in inflation. Foreign and domestic creditors alike would fail to obtain the full amount of goods and services they had expected. A burden in the form of failure to realize expectations would be shared by domestic and foreign creditors of the government with a real loss of goods to foreigners less than the real value of the external debt prior to the inflation.

Internally-held debt is assumed to be a component in wealth that affects aggregate demand, while external debt is not (taxes to repay the debt being ignored). In calculations of wealth for this purpose, and when considering the community as an aggregate, it is correct to exclude internal debt as a national liability. But in some contexts, clearly, it is as mistaken to exclude internal as to exclude external indebtedness in calculating the wealth of the community.

V. Some Factors Contributing to Confusion in the Literature

The word "burden" is widely used in a way different from the way in which we have used it so far. A burden is said to be borne by those who reduce their spending. This usage emphasizes the fact that resources are gone (except insofar as they are drawn into public capital formation). As we pointed out earlier, it is misleading in

11. See especially J. M. Buchanan, *Public Principles of Public Debt*, ch. 6.

one sense to say that those individuals (described in the first section) who free resources for the government's use by purchasing bonds bear the burden of public spending. They voluntarily move to preferred utility positions. Moreover, as our discussion of wartime finance attempted to make clear, it would be wrong to conclude that, if spending is reduced by someone at a particular time, the burden is necessarily taken care of once and for all.

The Keynesian model of the economy explains the level of aggregate demand and supply and economic activity in terms of the behavior of various groups and of the monetary and fiscal activities of governments. A new set of consequences is introduced into the analysis of these activities, and the possibility of an underemployment equilibrium provides a different perspective for evaluating fiscal policy.[12] Public spending has been said to be burdenless or almost burdenless, consequently, if it does not reduce private spending.[13] No one can quarrel with consistent use of this terminology, though the use of the word "burden" to refer to a reduction in private spending probably has worked against clarification of the matters of chief concern in this article.

Other factors have contributed to confusion on occasion. It is obviously important to distinguish carefully between questions relating to debt creation *before* the fact and questions relating to debts existing *after* the fact, to make explicit assumptions about anticipations, and to make the subject of discussion unambiguous. Reference was made in the preceding paragraph to the burden associated with public *spending*. In earlier sections we were concerned with burdens imposed by or shifted by public *debt creation*, in conjunction with public spending, or in and of itself. It is clear that one can look into the effect of all possible combinations of taxing, borrowing, and money creation *plus* spending, not spending, and retiring existing debt in terms of consequences investigated here as well as other consequences. Modigliani approaches the subject in essentially this fashion in a recent article concerned with the

12. The view that the economy would automatically attain full employment if prices were more flexible need not be considered here. We assume that they are not sufficiently flexible.

13. Various writers from Wright on have pointed out that deficits financed by debt creation impose a transfer burden on the economy (D. McC. Wright, "The Economic Limit and Economic Burden of an Internally Held National Debt," *Quarterly Journal of Economics*, LV (November, 1940), 129). Buchanan has recently argued for financing deficits by issuing currency to avoid unnecessary costs to the economy (Buchanan, *Public Principles*, pp. 125-34).

effect of alternative fiscal policies on private capital formation.[14]

VI. Concluding Comment

We examined in the first section of this paper one sense in which debt creation can shift a burden from present to future—borrowing by a public that fully anticipates taxes in order to equate benefits and taxes. What appears to be the most widely persuasive argument for public borrowing in a full employment economy is an argument for shifting a burden in this sense. Later we noted that the public would have no desire to engage in public borrowing to finance a war if every individual fully anticipated taxes with certainty, and the other circumstances discussed prevailed. This fact is surely of some interest. We emphasized subsequently that a burden can appear in the form of frustrated expectations. A burden of this sort has almost certainly been an important characteristic of wartime finance. These consequences and considerations relating to the rationale of public borrowing are obscured rather than illuminated by the prevailing analysis.

14. Modigliani, "Long-Run Implications."

Chapter Seven

REJECTION OF THE CONCEPT OF PUBLIC DEBT BURDEN

A/ THE LOGIC OF NATIONAL DEBT POLICY*

BY *Jack Wiseman*

This article will not be concerned to argue that any particular debt policy or policies should be pursued in Britain at the present time, but rather to make proposals as to the context in which such policies need to be considered. In particular, it will be argued that the national debt needs to be thought about in relation to more than one kind of policy aim, and that the relevant, distinct policy aims are not at present considered in a fashion conducive to satisfactory decisions about debt policy in general.

Before the Keynesian revolution, discussion of the economic implications of the public debt was conducted on the theoretical assumption that there was an inherent tendency to full employment, and was almost exclusively concerned with the question of whether or not the existence of such a debt imposed a "burden" on the community. Keynesian ideas changed this situation in two important ways. First, they shifted the emphasis of discussion towards the examination of the effects of changes in the size and structure of debt upon the level of aggregate demand and employment. Second, they stimulated a re-examination of the earlier ideas about debt burden, and the rejection of those ideas in favor of a new "debt orthodoxy."

The shift of emphasis towards questions of stabilization in dis-

* Reprinted by permission from *Westminster Bank Review* (August, 1961).

cussion of debt policy has persisted; some of the debate about the Report of the Radcliffe Committee, for example, appears to regard the existence of a national debt as an essential prerequisite for the successful operation of monetary (stabilization) policy, a socially valuable insititution that would have to be invented did we not already possess it. Undoubtedly, this persistence is to an important extent the direct consequence of the general change in intellectual attitudes generated by Keynesian ideas, which led in this field as in others to the relative neglect of questions of efficiency in resource-allocation and to concentration upon macroeconomic considerations. That is to say the emphasis was switched from consideration of decisions of individual consumers and producers to the *total* demand for and supply of resources. But whereas this over-emphasis has now largely disappeared in other fields of economic policy, it continues to exist in the case of the public debt. The reason for this is to be found in the fact that, while the Keynesian revolution encouraged a re-examination of earlier ideas about debt, it failed to change the context within which those ideas were propounded: the "new orthodoxy," like the old, has been concerned to make general propositions about the presence or absence of a "burden" of debt. This concept of "burden" is in my view useless and misleading; and its persistence, by obscuring the other issues of real importance to public policy, has resulted in an approach to debt policy that is unduly dominated by considerations of stabilization.

It is enlightening to compare the classical and post-Keynesian views on debt burden, and to examine both in relation to what seem to be the economic considerations relevant to decisions about public policy. Professor J. M. Buchanan, in his recent book *Public Principles of Public Debt*, suggests that the post-Keynesian discussion has produced three propositions which stand in contrast with earlier views about the burden of debt, which together constitute the essence of the new "debt orthodoxy," and which he believes to be erroneous. These propositions are: first, that there is an important sense in which the burden of a debt contracted now cannot be borne by future generations; second, that a public debt differs in all essential (economic) characteristics from a private (individual) debt; and third, that a public debt held internally has quite dissimilar economic ("burden") characteristics and implications from such a debt held externally.[1]

1. These propositions are much more fully criticized in Professor Buchanan's

The first proposition of the "new orthodoxy" is concerned with the "real primary burden" of debt. Those who make it do not deny that the raising of debt now may impose "frictional" burdens (administrative costs of making transfer payments, etc.) on future generations, or that the effects of debt finance *on individuals* now and in the future would be different from the effects of using taxation to finance the same public project. But, they argue, debt raised in the present creates no aggregate real burden *to the community* in the future, because the only obligation of the government is to make money transfer payments, and the claims and commitments of individual members of society must cancel out. When a government borrows, there is a transfer of purchasing power from individuals to the government. The use of this purchasing power in the same time period draws resources to government employment from other uses. That is, the real sacrifice (of resources from other uses) must be currently borne. The sacrifice is the consequence of the resultant public expenditures and not of the act of raising loans per se, it cannot be passed to future generations, and the use of debt to finance public projects thus differs little in its economic implications from the use of taxation for similar purposes. This position is in striking contrast with the bulk of pre-Keynesian writing, which saw the need to make interest payments on the existing debt as a real burden on future generations.

The refutation of the classical analogy between private and public debt proposed by post-Keynesian writers follows similar lines. To an individual, they argue, the interest-charge on a debt incurred in the past constitutes a real burden; it must reduce an individual's current standard of living or current savings. But it is improper to use the same reasoning in respect of a public debt, as the classical writers did, since if the debt is held internally, the debt-holders (interest receivers) must be the same people as the taxpayers. The distribution of the *community* income-stream over time is not significantly altered by the raising of debt, and the classical objection to debt, that it implies that the community is "living beyond its income," is without substance. Although this refutation of the analogy between private and public debt is put forward by the

---

book than will be possible here. Our analytical interpretations are essentially similar; the real difference between his position and mine is that, while Professor Buchanan sees his purpose as the rehabilitation of classical concepts of burden, it is my view that the whole discussion of burden has become pointless.

post-Keynesians as a general one, its bearing upon the special problem of unemployment is obvious. The argument has been used in particular to support the widely-accepted view that in time of unemployment an increase in debt could be used to increase the level of community income and employment. Future interest-payments could thus be met out of additional tax-yields obtained without need to increase tax rates, and it is held that no "burden" is therefore involved. For the community, "living beyond income" in such circumstances is not only not wrong; it is obligatory.

Finally, while the classical position on debt did not distinguish in principle between debt held internally and debt held abroad, post-Keynesian discussion has tended to support the view that the two have quite different economic implications. This view is implicit in the arguments already discussed, for the post-Keynesian position in respect of the two propositions already examined is based upon the unity of the economy being considered; taxpayers and interest-receivers are members of the same group. This is no longer the case if the debt is external. Now the debt burden can be shifted forward; borrowing abroad in the present implies the need to make interest payments abroad in the future, and this must reduce the future real income of the community.

The Shortcomings of The "Burden" Approach

These new propositions about debt burden have been widely accepted. This acceptance, which owes much to recognition of the fact that public debt can obviously be used to increase the level of community income and employment in time of recession, has had as its corollary a belief in the unimportance of the size and structure of the national debt outside the context of stabilization policy. On the other hand, there has been some uneasiness; Professor Meade and others, as well as Professor Buchanan, have felt the need to look at the question more closely. This uneasiness is not difficult to appreciate, for the "new orthodoxy" invites policy inferences which are *prima facie* implausible. To cite but one instance, the proposition above as to the difference between internal and external debt would seem to imply that it is *always* better to borrow at home, *whatever the interest rate that has to be paid*, rather than borrow abroad at any rate greater than zero.

Both acceptance and uneasiness are to be explained by the fact that the "burden" propositions, as formulated both by classical

writers and by supporters of the "new orthodoxy," are so vague as
to defy precise interpretation. This is due to the persistence, in debt
discussion, of general statements about burden which obscure the
diversity of the relevant economic considerations. The point can
be sufficiently demonstrated by asking two questions. The first is:
When debt is said to impose a burden, with what alternative situation is it being compared? The second is, simply: what kind of debt
are we talking about?

The first question draws attention to the fact that statements
about the "burden" imposed by any particular policy must be meaningless unless they compare the effects of that policy with those of
some alternative policy. Further, the alternatives chosen for purposes of comparison must be both relevant and possible if the propositions are to throw light on the practical problems of public
policy. In general the approach in the "burden" discussion has been
of a "partial equilibrium" kind, in that it has been assumed that it
is possible to compare the situation of a community with a public
debt and that of one in which debt does not exist *but in which
all other economic magnitudes and relationships remain unaltered.*
This procedure is objectionable on a number of grounds. In the
first place, there are some economic magnitudes that are so closely
related to decisions about the raising of debt that it is implausible
to proceed as though they could be unaffected by debt policy.
Again, the procedure is obviously unsatisfactory if the magnitude
of the debt operation under consideration is such that it must have
general effects on income and employment. In fact, to be realistic
and useful, discussion of debt policy must distinguish between the
raising and the spending of money by the government, and must
consider the raising of debt in relation to the other courses that the
government might have followed—e.g., meeting the expenditure
under consideration by the use of taxation, by currency inflation, or
by the reduction of other expenditures.

The diversities are increased when we turn to my second question—what kind of debt are we talking about? Inevitably, the "burden" discussion has proceeded on the assumption that the national
debt can be thought about as a single economic magnitude with
given properties. But the term is in fact a generic one covering many
kinds of debt: marketable securities, floating debt, National Savings securities, and so on; and there is a variety of reasons for public borrowing, of types of borrowing, and of sizes of loan. Also,

the general economic conditions in which debt is to be raised can themselves vary, and these differences must change the economic implications of particular debt policies. Thus, debt may be issued in conditions of full employment to give command over resources, and that command over resources may itself be intended for projects that are or are not self-liquidating. Or debt may be raised in time of unemployment and devoted to collective social investment. Debt may be raised on a scale such that its general economic implications cannot be ignored, or in quantities small enough not to affect prices and interest rates. There are many other possibilities, and there seems little chance of finding generalizations that will embrace them all.

Some Conclusions and Suggestions

The whole of the argument so far supports the view that discussion of debt "burden" has become pointless, and that we should do better to devote our time to the study of particular situations in which the raising or retirement of debt is one of the possible means of pursuing a specified objective. This conclusion is supported by a re-examination of the "new orthodoxy" of debt burden in the light of our methodological criticisms. Each of the propositions of the "new orthodoxy" in fact constitutes an invalid generalization from a special case, and the choice of special cases has clearly been influenced by the interest of those concerned in the problem of unemployment. This is perhaps most easily illustrated in the case of the distinction between internal and external debt. In time of unemployment it can be argued that the "real" cost of government borrowing at home is zero, as the resources over which the government gains control are not being used. Thus, any borrowing abroad would involve an unnecessary future sacrifice in the payment of interest, and such borrowing cannot be justified at any positive rate of interest.

But consider a situation of full employment. If the government borrows at home, it obtains claims on resources only by reducing current private consumption or investment. If the public investment is at the cost of private investment, any future increase in national income from the raising and spending of debt has been obtained at the cost of the lost income that the private investment could have provided. If we borrow abroad, no sacrifice of current private investment is involved. In the future, output has to be sent abroad to service the debt, *but the flow of income from which that output is provided is enhanced by the fruits of the relevant private investment.* In such circumstances, the respective interest rates at home and abroad are clearly pertinent to decisions as to where to borrow. The post-Keynesian distinction now made between internal and external debt is thus a special case concerned with unemployment situations, and not a proposition of general validity.

Recognition of the futility of the debt burden discussion does not of itself make decisions about debt policy easy, but it opens the way to a more satisfactory formulation of the policy issues. Once we accept that debt policy is concerned not with one problem (stabilization) but with many, and that there is need to keep a whole group of aims and potential policy means continuously and simultaneously under review, then useful discussion of the way the policy problem might be formulated becomes possible, and the examination of the kinds of statistical and other information that satisfactory policy-making demands becomes imperative. It is clear, for example, that the raising of debt to provide capital for the nationalized industries raises not only questions of stabilization but also questions concerned with the economic organization of such enterprises and of their access to the capital market. This particular problem was considered as a whole by the Radcliffe Committee, but elsewhere these considerations continue to be discussed in isolation from each other.

In the case of Britain, there are a number of ways in which the statistical information now provided about debt could be improved and concentrated, if it were desired to facilitate informed discussion of the "opportunity costs" of debt policies, and to enable debt-raising policies and questions of management to be considered together. Perhaps the most obvious of these concerns the provision of more information about the relative importance of "commercial" debt, which is used for purposes providing a monetary return to the government and "deadweight" debt which has no such attribute. The distinction is important because the economic considerations that are relevant to decisions to raise or retire debt for the one purpose may be very different from those that apply in the case of the other. It is also important for an understanding of what has in fact been happening to the debt. In money terms, the total of public debt is now more than forty times as large as before the first world war. But such information as is available (e.g., about interest receipts in the "below the line" accounts provided in the annual Financial Statements) suggests that the rate of growth of deadweight debt has been much slower than that of total indebtedness. It would be useful to have precise and accessible information about this. It would also clearly be valuable to have information about the magnitudes of domestic and of foreign-held debt (the latter distinguishing between sterling and foreign-currency obligations), and about intra-governmental debt holdings. These last (held by such bodies as the Exchange Equalization Account and the National Insurance Funds) are considerable in amount: their size affects the net transfers that have to be made from the Government to the private sector by way of debt service. We have too little information, both about the magnitudes involved and about the departmental policies affecting them.

Most of the information concerned is available from one source or another, or can be inferred with greater or smaller margins of error. But regular publication in a single and accessible form would do much to facilitate useful public discussion of debt policy and to wean economists from their present undue concentration on questions of stability or on barren concepts of burden. In the conclusions to the chapter on the national debt, the Radcliffe Report stated that "debt management lies at the heart of monetary control," and that the two things "are one and indivisible" (paragraph 603). The emphasis here may not command general agreement, but the theme might attract wider attention than it has so far received if better information were forthcoming and if there were a better understanding of the nature and complexity of the economic considerations that affect (or should affect) decisions about debt policy and debt management.

B/ HOW TO MAKE A BURDEN OF THE PUBLIC DEBT*

BY E. J. Mishan

I. Introduction

Writing on the subject of the national debt in 1947, the great Pigou expressed himself as follows: "It is sometimes thought that whether and how far an enterprise or enterprises ought to be financed out of [government] loans depends on whether and how far future generations will benefit from it. This conception rests on the idea that the cost of anything paid for out of loans falls on future generations while the costs met out of taxes are borne by the present generation. Though twenty-five years ago this idea could claim respectable support, it is now everywhere acknowledged to be fallacious. It is true that loans *raised* from *foreigners* entail a burden represented in interest and sinking fund on future generations in the borrowing country. But interest and sinking fund on *internal* loans are merely transfers from one set of people in the country to another set, so that the two sets together—future generations as a whole—are not burdened at all."[1] For a decade on either side of that year little dissent to this doctrine could be found in professional circles. Indeed, the propositions comprising it appeared so self-evident and inescapable that it is only by reminding ourselves of the circumstances in which they were enunciated that we can appreciate the solemn emphasis laid upon them.

Much of the Keynesian reflationary medicine envisaged continuous government expenditures in excess of tax receipts. If the deficit were to be covered by bond issues, a continuous increase of the public debt would result. Such a contingency was not, however, congenial to the Treasury mind of the thirties; indeed it was not congenial to any mind reared in the maxims of prudent business

* Reprinted by permission of the University of Chicago Press from *The Journal of Political Economy*, LXXI (December, 1963). Copyright 1963 by the University of Chicago.
1. A. C. Pigou, *A Study of Public Finance* (3d ed.; London, 1947).

management. Visions of a nation weighed down by debt, tottering toward bankruptcy, were by no means uncommon at that time. In view of the hold of such fears on the minds of influential people, and therefore of the real political danger which any bold government program would run into, such assurances of the innocuous, nature of the public debt could not be too frequently repeated.

It should be mentioned in passing that this view of the internal public debt as not being transferable to future generations was far from being novel among economists even in the thirties. In 1920, for instance, Jacob Viner, in the course of examining allegations of working-class hardship during the war, readily conceded the proposition that "the cost of the war for a country which . . . does not borrow from abroad must be borne from current income," this view being, in his opinion, one that was "generally accepted by economists."[2] Nevertheless, it was largely due to the efforts of Keynes and his followers that, in Britain at least, this doctrine finally penetrated the inner councils of the Treasury. And, indeed, to such effect that no inhibitions about the public debt being a burden on the economy remained to restrain the British government from, in fact, incurring huge budget deficits in its finance of World War II.

There is a dialectic in these things, however. The unquestioned ascendancy of this no-burden doctrine—what Buchanan refers to as the "new orthodoxy"—seems to have elicited a "negation of the negation." At any rate a rebellion took place in the late fifties in which—according to the impression conveyed by the leader of the first open revolt—the ramparts of the new orthodoxy were breached by the battering ram of a new burden construction. Though sharp counterattacks were soon to follow, rebel reinforcements began to appear from unexpected quarters. The Buchanan "mark one" burden may have become badly damaged, but it was not long before other ingenious burdens were brought into service.

The story has not yet ended, but perhaps we need not wait before making up our minds as to what is happening. It is only the incidental purpose, however, to entertain the reader with a short account of the campaigns so far conducted by the "new heretics." Its chief object is to provide a wide enough framework of analysis to enable the reader to decide for himself whether we are in the

2. "Who Paid for the War," *The Journal of Political Economy* (January, 1920).

presence of a genuine revolution in fiscal thought or whether it is all so much "sound and fury signifying nothing," a battle of words, no more. My impression, for what it is worth, is that there is no evidence yet of any genuine class of ideas. While there has been a repeated marshaling of forces and some elaborate maneuvers executed by the insurgents, they appear to have issued only in loud claims to positions that are apparently not being contended, nor indeed were ever contended, by the supporters of the new orthodoxy.

Lest this appears to the insurgents too unsympathetic an interpretation, I hasten to add that, by presenting as fairly as I can their own account of strategic positions taken, I will, I hope, enable the reader to pass judgment on the nature of the victories claimed. And though in each case I shall append my own critical observations I shall try to confine them, until the final section at least, within the context suggested by the pro-burden economists themselves.[3]

II. The First Blast of the Trumpet Against the Iniquitous Regime of Keynesians

The revolt flared up with the publication in 1958 of a slim volume, *Public Principles of Public Debt* by Professor James Buchanan.[4] With an impressive flourish he threw down the gauntlet. Not only did he challenge "the new orthodoxy" on each of its three main propositions, but he undertook to establish that "vulgar conceptions" of the national debt were, after all, "fundamentally

---

3. In chap. xxiii of R. A. Musgrave's *Theory of Public Finance* (New York, 1959) a different twist is imparted to this burden aspect. While the authors mentioned in the text of this paper tacitly condemn government loan finance on the alleged grounds of shifting a burden from the present to the future, Musgrave apparently approves of the shifting mechanism as a means of achieving a more equitable spread over generations of the cost of government-constructed assets whose benefits accrue over a long period. His thesis can be illustrated by supposing a government that decided to tax and borrow from the existing generations in equal proportions in order to finance a useful social asset, such as a bridge or pedestrian precinct. In thirty years' time extra taxes would be levied on the younger generation only in order to retire the bonds by the older generation. Putting aside the objection that the older generation would surely prefer to hold on to their bonds in any case (since otherwise they would have attempted to sell them), this device only illustrates the possibility of tax discrimination in favor of the *existing* older generation and against the *existing* younger generation. It does not purport to show, as does the argument of the authors mentioned in the text, that a burden may be transferred from the current generation to generations yet unborn.

4. Homewood, Ill., 1958.

correct and valid generally." More explicitly he proposed to demonstrate that, in the most general case, (1) the "primary real burden" of the public debt is indeed shifted to the future; (2) the analogy between public and private debt is fundamentally correct; and (3) external debt and internal debt are fundamentally equivalent.

Before launching the main attack Buchanan prepares the ground in three respects: (a) He enlightens us about the long history of the public debt controversy. The "new orthodoxy," he assures us, is not really new. Articulate statements about the difference between private and public debt hark back to the eighteenth century, and notwithstanding that they were challenged at the time, and again more effectively in the following century, the current no-burden view of the public debt became firmly established in the thirties and forties. (b) To convince us that he is not engaged in any petty skirmishes, he proposes to ignore all "secondary" effects of public debt creation. After all, no one would deny the possibility of disincentive to effort and enterprise arising from any increase in marginal tax rates necessary to service a large public debt. Also classified as a secondary effect is that arising from the asset-expenditure relation: for a given change in the price level the larger the public debt the larger the asset-expenditure effect. The "primary real burden" of which Buchanan speaks will emerge below. (c) Finally, he tells us of some of the special preparations necessary to achieve his objectives: (i) The economy he has in mind is one in a continuous state of full employment. (ii) The creation of debt by the government is, therefore, not undertaken as a measure to combat inflation. It is the financial counterpart of transferring real resources from the private to the public sector. (iii) These resources, however, can be employed by the government in any way it chooses, either "productively" or "wastefully" without in any way affecting his thesis. (iv) The funds used for the purchase of new government bonds are drawn wholly from private capital formation—a pretty strong assumption.[5]

5. As Ricardo pointed out, under stable conditions a person with foresight should realize that whether he paid a levy, say, of £2,000 now, or whether instead he bought a £2,000 bond entitling him and his heirs to £100 per annum in perpetuity, which future income stream would do more than exactly offset a perpetual tax liability of £100 per annum, his net worth would be equally reduced by £2,000.

This assumed indifference between loan finance and tax finance would apply also to all rational individuals in conditions of unchanging certainty, regardless of their income, in the presence of a loan market with access to all on equal terms. For example, a person who would choose *not* to buy a $100 bond in

We are now ready for the main revelation: the argument that a public project has to be paid for during its period of construction because alternative goods or projects must be foregone during that same period, say t_0, and not during any subsequent period, t_1, t_2, ... or t_n, is attacked by Buchanan as a misunderstanding of what is implied. Indeed, to talk of the economy as a whole enduring a sacrifice during period t_0 involves an organic conception of the state, alien to the liberal spirit. We must, instead, consider first the impact of the government's expenditure during period t_0 on the individuals in the community.

Now since no pressure is brought to bear on them, those individ-

---

order to offset certain additional future taxes of $5 per annum (p.a.) suffers the same $100 reduction in his net worth (if the government spends the loan "wastefully") as he does if, instead, the government taxes him $100. For in the latter event he would at once borrow $100 from the capital market, paying interest on it of $5 p.a. thereafter. But once we remove the perfectly accessible loan market, asymmetrical behavior may no longer be regarded as irrational for everyone. Thus, an individual who was taxed $100 might have no option but to reduce his consumption immediately. The alternative, loan finance, makes him liable, instead, to a future stream of taxes of $5 p.a. and he may then exercise the choice of meeting these tax payments when they fall due rather than investing at once the sum of $100 to yield $5 p.a., a stream of returns exactly equal to the anticipated annual taxes. Thus, whenever the government resorts to debt finance such people do not reduce consumption, whereas under tax finance they are obliged to. And though the wealthier members can afford to act rationally and to reduce consumption equally when taxes are levied as when instead, the government resorts to loan finance, the asymmetrical response of the remainder of the community results in private consumption expenditure being reduced more under tax finance than under loan finance.

Add to this consideration the difficulty any individual will have in singling out his future tax liability attributable to the loan in conditions of uncertainty, and one can appreciate his propensity to discount it. In the extreme case, loan finance will result in no reduction in current consumption, while tax finance will be met entirely from a reduction in current consumption. For simplicity's sake, however, we shall adopt this extreme assumption—although of course all pro-burden arguments require no more than a differential in the reduction of consumption when expenditure is covered by tax finance rather than loan finance.

Finally, not only do we require the assumption of irrationality, or else of uncertainty, and/or an imperfect capital market, in order to explain why a person's current purchases of private securities are not reduced by taxes but are reduced by his contribution to government bond issues (regardless of government's "wasteful" expenditure) it is also required (a) that the rate of interest not be stabilized, as in the Keynesian model (else additional government spending would lead to aggregate excess expenditure and, therefore, inflation) and (b) that the current saving schedule against the rate of interest be completely irresponsive along the relevant range; otherwise the value of additional sales of government bonds, which raises the rate of interest, would not entirely displace the sale of private securities, as required by Buchanan.

uals who elect to buy government bonds during the period in question cannot meaningfully be said to be making any sacrifice. Indeed they may be considered better off inasmuch as they choose freely to give up alternative ways of using their cash in favor of buying government bonds. However, "future generations" at periods $t_1, t_2, \ldots, t_n$ (these periods are quite arbitrary; Buchanan treats as "different generations" the *same* individual existing over different periods, $t_0, t_1, t_2, \ldots, t_n$) are *compelled* to pay taxes, and therein lies the burden on future generations.[6]

The reader will surely apprehend that there is nothing in this argument, if we provisionally accept it, that contradicts anything held by the new orthodoxy. It is still manifestly true that there is no method of finance available to any government enabling it to transfer real resources from the future into the present. It is also true that the government may have to redistribute some of the community's future output as between taxpayer and bondholder, and, as Buchanan reminds us, the taxpayer will feel the pinch. The question still remains, however, whether there is a good case for referring to this latter consequence as a burden of the public debt.

Several reasons may be urged against it. First, it is clearly not true that, irrespective of the government's disposal of the funds, this consequence follows. If, for instance, the government invested the funds in productive assets whose services could be sold profitably to the public, it would have no need to raise taxes on future generations to service the debt. We might even go further and suggest that if such services were not sold direct to the public but distributed on some other system, the tax payments required to service the debt could be more than offset by this increase in real income and the taxpayers as a whole made better off by this debt-financed government expenditure.[7]

6. As Carl Shoup has pointed out recently in *The Economic Journal*, LXXII (December, 1962), Buchanan regards the government as a force external to the individual. It is certainly not regarded for the purpose of his thesis as a part of the voluntary decision-making process in a democracy. Thus even if the electorate votes for debt creation and consequent future tax payments to service the debt, it is deemed to suffer a burden when complying with its own decision.

7. Buchanan would seem to concede this possibility, but for all that would segregate the future stream of taxes as a burden in its own right irrespective of benefits. But it is difficult to maintain this sort of dichotomy. We are called upon to represent future generations as shouldering a burden even when they are avowedly better off as a direct result of government debt-financed expenditures. Indeed, since every transaction involves a payment, all non-Crusoe economies necessarily engender burdens.

More important still, even if we assume that the government uses the funds in a "wasteful" manner, no tangible assets remaining, Buchanan's results do not follow; at least, not if we push his logic a little further. Recall that Buchanan alleges that those who subscribe to the bonds are thereby made better off, though insofar as they are compelled later to pay taxes to service the debt in the future they endure a burden. If we confine our attention to the existing number of persons in the community, we can with more justification obtain exactly the opposite result; namely, that, on familiar welfare premises, the community is always better off if the government creates debt to meet its expenditure on some project than if it raises taxes. But first we must object to the split personality with which Buchanan has invested his individuals.

If individual tastes change over time, or if they behave inconsistently over time, then economists are agreed that, in general, one cannot make acceptable welfare propositions. To say anything at all we must suppose a consistent and unchanged personality to exist over the period in question. Granted this much, it is hard to attach any sense to Buchanan's contention that a person who buys government bonds improves his welfare, unless that person is deemed to acknowledge the result that it will yield him a stream of income over time; unless, that is, we are permitted to infer that by his action in buying the bonds he has elected to reduce his expenditure at time t_0 in return for a stream of payments over future periods, $t_1, t_2, \ldots, t_n$.

Now suppose the government began by covering its expenditure by a tax levy, but on second thought transformed the levy into a legal obligation to buy bonds to the same amount. This compulsory purchase of government bonds is exactly equivalent to the tax alternative if we suppose the pattern of income to remain unchanged over time, since then each person receives, over the future, interest payments exactly equal to his tax liability. We can assume that everyone is fully aware of this when the government has the bright idea of allowing people to trade freely (at the fixed price) in these bonds. All those who avail themselves of the scheme to change the initial number of bonds allocated to them must be regarded as improving their welfare. Since all who trade will be better off, and those who do not trade will not be any worse off, we can legitimately say that the scheme has made the community as a whole better off. But this new position is exactly equivalent to that which would have been reached had the government in the first place financed its expenditure by debt creation. *Ergo* there is a loss of welfare in covering expenditure by taxation rather than debt creation. On Buchanan's arguments, the burden seems to fit the other situation better.

We return for the moment to Buchanan's treatment of the subject, in particular to his demonstration that the analogy between public debt and private debt is valid in all essential respects.

According to the new orthodoxy, we are told, whenever the public debt is increased the addition to the net worth of people resulting from anticipated interest payments is just offset by the reduction in net worth owing to anticipated tax payments. Now this is misleading, says Buchanan, as it fails to compare "relevant alternatives." For without any increase in the national debt an increase in net worth would have taken place since people would have invested their saving in private capital formation instead. In fact, then, it is only the decrease of net worth of taxpayers that may be attributed to the government's fiscal operations.

Put otherwise, the bondholder's net worth is *not* increased by government debt per se since future tax liabilities have to be set against interest payments. But the increase in government bonds goes to replace a *potential* increase of securities which would increase net worth.

This reasoning was later amended to read that the bondholder's final position depends upon the productivity of the government's project; that is, the reduction in the net worth, because of tax payments, may be offset, or more than offset, by the productivity of the public project. But this is an admission which effectively undoes the whole argument. It leads to a rather simple prescription, one that nobody would bother to challenge, namely, that the government should not spend "wastefully." Clearly if the funds could have been used more productively in the private sector, the government had no right to them in any case. And if by "more productively" we include even current expenditure by the government which has, by some established criterion, a greater social yield than that arising from private expenditure then surely the propounder of the doctrine of "relevant alternatives" would also find in favor of government expenditure. What is at issue then is not debt creation per se but potential malallocation of resources as between the private and public sector.

All this, be it noted is without prejudice to the relevant proposition put forward by the new orthodoxy, to the effect that debt held within the community is exactly analogous to debt held within the family group. Such a group taken as a whole, and ignoring secondary effects, is no worse off than another group identical to it in all respects, save that the latter has no internal debt.

Buchanan's final contention, that there is no essential difference between external and internal debt, need not detain us long. He points out that if a public loan is raised externally the real resources are financed by foreign saving, leaving domestic saving unchanged. In contrast the same loan raised internally would (on his assumptions) reduce domestic saving and therefore also domestic investment. Once this is recognized, says Buchanan, the public should be indifferent as between internal and external borrowing, at least provided that the external rate is equal to the internal rate on loans. Nevertheless, Buchanan acknowledges that the possible existence of a future transfer problem in the case of an external loan may provide a reason for preferring to raise a loan internally.

But, again, these considerations in no respect detract from the simple proposition that if an *existing* debt is internally held "we owe it to ourselves," while if it is held externally "we owe it to the foreigner." In the former case a redistribution of the community's real income is involved; in the latter case, a part of our real income has to be transferred abroad. From such ordinary facts of economic life nothing may be inferred about policy; whether a loan *should* in general be raised domestically or abroad involves many considerations, economic and political, in addition to the transfer problem.

III. New Burdens for Old

Buchanan's book came in for a rather dusty reception at the hands of some of the better-known economists.[8] Without dissecting his arguments in any detail, they pointed out rather wearily that he was engaged in a cardboard battle and as indicated above, nothing he had educed could be regarded as a refutation of these well-established, if rather empty, propositions of the new orthodoxy.

8. In particular see Abba Lerner's review in *The Journal of Political Economy*, XLVII (April, 1959), and Earl Rolph's review in *The American Economic Review*, XLIX (March, 1959).

Notwithstanding this scepticism, Bowen, Davis, and Kopf,[9] of Princeton University, were taken up with the burden idea as elaborated in Buchanan's book, and sought by the use of some slightly different ingredients to cook up a more acceptable burden of the public debt, one that would necessarily be shifted toward future generations.

The rough handling to which Buchanan's thesis had been subjected made them very cautious, however, and they began by granting that, if the real burden be defined as the total consumption given up by the country at the moment the borrowed funds are spent, then indeed the real burden must be borne by the generation alive at the time of spending. Nonetheless, they urged, there is a sensible definition of the term that permits the shifting of the burden.

In order to produce this sensible definition of a burden—to wit, total consumption of private goods foregone during the lifetime of the generation in question consequent upon government borrowing and attendant spending—the reader will require the following: (1) a full-employment economy, as in the Buchanan recipe, (2) a Generation I all of whom are exactly twenty-one years old at the time of the government's loan expenditure, say, in the year *dot*, (3) another Generation II all of whom are twenty-one years old in forty-four years time from the year *dot*, when, of course, the first generation are all sixty-five years old, (4) optional, a third generation, all twenty-one years old in another forty-four years, subsequent generations as required. We ignore, provisionally, the use to which the government's expenditure is put, and also the interest payments on the debt.

Now when Generation I buy the bonds, they will to that extent reduce consumption. But this is only a postponement of consumption, for in forty-four years the bonds are sold entirely to Generation II, the proceeds being spent by Generation I purely on consumption. Since their lifetime consumption is maintained, they cannot, on this definition, be said to suffer any burden. If these bonds are not retired during the lifetime of Generation II, lifetime consumption of II is not reduced either, since in another forty-four years they too will sell them to Generation III and use the proceeds

9. W. G. Bowen, R. G. Davis, and D. H. Kopf, "The Public Debt: A Burden on Future Generations?" *The American Economic Review*, L (September, 1960).

for consumption; and so we could go on. But suppose the bonds are retired in the lifetime of Generation II by a tax levy generating a budget surplus sufficient to buy up these bonds; then the cash that Generation II receive for their bonds is, alas, no other than the cash that is raised by taxing them. Thus the money they once paid to Generation I for the now-redeemed bonds is never recouped; their lifetime consumption is then reduced by the value of the bonds.

In general, conclude the authors, Generation I merely makes a loan of its initially reduced consumption, the eventual real reduction of consumption being borne by the generation alive at the time the loan is extinguished. It follows that the distribution of the community's private consumption between generations can, after all, depend on whether or not a public project is debt-financed.

Interest payments on the public debt are quickly dealt with as constituting a secondary burden. Since the bondholders regard these interest payments as adequate compensation for postponing consumption,[10] they are no worse off on this account. But they and all the other taxpayers do have to pay annual taxes to service the debt, and to this extent they are worse off, a proposition which holds for every succeeding generation that has to service the debt.

Finally, whether the government spends wisely or foolishly is irrelevant to the issue, we are told, since we are concerned with the distribution over generations of the real *cost* of debt-financed government expenditure, and not with the distribution of the *benefits* over time.

Two rather drastic qualifications follow. If, as in fact is generally supposed by the new orthodoxy, Generation II did not *buy* these bonds from Generation I, but, instead, *inherited* them the burden would be borne by Generation I after all. Second, from what has been said no prima facie case follows against debt finance. After all, public projects often benefit future generations, and it is fairer therefore that they contribute to the costs. But, say the authors, economists should not deny the possibility of shifting part of the real cost onto the future.

All this is very neat, but what is its significance? To generate a Bowen-Davis-Kopf burden it is not only necessary that Genera-

---

10. As already stated, however, bondholders must be deemed to be better off if they voluntarily choose to postpone consumption over a period in return for interest payments.

tion I *sell* its bonds to Generation II, but also that the government *retire* the debt during II's lifetime, or during III's or IV's lifetimes. But what if the government chooses *never* to retire the debt? In that case lifetime consumption is not reduced for *any* generation, no generation suffers the primary burden of the debt as defined.[11] Moreover, even the secondary, or additional, burden of tax payments necessary to service the public debt[12] need not arise if the government project yields sufficient income. Thus, contrary to the authors' initial allegation, how the government spends the bond proceeds does matter. Indeed, their suggestion that benefits be separated from costs in assessing the burden cannot be followed, for if the government project were productive of income such real assets could be sold on the market whenever the government wished to extinguish the debt. There would be no need to levy taxes in order to redeem the bonds, and the existing generation would not, in these circumstances, be compelled to suffer any reduction in their private expenditure.

Finally, even if the government did use bond proceeds "wastefully," and did retire the debt during the lifetime of future generations, it is not the public debt per se that is responsible for the Bowen-Davis-Kopf burden but the wasteful expenditure that has left no legacy for the future. For, as suggested above, had the government used the bond proceeds to purchase a productive asset, its full value could be realized on the market in the future. There would be no need to raise funds by a tax levy. If public expenditure can be wasteful, so can private expenditure: private enterprises

---

11. If, as suggested, the government does not retire the debt, it might still be argued—though Bowen, Davis, and Kopf do not take this up—that the procedure by which one generation sells its bonds to the next and *consumes* the proceeds is itself indicative of a burden. For by consuming these proceeds received from the younger generation, potential investment is foregone—investment which could have increased the real income of subsequent generations. This point is made more explicitly by Franco Modigliani and others, and we shall turn to it presently. Suffice it to point out here that, if the burden were to be defined in this sense, it could arise even in the absence of any public debt. All that is required to generate a burden in this sense is for one generation to sell its private securities to the future generation and use up the proceeds for personal consumption, in effect to "dissave."

12. It is interesting to notice in this connection that Bowen, Davis, and Kopf's "secondary burden" is Buchanan's "primary real burden." Buchanan does not consider the retirement of the debt and therefore does not deal with that eventuality—in which Bowen, Davis, and Kopf detect the "main burden" of the public debt.

are sometimes wound up and shareholders suffer losses as their assets turn out to be socially useless. There is perhaps little harm in saying that waste is a burden, whether the waste is public or private. But this innocuous statement, which seems to be all that can be salvaged from the Bowen-Davis-Kopf formula, is not something to which any adherent of the new orthodoxy would object.

IV. Modigliani Burdens, True and False

In a lengthy article in *The Economic Journal* for December, 1961, Franco Modigliani suggested that the burden proponents, though fundamentally right, failed to provide "an altogether adequate framework," in part because they paid too much attention to flow concepts and not enough to stock concepts. He therefore proposed a fresh approach which, unlike that of his predecessors, would lead to "a consistent and yet straightforward answer to all relevant questions." Straightforward the paper is, but, apart from attributing to notions of net worth the commonly accepted responses of taxpayers to tax and debt finance, it adds little to what had already been contended.

Modigliani finds the essence of the burden argument in a proposition that can be found lurking in Buchanan's book, a proposition developed in Musgrave's book, and one ascribed by Shoup[13] to the classical economists, in particular Ricardo; namely, that the burden of the public debt consists in the loss of potential capital formation, and consequent reduction of potential future income. Since Modigliani devotes a large part of his paper to suggestions for measuring this burden, he has to be a little more explicit about its definition. Whereas Buchanan, and some of the classical burden proponents, viewed the burden on future generations as consisting of interest payments on the public debt that have to be met by additional taxation, Modigliani boils this down to the loss of potential income associated with the loss of potential capital formation. There is, however, some ambiguity here: the impression in the first few pages is that *private* capital formation is the yardstick. Later on, the predominant impression is that *total* capital formation is what

13. It is also interesting to note that Viner, "Who Paid for the War," p. 48, made explicit mention of the effect on succeeding generations of the destruction of real assets and of the retardation of normal capital formation during wartime. However, he did not associate such losses with any particular method of finance.

really counts.[14] We can afford to be generous, though, and to concede the more tenable interpretation, that of total capital formation. Having adopted the key notion that government loan expenditure is at the expense of capital formation, Modigliani is rather fastidious over a minor matter. If people reduce their consumption by less than the reduction of their disposable income (by eating into their saving) every additional $1.00 of tax entails a loss of private saving, by some fraction of $1.00. Accuracy demands that we compare this fractional loss of saving associated with an extra $1.00 of tax with the loss of the whole $1.00 of private saving for every $1.00 raised by government bonds. If I mention this at all, it is only because Modigliani makes great play with it in his suggestions for measuring the burden, and because others, in defending the new orthodoxy, have dwelt on it heavily.[15] But the validity of the argument is independent of its quantitative significance. We shall have no difficulty in exposing the muddled state of mind that produces such chimerical burdens even if we suppose, as does Modigliani occasionally, that people, over their lifetime at least, use up all their income on consumption expenditure, so that (with a fixed population) the capital stock does not grow at all.

Indeed, there is a further consequence to be considered apart from the immediate loss of private capital formation when taxa-

14. The former interpretation is suggested by the Modigliani text on p. 734, where it is intimated that in order to estimate the net outcome of government debt expenditure we must subtract from the "gross burden" any benefit resulting. However, even if the benefits are greater than those of the private capital formation which it displaces, the classical argument, according to Modigliani, does imply that the expenditure of the government is being "paid for" by future generations. Nevertheless, on p. 751 he talks of an essential difference arising from the existing "deadweight debt" (a term used by James Meade to indicate government debt without any corresponding assets), and mentions this again in his policy implications on p. 755. These statements make sense only if the burden is defined in terms of total capital formation.

Indeed one could be driven into a corner quickly if one took up the former position, defining burden in terms of private capital formation. For if we had two communities, identical in every respect (including tax rates) save that in one of them all capital was privately owned and in the other the stock was partly owned by a government that met all interest payments on the public debt from the proceeds of marketing the products and services through its own agents, this latter community would have to be regarded as carrying a burden. This example serves to emphasize a point already made: despite allegations to the contrary, the burden argument is dependent directly on how the government spends its loans.

15. See in particular W. Vickrey and T. Scitovsky, *The American Economic Review*, LI (March, 1961).

tion is rejected in favor of deficit finance, namely, the effect of people's asset holdings on their willingness to save. Although in a full-employment economy these assets may be deemed to grow at much the same rate irrespective of the size of the deficit, if any (deficit expenditure merely causing people to subsititute additional government bonds for additional private securities), any apparent destruction of these assets increases the rate of current saving. If, on the other hand, the government simply presented a free issue of bonds to the community there would result a reduction in current saving and, therefore, also a reduction in the current rate of real capital formation. The significance of this asset-saving relationship is brought out in Modigliani's not unrealistic example of a total war at the end of which the real capital stock is independent of the method of finance employed. Nevertheless, the greater the holding of government bonds at the end of the war, the greater is the community's illusory holding of assets, and the smaller therefore will be the subsequent rate of current saving. As a corollary, future generations will not inherit so large a stock of capital as they would have done had the war been financed to a greater extent by direct taxation.

Not content with this, Modigliani moves out of the stable full-employment framework, within which Buchanan and Bowen, Davis, and Kopf conducted their campaigns, and carries his attack right into the camp of the Keynesians. If the government resorts to deficit expenditure in order to lift the economy out of a slump, a burden, in the shape of a reduced aggregate real income, is still passed on to future generations. For, as it happens, people prize these bits of government paper as though they were the real thing, and accordingly they continue gradually to reduce their rate of saving over time (just as they would have done if full employment had been maintained *without* any government deficit), notwithstanding that, in fact, the amount of real capital formation is smaller than the value of their accumulated holdings of securities by the amount of the growth in the public debt. True, if the government stood aloof and allowed the depression to run its course, real income would fall and, it would seem, some real saving would be lost. But, sooner or later, the economy does recover—with no illusory assets to induce complacency—and people make special efforts to catch up on their saving programs. If, as is assumed by Modigliani, these saving programs are designed to be completed in their lifetimes, they will eventually not only make good the amount of real private capital formation foregone over the depression period, but end up with a larger real stock of productive assets—larger by that amount of private securities which displaces the value of government bonds that they would have held if full employment had been, instead, maintained by deficit finance. Thus, although the government's refusal to administer the Keynesian medicine makes life pretty beastly for the existing generation, future generations will revel in the joys of a richer inheritance.

After this demonstration of virtuosity, Modigliani hastens to assure us that nothing he has said implies that government remedial action should not be undertaken; there are many other factors to consider. However, he voices the hope that "the tools we have developed may provide some insight into the problem" of counter-cyclical fiscal operations by reminding us that they involve inter-generation equity.[16]

It is about time we began to push these arguments of the burden-creators from their chosen terrain where, as we have already seen, they are far from being invulnerable, onto a soil that is more congenial to the traditional view of economics as a discipline that concerns itself with the disposal of scarce resources among competing ends.[17]

V. Is the Burden Really Necessary?

As a springboard to help us to a position of vantage, we can make use of the last of Modigliani's list of "substantive implications" of his "line of approach" summarized at the beginning of his paper, namely: "The gross burden may be offset in part or *in toto*, or may be even more than offset, insofar as the increase in the debt is accompanied by government expenditure which contributes to the real income of future generations, e.g., through productive public capital formation."[18]

16. Since the income of future generations is almost certain to exceed ours in any case, whether we add to our capital equipment or not, intergeneration equity would suggest to me that we should, at least, cease to accumulate any further capital.

17. A definition taken from Lord Robbins' celebrated essay *On the Nature and Significance of Economic Science* (London).

18. This is "substantive implication" No. 5 (p. 731). The other four are really attenuated out of the classical thesis that an increase in the national debt (whether internal or external) shifts the burden to the future, and that the burden can be measured by using the rate of interest as an approximation to the marginal productivity of capital.

It turns out that this is a qualification that gives away the whole show. For immediately one's attention is drawn to the fact that it is not really debt creation per se that is responsible for withholding potential lucre from future generations but simply government loan expenditure that does not issue in sufficiently productive assets. The existence of a "net" burden does after all depend therefore on just how the government disposes of its bonds proceeds, contrary to the initial allegation of the other writers.

But this rather pat solution brings us face to face with the more fundamental question: Even if the government's loan expenditure does *not* realize productive assets, how sensible is it to regard the loss of future potential income as a burden on future generations? After all, we could enormously increase provision for the future if we performed heroic feats of austerity during our lifetimes. Are we then not imposing a heavy burden on these future generations to the extent that we eschew these heroic feats of austerity and instead follow the path of our wonted self-indulgence?

Now economics is more than just verbal hair-splitting of this sort. It may not have an impressive record of quantitative prediction, but its concepts are often valuable in indicating the essentials of a problem. The concept of *opportunity cost* serves to remind us that the cost of something that uses up scarce resources is, in the last resort, the value of any of the alternative things that could, instead, have been produced with those same resources. The concept has a time dimension also: (*a*) the opportunity cost of increased aggregate consumption in the present must be regarded as a reduction of the potential aggregate consumption by our children. But considerations of symmetry also require that we recognize that (*b*) the opportunity cost of increased aggregate consumption by our children is no less a reduction of potential aggregate consumption during the present. If, in the light of statement (*a*), we wish to talk of a "burden" being imposed *on future generations* whenever we decide to consume rather than to invest, then in the light of statement (*b*) we are equally obliged to talk of a "burden" being imposed *on the present generation* whenever we take the opposite decision. Perhaps Modigliani would like to measure this also. Certainly, those with a flair for figures should derive some quiet satisfaction from the discovery that whichever way the wind blows a burden is left to be measured. But if pushing the meaning of "burden" to its logical conclusion lands us on this sort of seesaw, we cannot but infer that the burden that is being measured has no fiscal-policy implications whatever.[19]

Enough has been said in connection with the concept of opportunity cost to reveal the existence, however, of a genuine allocative problem, a problem that is all but evaded by the arbitrary procedure adopted by the burden-mongers, the problem of criteria for determining the flow of investment over time.

The traditional response to such a problem would regard the rate of interest as presenting terms—arising out of society's resources, technology, and subjective preferences—on which, temporarily or permanently, society may choose to defer current consumption. Of course, these important social decisions about how much to consume and how much to invest are taken by the existing generation without consulting future generations. It may well be an improvident generation, and may provoke the criticism that it is paying insufficient attention to "the needs of posterity."[20] However, in Western societies at least, the government has gradually assumed the role of watchdog over the nation's resources and of guardian of the future. It is possible, therefore, to criticize the government for not establishing an appropriate rate of interest in some sense, or for not consistently referring its own decisions to such a rate of interest.[21] But the government is not open to general criticisms for spending the loan proceeds in a particular way, say, on current goods or services. If the time preference of society is measured by 5 per cent, this implies that society is on the margin of indifference whether to use an additional $1.00 of its current income in a 5 per cent yielding investment or whether to spend the $1.00 on current consumption. Clearly, if the best investment project available yields only 4½ per cent, the government is not justified in undertaking it. On the other hand, using loan proceeds on certain ostensibly current needs, say, on educa-

19. Those whose ideas of game-hunting, like my own, do not extend beyond a reading of Adam Smith's famous passage on the subject will know at least that the opportunity cost of one beaver is exactly equal to that of two deer. This is useful information for the prospective trapper. But it is not enough to determine whether he should hunt deer or beaver. Before making up his mind, he must know, in addition, their relative prices.

20. In this connection, however, I confess to some sneaking sympathy with the irate Congressman who demanded, "What has posterity ever done for us?"

21. Since the government has complete control over the money supply, the full-employment rate of interest, as Professor Metzler has shown, is in the last resort open to arbitrary political determination.

tion or on student grants or on unemployment benefit, may be estimated to yield a return to society of over 5 per cent p.a. If so, no consideration bearing on tangible "productive" assets should deter the government from this sort of spending. In sum, that expenditure which is designated by Modigliani as a "burden" gross or net, is no more likely to be associated with a bad allocation than with a good allocation of the resources appropriated by the government.[22]

In general, measures to maintain price stability and full employment are undertaken simultaneously with those directed toward promoting allocative efficiency. If, for example, owing to an incipient economic decline, it is decided to incur a budget deficit, the government must also decide in the light of its allocative criteria whether to reduce taxes or to increase its expenditure on investment projects or on social services or otherwise. It may, in the event, choose unwisely and be justly accused of wasteful expenditure. But such wastful expenditure, or resource misallocation, has no affinity whatsoever with the increase in the public debt per se.

Put a little differently, the onus is on those who cry "burden" to impart acceptable welfare significance to the term by demonstrating, in general, that deficit finance results in a worse allocation of resources over time as compared with a system of balanced budget finance. Since there is small likelihood of their ever persuading us of this proposition, they would perform a service to the community by abandoning their efforts to establish a "burden."

VI. The Moral of the Story

There will always be those who will hold that nothing is involved here but theological disputation, and while the possibility of entering into a sophisticated analysis of the consequences of public debt policies without recourse to the word "burden" is readily

22. If the community were indifferent between devoting more of its income to current consumption and to investment at just under 5 per cent p.a. (say 4½ per cent), which 5 per cent p.a. is yielded by private investment, a government which is said to be misallocating resources by devoting proceeds of its loans to reducing taxation and thereby increasing consumption would be inflicting an annual loss which, on familiar welfare considerations, might be reckoned as equal to the value of these resources times ½ per cent, but not times 5 per cent, the figure that Modigliani would use. Thus, employment of some existing rate of interest, in the attempt to estimate approximately the loss of income to future generations, requires that we ignore entirely the value of current spending to the present generation in determining the extent of that loss.

conceded, they will argue that there is, on the other hand, nothing to prevent people like Buchanan; Bowen, Davis, and Kopf; Modigliani; and others from defining "burden" the way they see fit, and having so defined it, trace the conditions under which it may be generated and proceed to measure it. But there is also a case against the arbitrary coining of terms. It is hard even among academics to feel neutral about a word like burden. Surely, the only purpose of calling anything a burden is that it is one. And if so, it is something to be avoided. If increasing the public debt is to become associated in the minds of economists with a burden on the future, it is hardly likely that the interested public will look upon it with an open mind.

Bowen, Davis, and Kopf, at the beginning of their paper, quote Eisenhower as saying, "Personally I do not feel that any amount can be properly called a surplus as long as the nation is in debt. I prefer to think of such an item as a reduction in our children's inherited mortgage."[23] With all respect to a former president of the United States, he was perpetrating vulgar error when he uttered this sentence. And it does not help matters that Bowen, Davis, and Kopf claimed to vindicate this pronouncement by manipulating a fancy set of assumptions and definitions. *They* may realize that theirs was just an exercise in ingenuity, that no policy implications could be inferred or were intended. But presidents as well as former presidents, treasury officials, administrators, politicians, and journalists do not as a rule read ingenious arguments with professional vigilance, particularly if it seems, on the surface, to bear out a favorite prejudice. It soon becomes current that well-known economists have written a book, or a paper, "proving" that the public debt is, after all, a most grievous burden. In this way a presumption against increasing the public debt becomes established in respectable and influential circles, a presumption which may well act as a brake on swift remedial action by the government when it faces a decline in economic activity.

23. "State of the Union Message," January 7, 1960. Again, on May 14, 1963, he attacked President Kennedy's administration for an extravagent spending program involving deficit finance. "In effect," he asserted, "we are stealing from our grandchildren in order to satisfy our desires of today" (quoted by the *Daily Telegraph*, May 15, 1963).

Chapter Eight

COMMENTS ON THE PRECEDING ANALYSES

A/ DEBT FINANCING AND FUTURE GENERATIONS*

BY *Carl S. Shoup*

The question, whether debt financing shifts the burden from present to future generations, has been raised again, by what appear to be dissents from a received doctrine.[1] These dissents have stimulated comments to the effect that the dissenters are in error.[2] But the comments do not, I think, meet the dissenters (if

---

* Reprinted by permission from *The Economic Journal*, LXXII (December, 1962). I am indebted to my colleagues of the Public Finance Research Center at Columbia, and to the authors of the three analyses here examined, for comments on an earlier draft; but it is not to be assumed thereby that any of them are necessarily in agreement with my views.

1. William G. Bowen, Richard G. Davis, and David H. Kopf, "The Public Debt: A Burden on Future Generations?" *The American Economic Review*, L (September, 1960), 701-6; "Reply," *The American Economic Review*, LI (March, 1961), 141-43; and "The Distribution of the Debt Burden: A Reply" [to Lerner], *The Review of Economics and Statistics*, XLIV (February, 1962), pp. 98-99. Richard A. Musgrave, *The Theory of Public Finance*, pp. 562-65, 571-73. James M. Buchanan, *Public Principles of Public Debt*, especially Chapters 2-4. Professor J. E. Meade's article, "Is the National Debt a Burden?" *Oxford Economic Papers*, X (June, 1958), pp. 163-83 (and "Correction," *ibid.* XI (February, 1959), pp. 109-10) is not discussed here, since it does not contradict flatly, or ignore, the classical conclusion regarding the conditions under which a debt burden can be shifted to a future generation.

2. Abba P. Lerner, review of Buchanan's book, *The Journal of Political Economy*, XLVII (April, 1959), pp. 203-6, and "The Burden of Debt," *The*

they really are dissenters) on their own grounds, though they do strengthen our understanding of the relation of government borrowing to capital accumulation. I shall therefore attempt to hold strictly to the issue: what is it that Bowen-Davis-Kopf, Buchanan, and Musgrave are charging, or implying, is wrong with the earlier analysis? Have they, in fact, discovered an analytical error? If not, how have they reached conclusions that appear to differ from the older doctrine?

The first question to be settled is, what is the doctrine from which BDK, Buchanan, and Musgrave are apparently dissenting or departing? It is not the simple argument that since resources are used up at the time of government expenditure, the generation living at the time of expenditure will bear the burden. What the new analyses are opposing, or bypassing as unimportant or irrelevant, or supplementing, is the more sophisticated view that the burden can be passed on to future generations, but only insofar as the present generation responds to the Government's action by reducing its rate of saving. An excellent statement of this view is to be found in the second edition of Pigou's *Public Finance*, but its essentials had been set out long before by Ricardo.[3] It is this assertion,

---

Review of Economics and Statistics, XLIII (May, 1961), pp. 139-41. Franco Modigliani, "Long-run Implications of Alternative Fiscal Policies and the Burden of the National Debt," *The Economic Journal*, LXXI (December, 1961), pp. 730-55. Hans Neisser, "Is the Public Debt a Burden on Future Generations?" *Social Research*, (Summer, 1961), pp. 225-28. B. U. Ratchford, "The Nature of Public Debt" (a review article of Buchanan's book), *The Southern Economic Journal*, XXV (October, 1958), pp. 213-17. Earl R. Rolph, review of Buchanan's book, *The American Economic Review*, XLIX (March, 1959), pp. 183-85. William Vickrey, Tibor Scitovsky, and James R. Elliott, "The Burden of the Public Debt: Comment," *The American Economic Review*, LI (March, 1961), pp. 132-41.

3. A. C. Pigou, *A Study in Public Finance* (2nd ed.; London: Macmillan, 1929), Part III, Chapter I, "The Place of Loans in Public Finance," and David Ricardo, *Works and Correspondence*, ed. Sraffa, Vol. I, *On the Principles of Political Economy and Taxation*, p. 247, and Vol. IV, *Funding System*, pp. 187-8. See also Carl S. Shoup, *Ricardo on Taxation*, Chapter XI. Ricardo said that whether financing is by taxes or by government borrowing, the real resources used by the Government are lost to society at the time of use; but I do not think he can be interpreted as meaning that the present generation always bears the burden (cf. Modigliani, ". . . Ricardo's famous conclusion that the cost of government expenditure is always fully borne by those present at the time," p. 746, note 1), in view of the fact that he concluded that private capital accumulation would be less under borrowing, because of a failure by the present generation to reckon the present value of future taxes needed to pay the interest, when deciding whether to cut their consumption or their sav-

that the burden can be shifted only through a reduction in the rate of investment, that is attacked explicitly by Bowen, Davis, and Kopf, and more or less implicitly by Buchanan, or is supplemented by Musgrave.

The Ricardo-Pigou thesis is as follows: If the government expense is financed by taxation the first generation hands on to the second nothing but tax receipts; if by bond issue, the first generation bequeaths the bonds to the second generation, but, along with them, a tax liability represented by the annual charge on the debt for interest, and, if the bonds are not perpetuities, for redemption or amortization. The members of the second generation, like those of the first, pay the interest to themselves, and hence cannot gain by holding bonds rather than their forbears' tax receipts. The welfare of the second generation depends, not on whether it inherits tax receipts or government bonds, but on what it inherits in the way of real stock of capital; and this latter inheritance depends on the reaction of the first generation to the taking away of real resources by the Government. The first generation may well cut its consumption more and its investment less, if it receives only tax receipts from the Government, than if it recieves bonds, because it fails to give full weight to the task ahead of servicing the bonds. The failure is perhaps understandable, if only because no one individual can be sure of the amount of tax he will have to pay towards bond servicing each year in the future. Almost every individual may therefore pursuade himself that he is richer with bonds, plus an undefined future tax obligation, than he would be with tax receipts and no such future obligation. Feeling richer, he may cut his consumption less. Moreover, "large subscribers have good reason to hope that the interest on their holdings will exceed the contribution in taxes which they will have to make to provide this interest."[4]

Now the less the first generation decreases its consumption, the smaller is the capital stock handed down to the second generation. In

---

ing ("The war-taxes, then, are more economical; . . .", *Funding System*, p. 187). This result reflected, in Ricardo's view, irrationality, or at least short-sightedness: ". . . but if he leaves his fortune to his son, and leaves it charged with this perpetual tax, where is the difference . . .?" (*ibid.*); this statement reflects his own rational view, not the irrational view that he regretfully concluded held the stage (but cf. Neisser, "Is the Public Debt a Burden?" p. 228).

4. Pigou, *A Study in Public Finance*, p. 244.

this sense, and only in this sense, says the classic (Ricardo-Pigou) doctrine, can financing by bonds lay a burden on the second generation, relative to financing by taxes. The burden consists of inheriting a smaller stock of capital instruments than otherwise.

The Bowen-Davis-Kopf Thesis

Bowen, Davis, and Kopf postulate that under debt financing the community's private consumption falls, by the amount of the financing, from the level it would have reached in the absence of the government expenditure and financing. The fall occurs in the period when the government expenditure and financing occur, let us say in Year 100. This assumption, that subscriptions to the bond issue come entirely out of consumption, is not realistic, but it is appropriate, in view of BDK's analytical aims. It presents them with their most difficult case.[5] If they can show that under bond financing a part of the burden is shifted to a future generation, even in the event that the financing comes entirely out of current consumption, then indeed they have raised an issue that the traditional analysis must meet head-on.

BDK further postulate that 44 years later (a "generation" later) there occurs, within the economy, a simultaneous increase in consumption by one group and decrease by another group: increase or decrease from what each group's consumption would have been if the government expenditure and financing had never occurred. The increase and the decrease are each of the same size as the initial decrease in consumption 44 years earlier. Another pair of simultaneous changes takes place after another 44 years and so on. The increase in consumption is always by the older generation, the one just about to leave the stage; the simultaneous decrease in consumption is by the just-emerging newer generation. Thus in Year 144 Generation I increases its consumption and Generation II decreases its consumption by exactly the amount that Generation I had decreased its consumption in Year 100.

Meanwhile, during the 43-year interval, in Years 101-43, Generation I has been consuming no more and no less than it would have consumed if the government expenditure and financing had not occurred.

If the debt is retired in Generation II's lifetime the taxes to re-

---

5. That this is the reason BDK make their assumption seems not to have been recognized in any of the comments cited in note 3 above.

tire the debt come out of consumption, by BDK assumption. Even if the bond redemption proceeds are spent at once on consumption, Generation II will have experienced a net decrease in lifetime consumption, and it is in terms of a decrease in lifetime consumption that BDK test for the existence of a "burden."

Since the community's private consumption decreases in Year 100, the year of government expenditure, by an amount equal to that expenditure, and does not alter in any subsequent year, total private investment is in no year any different from what it would have been if the government expenditure had not been incurred. Each year there exists just as much capital equipment as there would have existed, had the Government not made the expenditure. Yet, assert BDK, part of the burden of the Government's expenditure rests on Generations II, III, etc. The following seems to me to be the heart of their thesis: it is "the otherwise unrecognized fact that even if loan finance fails to dampen private investment [that is to say, even if loan finance is met entirely by reducing consumption], the present generation can still shift at least a part of the burden of government spending to future generations."[6] Only "a part," because the deferment of consumption by Generation I from Year 100 to Year 144 is a sacrifice that this generation never recoups; similarly, Generation II never makes up for the delay in its consumption, from Year 144 to Year 188; and so on. The sacrifice represented by the deferment of consumption runs on, through generation after generation, until the bonds are redeemed. The generation that redeems the bonds restricts its consumption in its opening year, say Year 144, and never in any later year increases its consumption above the level it would have enjoyed if the government expenditure and financing had never taken place.

This thesis may at first appear to run counter to the older analysis, which asserted that a future generation could be burdened only if its patrimony were impaired by the generation during whose lifetime the government expenditure was incurred. Under the BDK scheme, to repeat, Generations II and following possess just as much capital equipment as they would have possessed if no government expenditure and financing had occurred; yet BDK conclude that they are bearing part of the burden.

If we look at this conclusion closely we see that it does not contradict the traditional analysis. In real terms, and disregarding

6. BDK, "Reply," p. 141.

the paper transactions that evidence them (whether bonds, tax receipts, or what not), BDK's Generation I does impair the capital of the economy. It does pass on to Generation II a smaller amount of capital equipment than would have been in existence if the government expenditure had not been made. Generation II makes good this impairment, right away, by restricting its own consumption in the very year that Generation I is enjoying its increment of consumption. Generation II thereupon *possesses* the same stock of capital that it would have possessed if there had been no government expenditure; but it does not *inherit* the same stock.[7] Suppose, for simplicity, that the capital stock consists entirely of growing timber. In Year 100 let the Government cut j units of timber and use it up in war, or reparations. Generation I responds at once to this government action by cutting j fewer units for private consumption than it would have done. Consumption in the remaining years to Year 144 remains as it would have been otherwise, and the capital stock at the start of Year 144 is just what it would have been if the Government had not made the expenditure of Year 100. Generation I dies off in Year 145, after having gone on a consumption spree in Year 144, consuming j units more than normal. It bequeaths to Generation II j units less than it would have bequeathed if no government expenditure had been made. To this estate there is at once added the j units that Generation II is postulated to save, above what it would have saved if no government expenditure had been made in the first place. Thus Generation II, by cutting its consumption in Year 144, brings the capital stock back up; there is no impairment of capital stock resulting from the Government's expenditure.

Accordingly, no conflict exists between the findings of BDK and the traditional theorem that future generations can be burdened only if, and to the extent that, they inherit a smaller stock of real capital than otherwise.

Generation I, in the BDK illustration, bears part of the burden by deferring its consumption. By reminding us of this possibility, BDK make a significant contribution. Had Generation I not deferred its consumption at all, had it gone on consuming in Year 100 just as it would have done otherwise, and also not expanding its consumption in Year 144, a still smaller stock of real capital

---

7. This distinction between possession and inheritance of real capital is not drawn explicitly in any of the comments on BDK cited in note 3 above. Elliott, "Comment," p. 139, perhaps comes closest to doing so.

would have been passed on to Generation II. Fewer trees would have been growing in the period, Years 101-43.

The mechanism by which the inheritance is impaired can be any one of several. For example: if the Government finances the expenditure in Year 100 by taxation Generation I may possibly react in just the same way as is postulated for the bond case: they may cut their consumption by the full amount of the government expenditure in Year 100, maintain their consumption as it otherwise would have been in Years 101-43 and decide to make up for their earlier deprivation, in Year 144, by increasing their consumption by the amount of the decrease in Year 100. They pass on to their heirs, Generation II, j units of timber less than otherwise and a tax receipt. The tax receipt is no less and no more valuable to Generation II than would have been a parcel of bonds of the same face amount, for the bonds would have yielded only interest that would have had to be paid to Generation II by levying taxation on itself.

For purposes of policy we need to know, of course, whether tax-payers will react differently from lenders, whether, at the moment of finance, it is consumption or investment that is reduced, and whether a backlash, or reverse reaction, follows in a later year. BDK consider it an "important point that, regardless of whether loan finance reduces C or I, loan finance can result in intergeneration transfers of burden."[8] This statement is, of course, correct, if "reduces C or I" refers to the reaction in the year of finance, and if the word "can" implies that we may add, "but also may not." The next sentence, however, seems more positive, and hence in error, in predicting the actual outcome. "No matter what happens to C and I, Generation I (the present generation) is going to enjoy a higher level of lifetime consumption relative to the consumption of future generations if government expenditures are financed by issuance of debt instruments than if taxes are employed."[9] The phrase "is going to" seems a little too strong. The BDK argument is that, with more financial assets in its hands, Generation I is going to be more able to step up its consumption towards the end of its life. But when one thinks of the mass of capital instruments that Generation I owns, and which it can sell to Generation II in exchange for consumption goods that

8. BDK, "Reply," p. 141.
9. BDK, "Reply," p. 141.

Generation II was going to consume, does the existence of an extra block of financial assets—assuming that interest rates are not driven so high by the issuance of debt that the total value of all debt does not increase—really make an appreciable difference? Perhaps it does; Vickrey attaches some importance to this point:

> . . . the reverse option, *i.e.*, that of taking individual action, where the project is tax-financed, which would impose a burden on the future generations [presumably: stepping up consumption in the later years by the generation that has foregone consumption in the first year], is less completely available: it is often difficult to arrange to leave a negative estate when the estate was originally zero or very small.[10]

But Elliott puts it well:

> The older members of any economy which incorporates the principles of private property and the right of transfer are always free to sell their creditor claims. The sale may be made to other members of Generation I or to those of Generation II. If, during the lifetime of Generation I, there had been no deficit finance, they would still be free to liquidate *other* forms of creditor claims—life insurance, industrial bonds, common stock, etc. [11]

The Musgrave Inter-Generation Example

Although Musgrave explicitly recognizes the validity of what is here called the Ricardo-Pigou argument, in the setting that they assumed,[12] he goes on to construct a case in which, regardless of the reaction of Generation I to tax finance or loan finance, loan finance always divides the cost among generations, and tax finance never can do so. Evidently, there must be some special assumptions here; as it turns out, the most important assumption is largely implicit.

In this case, Musgrave is concerned with a long-lived government facility, the cost of which is to be distributed equitably among those who make use of it. He has in mind chiefly the prob-

10. Vickrey, "Comment," p. 136.
11. Elliott, "Comment," p. 139. BDK restate their thesis in their reply to Lerner: "Our proposition is that the use of debt finance permits, by the process described in our original paper, a relative improvement in the lifetime economic position of Set I persons, *vis-à-vis* a situation in which taxation was employed at t_0 [when the government expenditure was incurred] . . . had World War I been financed entirely by taxes, the lifetime consumption of the 1917-18 population would have been lower, apart from any effects of debt finance on the consumption-investment mix." *Loc. cit.*, pp. 98, 99.
12. Musgrave, *Public Finance*, p. 559.

lem that arises from shifting residence; not all those who are in a certain city when the facility is financed will be there to enjoy the services of the project throughout its life, and others, not in the city in the year of finance, will move in later, and enjoy some years of service from the facility. But Musgrave also speaks of "life span," and implies that his argument applies equally to successive residency spans and life spans.

His assumptions about the reactions of lenders and tax-payers differ radically from those of BDK, but the point at issue remains the same: can the burden be shifted among generations by the method of financing, without reference to the traditional analysis that looks to stock of capital inherited by one generation from its predecessor? Musgrave's answer is, yes. Let us see what makes this affirmative answer possible.

The project has a life of three "periods," which for Musgrave can evidently be as short as a year, or as long as a decade or more; at least, he does not suggest how long a period may be. Each generation has a life span (or residency span) of three periods. As period I opens, Generation I, already in its last period, is on the scene; so also is Generation II, with one more period to go, and Generation III, in its initial period. In the second period there exist Generations II, in its last period, III and IV. In the third period we find Generations III (in its last period) and IV (in its second period), and a new Generation V.

The problem is: how to take from Generation I just one-ninth of the cost of the project; from Generation II, just two-ninths; Generation III, just three-ninths; Generation IV, just two-ninths; and Generation V, just one-ninth. Musgrave's solution is to require Generation I to pay one-ninth of the cost in taxation and so on. As to financing the project in its year of construction, six-ninths must be covered by loan; but no part of the loan can be demanded from Generation I, since it is already in its last period, and thus could never be repaid. We may think of Generation I as vanishing at the end of the first period. At least this seems to be what is behind Musgrave's stipulation that "loans advanced by any one generation must be repaid within its life span."[13] So, the six-ninths is financed by loans from Generations II and III, who are repaid before they vanish. Thus everybody gets his money back, except to

13. *Ibid.*, p. 563.

the extent that he is required to pay tax, and the tax is distributed over time in accordance with degree of service use.

Musgrave stipulates that the loan finance comes completely out of private capital formation (at the opposite pole from the BDK assumption), and that each tax dollar comes 75 per cent from consumption and 25 per cent from private capital formation (BDK: 100 per cent from consumption). But Musgrave could vary these percentages without at all affecting his conclusions about how the burden is distributed among the generations.[14] Evidently, the economic position of Generation II depends not at all on how Generation I reacts to the finance measure. It does so depend, of course, in the BDK analysis, and in the traditional analysis. Musgrave, in effect, abstracts from the fact that Generation I may pass on part of its real capital to Generation II; there is no passage of property from one generation to a later one in this part of his analysis.[15] The implicit assumption of no inheritance is the key to this analysis.

This assumption seems to be quite reasonable as long as the analysis is confined to frequently shifting groups of residents. A San Franciscan, let us say, is spending his last period in New York before returning home; an earlier Chicago resident, perhaps the same age as the San Franciscan, has come to New York to stay two periods; he is Generation II, even if he is the same age as Generation I (the San Franciscan); a third man of, say, the same age, is starting the first of three periods of residence in New York—and so on. We have no grounds for supposing that the ex-Chicagoan will benefit if the returning San Franciscan possesses more capital, by the time he leaves for home, under one plan of financing than he would under another. Musgrave, indeed, stipulates that "each generation consumes its assets while still present";[16] perhaps this somewhat cryptic condition is just another way of saying that in his model there shall be no passage of property from one generation to another.

Generation I pays its 11.1 per cent tax (out of the total 100 per

14. In the "compensatory system," where private investment is a fixed amount, all of the tax or loan must come out of consumption; here, distribution of the burden among generations according to use must be accomplished by taxation, of a kind that discriminates among the coexisting generations. *Ibid.*, pp. 572-73.

15. So far as I am aware, no comments on Musgrave's debt analysis have called attention to the fact that, in the case here considered, he allows no inheritance.

16. Musgrave, p. 563.

cent needed for finance), 8.3 per cent by cutting consumption and 2.8 per cent by cutting its saving below the levels they would otherwise have reached. It "dies," or leaves, 2.8 per cent the poorer; but none of the other four generations is held to be affected by this fact. Consequently, Musgrave's analysis has no application to the ordinary case of intergeneration equity, where the generations are connected by inheritance. What Musgrave has done is to state, more explicitly than has been done before,[17] the case for loan finance in a geographic area marked by considerable immigration and emigration over the life span of the project that is being financed.

Even here, as Vickrey has reminded us in his discussion of the BDK thesis,[18] Generation I may find its net worth impaired by more than the tax it pays, less its restriction of consumption, for if it owns property in the taxing city the promise of higher property tax over the life span of the project may result in a fall in value of that property as of the start of Period Two, relative to what it would have been if the project had been completely tax financed in Period One. But of course the owners of property in the taxing city may be anyone, in or outside the city. The burden may fall on some who will never benefit from the project, unless, in turn, we assume that the project gives off services of a kind that enhance property values. Indeed, once we begin dealing in a wide-open economy, the possible variations on the burden theme become numerous.

The Buchanan Thesis

In his *Public Principles of Public Debt*, Buchanan argues that debt financing, as compared with tax financing, does shift the burden from the present generation to a future generation. The argument runs as follows. In the year of financing, the year when the resources are diverted from the private sector of a full-employment economy to public use, no individual can be found who feels that he is undergoing a sacrifice, whereas in the future year, when the bonds are redeemed by taxes, it is very easy to discover someone (the tax-payer) who is experiencing real sacrifice, while no one can be found who is thereby experiencing a gain. Since the sacrifice

17. Cf. Robert M. Haig and Carl S. Shoup, *The Financial Problem of the City of New York*, 1953, Chapter XIV, "New York City's Debt," pp. 539-41.
18. Vickrey, "Comment," p. 135.

of a generation can exist only through the sacrifice of one or more of the individuals who comprise it, we must conclude that bond financing postpones the sacrifice to a future generation. The nature of the government expense is not relevant to the argument, but to remove any doubts, Buchanan is willing to talk in terms of a wasteful expenditure.

Buchanan, in the initial stages of his argument, assumes that "the funds used to purchase government securities are drawn wholly from private capital formation."[19] As we shall see, this assumption is not central to his argument. He does not expressly stipulate that, if taxes were used instead, the funds would be drawn wholly from private consumption, so we cannot be sure that in his community the use of debt finance will burden the future generation, relative to tax finance, in the sense of causing them to inherit a smaller stock of capital goods. But let us assume that, if taxation were employed, the tax would come wholly out of consumption.

To centre on the point at issue, let us also assume that the Government's expenditure does not create an asset of value to anyone in the economy.

At the time of withdrawal of resources for government use, Generation I must make a decision, a decision that has important consequences for Generation II. Shall Generation I reduce its lifetime consumption below the level it would have reached if there had been no such withdrawal of resources for governmental use? Or shall Generation I reduce (in the same sense) its capital equipment?

Whichever decision Generation I makes, it makes voluntarily. No one decrees that it must take the one road or the other. Each individual in Generation I makes up his own mind. Consider first the case where the Government finances by a bond issue. Each purchaser of a bond decides for himself whether, upon receipt of the bond, he shall restrict his consumption spending or shall divest himself of an asset (or, for that matter, shall work harder). Suppose, in contrast to Buchanan's assumption, that each bond purchaser decides to meet the cost by restricting his consumption spending. In the spirit of Buchanan's analysis, we may still say that this reaction to the bond issue represents no sacrifice to anyone in Generation I. No one in that Generation is moved to a lower indifference surface than if he had not participated in the financing

19. Buchanan, *Public Principles*, p. 32.

by restricting his consumption. Note that the Government's withdrawal of resources is here a datum, and so is the issuance of bonds. The Government offers the bonds for purchase, but does not compel anyone to buy them. The bonds are so attractive, and (we assume) the desire to maintain one's other assets so strong, that the individuals of Generation I willingly cut their consumption in order to buy the bonds. By doing so, they move, indeed, to a higher indifference surface than if, in the face of this bond issue, they had continued to consume and had not bought the bonds—this must be so, by our assumptions about their preferences. In Buchanan's sense there is no sacrifice by any member of Generation I, given the fact of the Government's withdrawal of resources, and the offering of bonds.

Yet it is equally clear that Generation II now inherits a capital equipment larger than it would have inherited if Generation I's voluntary decision had gone the other way, that is, if Generation I had decided to pay for the bond issue by lowering the rate of capital formation during the lifetime of that generation instead of restricting consumption. By restricting consumption, Generation I voluntarily sacrifices in favor of Generation II, if by sacrifice we mean simply: enjoy less consumption. Whichever way Generation I's decision goes, that decision imposes no burden on it in Buchanan's terminology, for Generation I makes that decision freely.[20] But Generation II is obviously better off, in some economic sense, if Generation I decides to restrict consumption than if it decides to restrict capital formation. This apparent asymmetry

20. None of the commentators in note 2 above explicitly recognizes that Buchanan is dealing with sacrifice in terms of freedom of choice of the individual, except Modigliani, in passing ("Long-run Implications," p. 734, and p. 746, note 1), and Ratchford, who remains unpersuaded ("The Burden of Debt," pp. 214-15). As Modigliani interprets this argument ("Long-run Implications," p. 734), the existence of a net burden on society from taxes to service the debt depends on an assumption that subscriptions to the government bonds come out of private investment. As I understand the free-choice argument, a net burden on society exists because of the debt-service taxes, no matter what is assumed about the source of the bond subscriptions. Scitovsky ("Comment," p. 138) uses the free-choice argument in commenting on BDK, but this is not the point they are making. Ratchford, agreeing that "Taxes are more readily identified and thus psychologically more burdensome [than the interest charges on investment, paid by consumers in the prices of goods]," discerns that "the major question is whether these differences in psychological behavior and financial practices constitute a real economic burden. In my opinion they do not" ("The Burden of Debt," p. 215). But Buchanan would presumably reply that taxes are not only more easily identifiable, they are compulsory.

arises from the fact that among the factors that influence Generation I's welfare (the shape of its indifference surfaces) is the fate of Generation II, a fate in which Generation I may well take a lively interest, whereas Generation II's attempts to maximize its welfare cannot take into consideration the fate of Generation I; time cannot run backward. Thus Generation I can gain, in a welfare sense, by sacrificing, in the consumption sense, thus leaving Generation II on as high an economic level as if the Government had never diverted resources to a wasteful purpose.

Let us suppose that during the lifetime of Generation II the bonds are redeemed by taxation.[21] In Buchanan's sense a sacrifice has occurred, because somebody has been forced to do something; those who pay tax in Generation II do not voluntarily hand over cash to the bond-holders of Generation II in order that the bonds may be torn up. If the debt is not redeemed a smaller sacrifice, taxation to pay the interest, is repeated indefinitely.

If we view Generation I as holding a town meeting, in which everyone agrees that he prefers to have bonds issued, although knowing that in this case he and those who come after him will have to contribute taxes towards the interest, rather than paying for the resource diversion by a big tax effort at once, we are pushing Buchanan's type of analysis, viz., welfare as influenced by free choice, back and up one level, to government. The annual tax payments for the interest now impose no sacrifice, for they are but part of a package deal agreed to by all. And if the town meeting's decision had been to the contrary, i.e., that heavy taxes should be levied at once to pay for the resource diversion, these taxes, too, would not be said to impose a sacrifice (given, always, the fact of government diversion of resources), for each person would be placing himself on a higher indifference surface by choosing to pay heavy taxes now rather than accept the less-attractive alternative of light annual taxes to be paid forever by him and those who were to come after him. But Buchanan's analysis, perhaps more realistically, does not carry the free-choice assumption back to those levels. Anyone who is required to pay taxes is moved thereby to a lower indifference surface. The Government is a force external to him, requiring him to surrender something.

21. On this point, see Pigou, *A Study in Public Finance*, p. 238: "Thus, though it is true, as Professor Seligman asserts, that the bondholder gets no benefit from debt repayment, it is also true that the taxpayer suffers no loss."

The fact that Generation II is better off, materially, if Generation I has saved rather than consumed is of no interest to Buchanan's analysis. But it is of overwhelming interest to the traditional school. To them, the fact that nobody in Generation I is forced to do anything, while somebody in Generation II is forced to do something, is of no consequence. Or perhaps we must say that the traditional view implies that there is no forcing at all, in the taxing process; that there is implied a collective agreement on the financial policy selected. The bond issue plus the annual tax for interest is selected, by the individuals, acting through their political representatives, because it is preferred to no-bond plus heavy immediate taxes—or vice-versa. Without this implication, indeed, the traditional view is in an embarrassing position vis-à-vis Buchanan and welfare economics. With this implication, they escape this embarrassment, if we can assume that Generation I can act for those who come after them.

Buchanan, who deems of no consequence for the argument on sacrifice the fact that Generation II possesses greater material wealth if Generation I reacts one way to the bond issue rather than another, does seem thereby to be in a somewhat difficult position vis-à-vis the traditional view. It seems awkward to disregard the material inheritance of Generation II when speaking of burden.

Summary

In conclusion: if, although capital is never impaired, inheritance is impaired; or if inheritance is not allowed; or if freedom of choice rather than level of consumption is the test of well being—then the traditional conclusion, that the burden is passed on to a future generation only insofar as the government outlay is not met at once by increased saving, is either incomplete, or not applicable, or irrelevant. But it is still to be judged correct, in the setting its formulators assumed for it, which is probably the setting that most of us have inferred as we studied it.

B/ TEMPORAL UTILITY AND FISCAL BURDEN*

BY James M. Ferguson

I

Issuing bonds rather than using taxes to finance public expenditures does not insure that more of the cost of the expenditure will be shifted to future time periods or to later generations of taxpayers. Postponing the reduction in taxpayers' consumption of private goods and services required by the withdrawal of resources from the private sector depends on the decisions of taxpayers who legally bear the cost of all public expenditures in a democratic society. All of the shifting analyses presented in the preceding pages suffer from a common defect. They have either not dealt explicitly with the determinants of individual utility, or they have attempted to include both stock and flow items in the utility function. To understand the temporal distribution of the reduction in private consumption required by the withdrawal of resources from the private sector for the government project requires understanding of the effects of reducing consumption and investment on the individual taxpayer's utility in the current period and in future periods. Is utility in any period a function of consumption in that period, of net worth, or of some combination of stock and flow items? The authors who suggest that reductions in saving do not impose a burden at the time they occur implicitly assume that people invest only to consume in future periods and that current utility is not a function of current investment. The present analysis develops the individual's utility function and uses it to determine the effects on current and future periods' utility of alternative taxpayer decisions under tax and bond financing.

The participants in the shifting debate also have not asked whether there are costs (or a burden) connected with the use of

* The author thanks Professors James Buchanan, John Hause, and Gordon Tullock for their cordial efforts to improve the author's analysis.

debt financing of a given public expenditure which do not occur
with taxation. Using a utility measure of burden, it is possible to
identify an additional burden borne by taxpayers under debt financing which is attributable to the debt method of financing not to
the withdrawal of resources from the private sector caused by the
expenditure. The additional burden or loss of utility borne by taxpayers under debt financing relative to taxation is due to factors
inherent in the institution of public debt, which are described by
the term "public debt illusion." These factors, which include uncertainty concerning future taxes and limited time horizons, cause
people to treat the government bonds as assets but to underestimate their liability as taxpayers to pay additional taxes in future
periods to service and retire the debt. Feeling more wealthy than
they actually are, taxpayers consume more private goods and services and save less in the period of the government expenditure
than they would in the absence of the illusion. Taxpayers must
then consume fewer private goods and services in future periods
when they are taxed to service and retire the debt. Assuming the
temporal distribution of lifetime consumption in the absence of illusion would have been more nearly optimal, these changes in
taxpayers' consumption patterns will reduce taxpayers' lifetime
utility under debt financing relative to tax financing.[1] No such distortion in lifetime consumption occurs under tax finance because the
taxes are levied in the initial period, when the government expenditure occurs. (Any distortions in resource allocation caused by using
non-lump sum taxes will also occur in future periods under debt
financing when taxes are levied to service and retire the debt.) Not

1. As in the comparison of the welfare costs of income and excise taxes, the
initial position has an important bearing on the findings. If at the outset conditions exist which lead taxpayers to underestimate their wealth, and as a result
to plan to save too much in the current period, the use of debt finance in the
presence of uncertainty concerning future tax liability may result in taxpayers
increasing current consumption *and* increasing their lifetime utility.
People may plan to save too much if they underestimate the benefits from
the public expenditure. If the public goods and services are substitutes for
private goods and services, then with correct foresight it is likely that they
would pay more of current taxes out of investment funds. In such a situation
using debt finance with its accompanying underestimation of future taxes may
lead people to save less and increase their lifetime utility compared to tax
finance. However, if public goods and services (such as defense) are not considered substitutes for private goods and services, then underestimation of benefits will not affect private saving-consumption decisions. In this context use of
debt finance will lead taxpayers to increase their current consumption and will
distort their temporal consumption pattern and reduce lifetime utility.

only the total amount of consumption, which will be the same under the two methods of finance, but also its temporal distribution can affect the welfare of the individual.

Finding a burden of the debt method of financing is the basis of a reply to Vickrey and Mishan who ask whether on welfare grounds debt financing is always preferable to tax financing because it allows individuals a wider range of alternatives. A negative answer is possible if the loss of utility from distortions in the timing of taxpayers' consumption under debt financing is greater than the gain in utility from the wider range of choice.

II

In a democratic society the burden of all government expenditures is borne by taxpayers. This section discusses the alternatives open to taxpayers under tax and debt finance and the various measures of how much of the burden is borne in the period of the expenditure and in future periods. Society is assumed to be composed of a fixed population through time. Shifting part of the burden of public expenditure to later generations of taxpayers is not considered. Suppose we start by defining the gross burden or objective cost of a public expenditure to be the reduction in private consumption required by the withdrawal of resources from the private sector. An individual taxpayer suffers a burden in any period of time in which his private consumption is less than it would have been in the absence of government borrowing (or taxing) and spending.

Consider the alternatives facing the individual taxpayer under debt financing.[2]

1. If he reduces current private consumption and buys bonds sufficient to cover the expected additional future taxes to service and retire the debt, he bears the burden entirely in the present and bears no burden in the future. Future periods' private consumption remains the same as before.

2. If he keeps current private consumption the same, future periods' private consumption will be less than before by an amount equal to the additional future taxes to service and retire the debt.

---

2. While the decisions of citizens in their other capacities are not explicitly considered, it is assumed that saving occurs for reasons other than to meet future taxes. Any public debt which is issued and not purchased to meet future taxes will still be absorbed.

The burden of the debt in terms of the required reduction in private consumption necessitated by the additional government project will be entirely shifted or postponed until future periods.

3. If he engages in some combination of the above, to the extent that he chooses alternative one he will bear a current burden, and to the extent that he chooses alternative two he will bear a future burden.

Government financing of the project yields withdrawal of resources from the private sector which must place a real burden of reduced lifetime consumption on taxpayers. However, the individual may choose to bear this burden now or later, and when the burden is actually borne will depend on individual decisions.

Some issues can be brought to the fore by considering the alternatives open to the taxpayer if the government should decide to use tax finance:

1. He can reduce current private consumption by the full amount of the current taxes, thereby keeping current private investment and future periods' consumption the same as before. As with alternative one under bond financing the individual bears the entire burden currently.

2. He can maintain current private consumption and reduce current private investment by the full amount of the taxes—thereby reducing consumption in future periods.[3] The burden will be borne entirely in the future. No current burden occurs with the reduction in current private investment. (We shall return to this matter in a moment.)

3. He can maintain both his current private consumption and his investment by borrowing the funds to pay the current taxes. Again the burden will be postponed until future periods when reduction in consumption occurs with repayment of the loan. The addition of a liability in the current period causes no burden currently.

4. The individual can engage in some combination of the above with the burden borne partly in the present and partly in the future.

Perhaps the most interesting result of this analysis is the postpon-

3. The individual can also sell certain assets (wealth items) to pay the taxes. Again consumption would be reduced in future periods, although to the extent that these assets would have rendered consumption services in the current period a burden is also borne currently. Money is such an asset—it yields utility while held and when exchanged for goods and services.

ing of the burden of current taxes if they are paid out of current investment funds. This result, of course, would not follow if burden were defined in terms of changes in net worth. Obviously implicit in this analysis is some concept of the individual's utility function and the determinants of utility.

In one sense the problem is how to combine stocks and flows in the utility function. One alternative is to make utility in each period only a function of consumption in each period. But such a function excludes the effect of expectations on current utility. A second alternative is to specify that utility in each period is a function of net worth in each period. With such a utility function the burden (loss of utility) occurs currently under taxation regardless of whether the individual reduces current consumption or current investment. But why does reducing current investment or incurring obligations to pay in future periods reduce current utility?[4]

Rejecting both of these alternatives, a third utility function is suggested which "explains" the relationship between future decreases in consumption and decreases in current utility. Utility in each period is specified to be some function of consumption in each period and of expected consumption in all future periods. Such a relation means that utility in each period is affected by anticipation of consumption in future periods. The individual receives a flow of satisfaction during the current period anticipating future consumption. This solution eliminates all stocks from the utility function. Investment and wealth (apart from the services of assets consumed in each period) enter the utility function through their effect on future periods' consumption. A decrease in current investment will

---

4. Assume correct foresight and suppose people decide, with government debt financing, not to reduce current consumption and buy bonds to pay the extra future taxes required to service the debt. Rather they decide to pay these taxes and reduce future periods' consumption of private goods and services. This anticipated future obligation will reduce net worth and therefore utility in the current period. Will there be no reduction in utility in the future when the actual reduction in consumption occurs? It appears that this treatment of the burden is equivalent to defining the burden to be the decrease in the present value of an expected lifetime utility stream. Such a burden is always borne in the present, unless a public debt illusion exists and future taxes are underestimated. These concepts confuse a (inaccurate) measure of the size of the burden with the burden itself. If a person knows that he will receive fifty lashes next week, will he feel pain now but not in the future when he receives the lashes? Our knowledge of human psychology and behavior does not support such a finding. The present value may provide a measure of the size of the burden, but it does not mean that the entire burden is borne currently.

mean a decrease in the individual's stream of utility in future periods when private consumption is lower than it would otherwise have been. There will also be some decrease in the current period's utility stream due to anticipation of the later reductions in consumption.

Suppose when public debt is issued that the taxpayer foresees the additional future taxes necessary to service and retire the debt. The resulting decrease in future periods' private consumption will reduce his utility stream in future periods. Some decrease in the current period's utility stream will also occur because of anticipation of the future reduction in consumption. Introducing the effect of anticipations, however, makes the size of the total burden indeterminate. Furthermore, it is difficult to specify how much of the gross burden of public expenditure is borne in any particular period.

Let us re-examine our findings in the bond case:

1. If the taxpayer reduces current private consumption and buys additional bonds sufficient to cover the expected future taxes to service and retire the debt, the entire loss in utility occurs in the present and the individual bears no burden in the future.

2. If the taxpayer maintains current private consumption, future periods' consumption (of private goods and services) and utility will be reduced. Anticipation of the reduction in consumption in future periods will make the individual feel worse off currently.

3. Any combination of the above two will result in some reduction in the taxpayer's utility in the current period and in future periods.

III

Vickrey and Mishan argue that taxpayers' consumption-saving decisions will not be the same under debt and tax finance. They argue that debt finance offers certain advantages to taxpayers which can result in less reduction in their private consumption. In fact they argue that on welfare grounds debt financing is always preferable to tax financing because it allows individuals a wider range of alternatives. A counter argument will be made that the use of debt financing, rather than current taxation, may result in distortions in the timing of taxpayers' consumption with a resulting loss of utility which is greater than the gain in utility from the wider range of choice.

Mishan mentions that poorer members of the community facing a current tax may have no alternative but to reduce current consumption, because of very high private loan rates due to imperfections in the capital market. Debt finance overcomes these imperfections in the capital market and makes available to all taxpayers at equal rates the opportunity of postponing the required reduction in consumption. The lower rate to the poorer borrowers (taxpayers) will, according to Mishan, lead them to postpone more of the required reduction in consumption. Current consumption will fall less and current investment more under debt finance compared to tax finance. In Mishan's analysis the taxpayer appears to be a borrower and the government bond purchaser a lender. The taxpayer is able to postpone reducing consumption under debt finance by implicitly borrowing from the government bond purchasers. The latter voluntarily surrender the resources for the project in return for resources in future periods.

Mishan [17] (references on page 229) expands this point in defense of the proposition

. . . that, on familiar welfare premises, the community is always better off if the government creates debt to meet its expenditure on some project than if it raises taxes [p. 533].

. . . .

Now suppose the government began by covering its expenditure by a tax levy, but on second thought transformed the levy into a legal obligation to buy bonds to the same amount. This compulsory purchase of government bonds is exactly equivalent to the tax alternative if we suppose the pattern of income to remain unchanged over time, since then each person receives, over the future, interest payments exactly equal to his tax liability. We can assume that everyone is fully aware of this when the government has the bright idea of allowing people to trade freely (at the fixed price) in these bonds. All those who avail themselves of the scheme to change the initial number of bonds allocated to them must be regarded as improving their welfare. Since all who trade will be better off, and those who do not trade will not be any worse off, we can legitimately say that the scheme has made the community as a whole better off. But this new position is exactly equivalent to that which would have been reached had the government in the first place financed its expenditure by debt creation. *Ergo* there is a loss of welfare in covering expenditure by taxation rather than debt creation [pp. 533-34].

Vickrey emphasizes a second advantage developed by Bowen, Davis, and Kopf, namely that it is easier to leave a negative estate under debt finance. When debt is issued, the initial generation of taxpayers can shift part of the required reduction in consumption onto later generations of taxpayers born after the period of the government expenditure who are present when taxes are levied to service and retire the debt. Selling the bonds to the later generations, consuming the proceeds, and giving them the tax liability increases the lifetime consumption of the first generation and reduces the capital stock inherited by, and therefore the lifetime consumption opportunities of, the later generations. Under tax finance, Vickrey [28] points out, the individual finds it hard to take action which will impose such a burden on future generations. ". . . it is often difficult to arrange to leave a negative estate when the estate was originally zero or very small. On this basis one could even argue that debt financing is the preferable policy in the abstract, in that it leaves a wider range for individual choice . . ." [p. 136]. The importance of this second advantage of debt finance, mentioned by Vickrey, is questionable given all of the other assets which generation 1 can consume instead of leaving for generation 2. This shifting among generations of people depends on the presence of people in the initial generation who originally planned under taxation to leave no estate. Everyone who planned to leave a positive estate under tax finance may plan to leave an even larger estate under debt finance so that their heirs can meet the additional tax liability. There is nothing in the use of bonds which will cause these people to increase their lifetime consumption. If every taxpayer in the present generation plans in the tax case to leave a positive estate, then no shifting to later generations of taxpayers will occur. Thus the amount of this type of shifting depends upon the number of taxpayers in the initial generation who plan to leave no estate.[5] Debt financing will in effect allow these people to leave a negative estate. Lacking evidence on the importance of this type of citizen, attention in the remainder of the paper will be directed to the first advantage, mentioned by Mishan. It is, of course, possible that if members of the initial generation of taxpayers find that they must consume less than they had anticipated in future periods due to underestimation of the taxes to service the debt, they will reduce the estate to be left for their heirs to avoid this reduction in consumption. But the basic determinants of this pattern of behavior are the factors which cause the underestimation.

5. Nevertheless the over-all inter-generation effect cannot be positive. The lifetime consumption opportunities of later generations cannot be increased when debt finance is used and may be reduced.

Almost everyone in the shifting controversy refers to a "public debt illusion," which is a collective term including all of the factors which cause people to treat government bonds as assets but to underestimate their liability as taxpayers to pay additional taxes in future periods to service and retire the debt. Uncertainty concerning future taxes (tax rates, number of taxpayers, general economic conditions) can result in underestimation. As a result under debt financing taxpayers feel wealthier and consume more and save less in the period of the government expenditure than they would under tax financing. Taxpayers must then consume less in future periods when they are taxed to service the debt. The illusion under debt financing causes taxpayers to deviate from their optimal planned lifetime consumption pattern, and they suffer a loss of utility from these distortions.[6] It is important to emphasize that the later periods' lower consumption is not the burden, as there was higher consumption in the initial period. Not only the total amount of consumption but also its temporal distribution can affect the welfare of the individual.

To say debt financing imposes a greater loss of utility than tax financing, taxpayers' position under debt with illusion must be less preferred not only to the position achievable under debt without illusion but also to the position achievable under tax financing. To the extent that debt finance provides equal access to the capital market by providing lower interest rates to poorer taxpayer-borrowers as mentioned by Mishan, resulting changes in consumer behavior by taxpayers cannot be said to represent a movement to a less preferred position or deviations from a preferred pattern. Rather they suggest a movement to a more preferred position.

Therefore, the differences in taxpayers' consumption-saving patterns under the two methods of finance do not necessarily indicate that they are worse off under debt financing. What can be said is that in the presence of a perfect capital market, uncertainty concerning future taxes can cause adverse differential behavior under debt finance. In this context the burden or welfare cost of the debt method of financing is then the loss of utility by the initial generation of taxpayers due to deviations from the temporal consumption pattern which they would have enjoyed in the absence of the

6. Tax uncertainty and its effect on the temporal distribution of private consumption depends on the use of debt finance. If current taxes are levied instead of issuing debt, no tax uncertainty occurs.

uncertainty. It follows that taxpayers are better off under debt financing without uncertainty concerning future taxes than they are with debt finance in the presence of this uncertainty. Taxpayers will be better off under tax finance if both uncertainty and imperfections in the capital market are present, and if under debt finance taxpayers' loss of utility from the distortion due to uncertainty is greater than the gain from overcoming imperfections in the capital market.

BIBLIOGRAPHY

1. Bowen, William G., Richard G. Davis, and David H. Kopf. "The Burden of the Public Debt: Reply," *The American Economic Review*, LI (March, 1961), 141-43.
2. ———. "The Distribution of the Debt Burden: A Reply," *The Review of Economics and Statistics*, XLIV (February, 1962), 98-99.
3. ———. "The Public Debt: A Burden on Future Generations?" *The American Economic Review*, L (September, 1960), 701-6.
4. Buchanan, James M. *Fiscal Theory and Political Economy: Selected Essays*. Chapel Hill: The University of North Carolina Press, 1960.
5. ———. "Public Debt, Cost Theory, and the Fiscal Illusion" [article written for this volume].
6. ———. *Public Principles of Public Debt*. Homewood, Illinois: Richard D. Irwin, Inc., 1958.
7. Elliott, James R. "The Burden of the Public Debt: Comment," *The American Economic Review*, LI (March, 1961), 139-41.
8. Ferguson, James M. "Temporal Utility and Fiscal Burden" [article written for this volume].
9. Hansen, Alvin H. (Review of 6, 14, and 15), "The Public Debt Reconsidered," *The Review of Economics and Statistics*, XLI (June, 1959), 370-78.
10. Lerner, Abba P. "The Burden of Debt," *The Review of Economics and Statistics*, XLIII (May, 1961), 139-41.
11. ———. "The Burden of the National Debt," in Lloyd A. Metzler and others (eds.). *Income, Employment, and Public Policy: Essays in Honor of Alvin H. Hansen*. New York: W. W. Norton & Company, 1948. Pp. 255-75.

12. ———. (Review of 6), *The Journal of Political Economy*, XLVII (April, 1959), 203-6.
13. Maffezzoni, Federico. "The Comparative Fiscal Burden of Public Debt and Taxation," *International Economic Papers No. 11*. New York: The Macmillan Co., 1962. Pp. 75-101.
14. Meade, James E. "Is the National Debt a Burden?" *Oxford Economic Papers*, X (June, 1958), 163-83.
15. ———. "Is the National Debt a Burden: A Correction," *Oxford Economic Papers*, XI (June, 1959), 109-10.
16. Miller, H. Laurence, Jr. "Anticipated and Unanticipated Consequences of Public Debt Creation," *Economica*, XXIX (November, 1962), 410-19.
17. Mishan, E. J. "How to Make a Burden of the Public Debt," *The Journal of Political Economy*, LXXI (December, 1963), 529-42.
18. Modigliani, Franco. "Long-Run Implications of Alternative Fiscal Policies and the Burden of the National Debt," *The Economic Journal*, LXXI (December, 1961), 730-55.
19. Musgrave, Richard A. *The Theory of Public Finance*. New York: McGraw-Hill Book Company, Inc., 1959.
20. Neisser, Hans. "Is the Public Debt a Burden on Future Generations?" *Social Research* (Summer, 1961), pp. 225-28.
21. Peacock, Alan T. (Review of 6), "The Rehabilitation of Classical Debt Theory," *Economica*, XXVI (May, 1959), 161-66.
22. Prest, A. R. (Review of 6), *The Economic Journal*, LXIX (June, 1959), 358-60.
23. Ratchford, B. U. (Review of 6), "The Nature of Public Debt," *The Southern Economic Journal*, XXV (October, 1958), 213-17.
24. Rolph, Earl R. (Review of 6), *The American Economic Review*, XLIX (March, 1959), 183-85.
25. Scitovsky, Tibor. "The Burden of the Public Debt: Comment," *The American Economic Review*, LI (March, 1961), 137-39.
26. Shoup, Carl S. "Debt Financing and Future Generations," *The Economic Journal*, LXXII (December, 1962), 887-98.
27. Tullock, Gordon. "Public Debt—Who Bears the Burden?" *Rivista di diritto finanziario e scienza delle finanze*, XXII (June, 1963), 207-13.
28. Vickrey, William. "The Burden of the Public Debt: Comment," *The American Economic Review*, LI (March, 1961), 132-37.
29. Wiseman, Jack. "The Logic of National Debt Policy," *Westminster Bank Review* (August, 1961), pp. 8-15.

INDEX